ELISHA'S PROFILE IN THE BOOK OF KINGS

Elisha's Profile in the Book of Kings

The Double Agent

KEITH BODNER

OXFORD

UNIVERSITY PRESS

OXFORD
UNIVERSITY PRESS

Great Clarendon Street, Oxford, OX2 6DP,
United Kingdom

Oxford University Press is a department of the University of Oxford.
It furthers the University's objective of excellence in research, scholarship,
and education by publishing worldwide. Oxford is a registered trade mark of
Oxford University Press in the UK and in certain other countries

First Edition published in 2013

Impression: 1

British Library Cataloguing in Publication Data

Data available

ISBN 978-0-19-968117-4

Printed by CPI Group (UK) Ltd, Croydon, CR0 4YY

Acknowledgments

For centuries Oxford University Press has been among the finest publishing houses in the world, and I am extremely grateful to Tom Perridge and his team for unflagging support, and to the Delegates of the Press for their commitment to impressive standards without compromise.

Several institutions provided me with opportunities to lecture on this material, including Tyndale University College and Seminary in Toronto, with thanks to Dan Scott, Larry Hopperton, and Janet Clark, and Crandall University, where I am deeply appreciative of inquisitive students who patiently study ancient literature, along with the consistent support of President Bruce Fawcett and Academic VP Seth Crowell.

Every year at the university we host the annual Murray Lecture, and Nicholas Wolterstorff deserves a twenty-one-gun salute for his rich encouragement, careful questioning, and thoughtful conversation around the topic of this book.

Various colleagues rendered assistance along the way, including Brian Aucker, Walter Brueggemann, Mark Leuchter, Ian Young, Erin Vearncombe, David Lamb, Deven MacDonald, Jon Vickery, Ellen White, Brent Strawn, Edith Humphrey, Louis Stulman, Jacob Wright, Paul Evans, Jeff Greenman, and Jeremy Hutton. Lots of editing took place in Shanghai on a lecture tour with my great friend John Stackhouse, mentor and model to all. I also value the opportunity to serve the *Journal for the Study of the Old Testament* and the chance to read the highest quality of current scholarship on the Hebrew Bible, so John Jarick, Yvonne Sherwood, Duncan Burns, and the editorial board deserve a word of thanks.

Like the fellow who loses his grip in 2 Kings 6:5, every day I experience some *random axe of kindness* from my family. Gratitude should be expressed to Coreen, Evelyn, Victoria, Jeff, not least because they remind me that Elisha's miracles anticipate the arrival of a later Agent who binds up the brokenhearted and sets the captives free.

Contents

Abbreviations

AB	Anchor Bible
ABD	*Anchor Bible Dictionary*
ABR	*Australian Biblical Review*
BibInt	*Biblical Interpretation*
BIS	Biblical Interpretation Series
BN	*Biblische Notizen*
BZAW	Beihefte zur Zeitschrift für die alttestamentliche Wissenschaft
CBC	Cambridge Bible Commentary
CBQ	*Catholic Biblical Quarterly*
CBR	*Currents in Biblical Research*
ESHM	European Seminar in Historical Methodology
FOTL	Forms of the Old Testament Literature
HCOT	Historical Commentary on the Old Testament
HUCA	*Hebrew Union College Annual*
ICC	International Critical Commentary
JBL	*Journal of Biblical Literature*
JETS	*Journal of the Evangelical Theological Society*
JHS	*Journal of Hebrew Scriptures*
JJS	*Journal of Jewish Studies*
JPS	Jewish Publication Society
JSOT	*Journal for the Study of the Old Testament*
JSOTSup	Journal for the Study of the Old Testament: Supplement Series
KJV	King James Version
LHBOTS	Library of Hebrew Bible/Old Testament Studies
LXX	Septuagint
MT	Masoretic Text
NCB	New Century Bible
NIBC	New International Biblical Commentary
NRSV	New Revised Standard Version
OTL	Old Testament Library

SBL   Society of Biblical Literature
SBT   Studies in Biblical Theology
SBLDS   Society of Biblical Literature Dissertation Series
SR   *Studies in Religion*
TynBul   *Tyndale Bulletin*
VT   *Vetus Testamentum*
VTSup   Supplements to Vetus Testamentum
WBC   Word Biblical Commentary
ZAW   *Zeitschrift für die alttestamentliche Wissenschaft*

Prologue: Double Vision

The life and times of Elisha the prophet in 1 Kings 19 and 2 Kings 2–13 make for an exceptionally absorbing study, containing many of the ingredients of a classic drama. The main character is both compelling and elusive, and as Elisha emerges from his master's shadow his rugged individuality is the subject of a great deal of narrative attention. In the stretch of text where Elisha is a central character, a host of interesting plotlines and unexpected events unfold, at once engaging the reader but also creating a puzzle in terms of how the episodes fit together. Further, there is a unique variety of supporting actors and minor figures in the narrative, adding both to the quixotic flavor of the story and its occasional difficulties. The story is temporally located during a most turbulent period in Israel's history, with plenty of international players appearing on the stage, and moments when the reader is whisked away on a foreign excursion. So for these and other reasons a study of Elisha's career can be a taxing but profitable undertaking, and I will suggest below that the present interpretative climate makes this a congenial time to embark on such an enterprise.

BAD NEWS BEARS

To prepare the table, I would suggest that a fairly bizarre scene in 2 Kings 2:23–5 is an ideal introduction to my reading of the Elisha story. On the surface this short episode is straightforward: the prophet is mocked by a group of youths, he curses them, and the youths are attacked by two bears. Yet even the most cursory survey of commentators reveals that a good number of scholars have been deeply disturbed by the violence of this account. For instance, Wesley Bergen samples the opinions of John Gray and Gwilym Jones, and notes: "Gray says the story is 'in every respect a puerile tale' and goes on to heap derision on the sons of the prophets who presumably are responsible for it. Jones feels similarly, saying that the story 'cannot have a serious point, and it does no credit to the prophet.'"[1] Given such hostility from these eminent commentators, it might be wise to pause and further consider the scene:

> He went up from there to Bethel, and as he was going up on the road some little lads marched out from the city and jeered him. They said to him, "Go up baldy! Go up baldy!" He turned around, looked at them, and cursed them in the name of the LORD. And two female bears marched out from the forest and tore up forty-two of them, youths. He walked off from there to Mt Carmel, and from there he returned to Samaria.[2]

After a more detailed reading of this episode, one guesses that the source of the struggle for scholars Gray and Jones lies in the reaction of Elisha more than in the taunting of the lads. In a fit of pique after a personal insult, Elisha invokes *the divine name* in a curse that results—though recognizing that the causal connection between the prophet's curse and the bear's assault is assumed rather than stated directly in the text—in the vicious attack against a sizeable group of children. Yet it is possible that, for every scholar who finds this scene unbearable, there are other readers—perhaps even some who have suffered the taunts and torment of bullies—who are not quite so scandalized in the same way as some modern academicians, and have a rather different take on the prophetic puerility offered here. These readers, perhaps acquainted with William Golding's contribution to English literature in *Lord of the Flies*, may be tempted to applaud privately even if they ought to be publicly repulsed.

At the very least this scene is worthy of careful scrutiny. As we will discover in the course of our analysis later in this book, there are other

---

[1] W. J. Bergen, *Elisha and the End of Prophetism* (JSOTSup 286; Sheffield: Sheffield Academic Press, 1999), 68, citing J. Gray, *I & II Kings*, 2nd edn (OTL; London: SCM, 1970), 428, and G. H. Jones, *1 and 2 Kings* (NCB; Grand Rapids: Eerdmans, 1984), 389. Cf. the related comment of V. Fritz, *1 & 2 Kings* (Continental Commentary; Minneapolis, MN: Fortress, 2003), 239: "Elisha answers their jibes with a curse that is effectively out of proportion."

[2] Unless otherwise indicated, all translations from the Hebrew text throughout this book are my own.

issues that arise in this episode early in Elisha's career. Further thought will be given, to begin a list of a few examples, to the geographical symbolism at work in this episode as the prophet enters the orbit of Bethel.[3] Not so long ago in the narrative, Bethel was established as a cultic center of Jeroboam I, where one of two golden calves was unveiled and became a snare for the northern kingdom. Bethel is the vicinity where a powerful but peculiarly self-controlled lion attacks a man of God (but refrains from eating a nervous donkey) in 1 Kings 13, so it is conceivable that there may be a comparable use of wild beasts for divine judgment in these two episodes. In terms of the taunt directed at the prophet, one wonders at the exact nature of Elisha's baldness (involuntary versus some sort of religious tonsure), and whether this lack of hair is intended as a contrast with the comparatively more hirsute Elijah, who is referred to as a "master of hair" (בעל שער) in 2 Kings 1:8. What exactly do the miscreants mean when they say "go up," and is this related to the use of the keyword "go up" (עלה) elsewhere in the Elijah–Elisha transition? Still with the group of lads, the question of their age has evoked vigorous debate among the commentators, enhanced by an internal textual discrepancy: they are referred to as "small young men" (נערים קטנים) in v. 23, but forty-two "children" (ילדים) are ripped apart in v. 24. After the mauling, Elisha is not recorded as doing anything in Bethel, but proceeds to Mount Carmel, and then returns to Samaria. Is this to copy the itinerary of Elijah or to introduce the next episode (in 2 Kings 3) that features Jehoram as king of Israel?

These are the kinds of questions that will be engaged in due course, but, as an introductory discussion and an overture to the analysis to come, consider for a moment the placement of this scene featuring the beasts of Bethel with respect to the larger structural design of the Elisha story. In other words, does this episode occur somewhat randomly at this particular point in the story, or does it occupy a more strategic position within the overall narrative architecture? As one recalls, the encounter in Bethel comes immediately on the heels of another equally brief account where Elisha heals the waters of Jericho in 2 Kings 2:19–22. Perhaps these two scenes have no points of intersection. In his summary of scholarship on this section of 2 Kings, Burke Long admitted that there is "a virtual consensus

---

[3] J. S. Burnett, "'Going Down' to Bethel: Elijah and Elisha in the Theological Geography of the Deuteronomistic History," *JBL* 129 (2010), 281–97.

among scholars that this unit consists of two originally independent traditions."[4] From a certain perspective it could be said the scenes do appear entirely unrelated. However, I would propose that reading these two episodes together with the assumption that there is an essential literary coherence might reveal an intentionality in the structural design of the narrative, and that possibility will now be probed.

As Elisha is staying in Jericho in 2 Kings 2:19, the residents of the city bring a serious problem to the prophet: despite an optimal location for the town, "the water is evil and the land causes bereavement." Now the most common use of the term "bereavement" (משכלת), of course, is the loss of children, as in the classic warning of Leviticus 26:22, "I will send forth wild creatures among you, and they will bereave (שכל) you."[5] In response to this crisis Elisha—by means of the unexpected instrument of a bowl of salt—heals the waters whereby life can continue. When reading the episodes of the healing waters and the destructive she-bears sequentially, one notices some opportunity for thematic evaluation. In the first scene Elisha heals the water and banishes sterility so that the "land" can bear fruit and the women bear children. In the next scene Elisha calls forth a curse, and two bears rob the Bethel women of their progeny.

One purpose for ordering the scenes in this manner, potentially, could be for comparison: a story of life is followed by its antithesis. A point of contrast subsequently emerges between Jericho's healing of bereavement (through supplication of the prophet) versus Bethel's bereavement (that is, loss of children) through insults directed at the prophet: Jericho recovers offspring while Bethel loses offspring. Despite the "virtual consensus"—and Burke Long certainly appears to be faithfully reporting the facts here—one could begin to make the case that there is a structural rationale for juxtaposing these two scenes, and my analysis in this book will endeavor to test such hypotheses. This present book, then, has an experimental quality: there have been a number of interesting and useful studies recently on this extended narrative, several of which are introduced in the next section of this prologue. The proliferation of such works allows us to conclude that

---

[4] B. O. Long, *2 Kings* (FOTL 10; Grand Rapids: Eerdmans, 1991), 33.
[5] W. B. Aucker, "Putting Elisha in his Place: Genre, Coherence, and Narrative Function in 2 Kings 2–8" (Ph.D. diss., University of Edinburgh, 2000), 92–3.

the last words on the Elisha material certainly have not been spoken and that ample scope remains for further research and reflection.

SOME RECENT INQUIRIES

Of late there have been some promising forays into the Elisha material in 1 and 2 Kings, and a variety of this secondary literature will be consulted and referenced over the course of this book. As part of this prologue, several of these works are briefly mentioned here, drawn from four standard categories of scholarly publication: dissertations, monographs, commentaries, and articles in academic journals. By no means are the following meant to be an extensive listing, but are only typical of contemporary trends in research, and are used here to illustrate the manner in which such works are incorporated into my analysis of the narrative. To start with doctoral dissertations, two particularly helpful works have been written by James Mead and Brian Aucker.[6] Recognizing a lacuna in Elisha studies, both scholars focused their doctoral energy on these texts with successful results. Both works begin with a *de rigueur* survey of the history of interpretation, especially in the modern era, and are keen to generate literary observations throughout their studies. Researchers can especially benefit from the bibliographies in both dissertations, and these works each have a number of useful local insights that I will reference along the way.

Two commentaries that are used extensively in this study can be cited here in this prologue as examples of other recent directions in the field. First, Robert Cohn's contribution to the Berit Olam series should be noted for its literary sensitivity and holistic approach to the

---

[6] J. K. Mead, "'Elisha Will Kill'? The Deuteronomistic Rhetoric of Life and Death in the Theology of the Elisha Narratives" (Ph.D. diss., Princeton Theological Seminary, 1999); Aucker, "Putting Elisha in his Place." Limitations of space and scope have curtailed the number of references in this book, but note the useful bibliographic compilation of M. Avioz, "The Book of Kings in Recent Research (Part II)," *CBR* 5/1 (2006), 11–57. Avioz is particularly helpful in outlining work from redaction-critical methods and the contribution of European scholarship, and the reader is referred to Avioz's discussion of numerous studies. Note also the perspective of Susanne Otto, "The Composition of the Elijah–Elisha Stories and the Deuteronomistic History," *JSOT* 27 (2003), 487–508.

Elisha material in 2 Kings. Cohn deploys a method that seeks to explore the literary angles without neglecting the results of earlier scholarship. As he puts it: "A literary perspective, let me be clear, in no way vitiates the importance of historical criticism, for more than a century the main approach to 2 Kings," but by "paying close attention to the way in which a writer has constructed a narrative world, we can see more clearly its historical, ideological, and esthetic dimensions."[7] As one practical example, consider Cohn's reflections on the larger organization of Elisha's biography, and especially the prophet's resurfacing after what appears to be the end of his career: "But after Elisha is memorialized and his great deeds recounted as if he were dead (8:1–6), he enters the narrative again, this time to challenge the political order directly by triggering revolutions in Aram, Israel, and, by extension, Judah. His fleeting appearances frame," Cohn continues, "what I have defined as the second part of 2 Kings (8:7–13:25). The variety of traditions about Elisha thus contribute to a multi-faceted portrait of a prophet playing a critical role in the lives of common people and in the destiny of the nations."[8] With due respect to F. Scott Fitzgerald, who famously said that there are no second acts in American lives, some Israelite prophets may prove to be an exception.

Another commentary to be noted here is Marvin Sweeney's volume in the Old Testament Library series, a replacement and updating of John Gray's earlier (though still helpful) contribution. An immediate strength of Sweeney's commentary—besides its erudition and breadth of scholarship—is the location of his exegetical work firmly within the contours of the Deuteronomistic History (a theoretical construct further discussed in the next section of this prologue). Even if one has a slightly different understanding of the lineaments of the theory, it is still an eminently *useable* discussion, and Sweeney consistently advocates that readers attend to both the synchronic and diachronic dimensions of the text. There is an undeniable value in reading the parts in view of the whole, and appreciating where the Elisha narratives fit in the larger scheme of the storyline: "This highly theologized account of Israel's and Judah's history attempts to explain why Judah and Israel—or more properly, the Davidic monarchy—

---

[7] R. L. Cohn, *2 Kings* (Berit Olam; Collegeville, MN: Liturgical Press, 2000), pp. xii–xiii.

[8] Cohn, *2 Kings*, p. xv.

came to an end and how this lesson might influence any attempt to restore Israelite or Judean life in the land."[9] A significant advantage, in my view, is that Sweeney has the luxury of reading Elisha in the context of both 1 and 2 Kings, and therefore he is able to draw connections from both earlier and later textual units. So, for instance, consider his remarks on the episode in 2 Kings 2:23–5 with the curse on the bears: "Focus on the typical character of the pericope prompts readers to overlook its specific function in the immediate literary context: it is placed here to validate Elisha's role as Elijah's prophetic successor by demonstrating that Elijah's powers have passed to Elisha. The passage thereby functions," Sweeney concludes, "as a part of the larger unit in 1–2 Kings to prepare the reader for Elisha's role in overthrowing the Omride dynasty and installing Jehu as an act of YHWH."[10] We will have occasion to explore further this ideological component at multiple junctures along the way.

A pair of monographs should also be mentioned in this short survey of recent work on the Elisha material in Kings, starting with Rick Dale Moore's 1990 book *God Saves: Lessons from the Elisha Stories.* After a lengthy conversation with the pioneering form criticism of Hermann Gunkel and others, Moore explicates his own interests, namely "the stylistic features and literary artistry of biblical texts in their wholeness. Over the past decade," says Moore, "this approach has gained particular distinction in the study of biblical narrative," and he proceeds to cite the seminal work of Alter, Berlin, and Sternberg as complementary endeavors.[11] When it comes to textual samples, Moore restricts his coverage to the Aramean material of 2 Kings 5–7:

A certain set of features distinctly shared by these stories suggests a basic kinship among them. All three stories (1) are set in the context of Aramean warfare against Israel, (2) refer to the current Aramean and Israelite kings without giving them specific identification, and (3) present dramatic miracles

---

[9]   M. A. Sweeney, *I & II Kings* (OTL; Louisville, KY: Westminster John Knox Press, 2007), 5.

[10]   Sweeney, *I & II Kings*, 275.

[11]   R. D. Moore, *God Saves: Lessons from the Elisha Stories* (JSOTSup 95; Sheffield: JSOT Press, 1990) 70, citing R. Alter, *The Art of Biblical Narrative* (New York: Basic Books, 1981), A. Berlin, *Poetics and Interpretation of Biblical Narrative* (Bible and Literature Series; Sheffield: Almond Press, 1983), and M. Sternberg, *The Poetics of Biblical Narrative: Ideological Literature and the Drama of Reading* (Indiana Studies in Biblical Literature; Bloomington: Indiana University Press, 1985).

which do not constitute the climax of the story but rather point beyond themselves in each case to serve a larger message.[12]

Moore's work has value, then, for the Aramean component of Elisha's career, even though there is not much consideration of the material from the point of view of the larger Deuteronomistic History. For instance, Moore makes a nice observation about the characterizations of Naaman and the little Israelite girl in 2 Kings 5, given that Naaman is described as a great man "before" (לפני) his master, and the little girl is serving "before" Naaman's wife:

The preposition לפני conspicuously follows the generic designation of each character. Parallel wording invites juxtaposition of these two figures, and juxtaposition yields a nearly perfect antithesis, an entire series of contrasts: great (גדול) vs small (קטן), Aramean vs Israelite, conqueror vs captive, male vs female, adult vs child, and ruler vs servant.[13]

Wesley Bergen's book *Elisha and the End of Prophetism* has already been quoted above, and will be extensively referenced throughout this study. Unlike Moore, Bergen treats every pericope of the Elisha material, and, even more unlike Moore, has a rather negative view of what he defines as "prophetism." Bergen understands Elisha as a deeply problematic character, yet, because each interpretative move is explicitly reasoned, his nuanced literary analysis needs to be taken into account at every turn. The healing of the Jericho waters in 2 Kings 2:19–22 furnishes a good example, where Bergen notes a subtle shift in language: "Thus says the LORD" (כה־אמר יהוה) is used in v. 21, but there is a shift to "according to the word of Elisha" (כדבר אלישע) in v. 22. For Bergen, this detail is telling: "The result is not a prophet who is directly discredited in the minds of readers, but one which makes readers uncomfortable with this prophet in particular, and prophetism in general. The narrator has already established in readers a suspicion of any character or event that takes away from the centrality of YHWH." He concludes: "Here the readers' suspicion is subtly turned toward the prophet, specifically in regards to the source of his power, without a direct assault being launched against this venerable institution."[14] Even though one may not entirely agree with

---

[12] Moore, *God Saves*, 70. [13] Moore, *God Saves*, 71–2.
[14] Bergen, *Elisha and the End of Prophetism*, 67–8. This critical stance toward Elisha is typical of Bergen, who has a consistently negative reading of the character (e.g., p. 42: "This study will read the presentation of the character of Elisha as a belittling portrayal of the prophet").

this conclusion, because some key issues pertaining to Elisha's characterization are so often at stake, Bergen's interpretation must be considered from start to finish.

There has been a wave of articles in various journals on the Elisha material in recent years. Among the many that will be appropriated in this book, two are mentioned here as part of the introduction to my own approach. First, Philip Satterthwaite published an essay in 1998 that contains many suggestive insights. His primary interest, as is evident from the title, is a quest for coherence in 2 Kings 2–8, seeking to discern the place of both the political episodes and the miracle stories in a meaningful whole. While every proposal may not finally be persuasive, Satterthwaite at least challenges the reader to consider the potential role of each episode in the account. A case in point is his brief treatment of the floating axe-head scene in 2 Kings 6:1–7, a cryptic episode that even Rick Dale Moore—whose focus is only on chapters 5–7—labels a "short 'interruption'" and comments no further.[15] Satterthwaite, in contrast, inquires about the placement of this scene in the midst of the Aramean conflict, and points to the minor characters (the sons of the prophets) and the spatial setting of the Jordan River: is there any connection with the account of Naaman's healing that precedes the floating axe-head? Satterthwaite suggests the following resonances: "the king of Aram has *lost his axe-head* (Naaman, his victorious general, incapacitated through leprosy), which is *restored* to him after *immersion in the Jordan* when Naaman *does what Elisha says*," but cautions: "if the broad outline of the episodes is similar, there is also a significant difference: the Naaman episode was ambiguous as regards YHWH's commitment to Israel's welfare; but here his power directly aids the (Israelite) 'sons of the prophets.' The next episode will take this development further."[16] Thus the quest for coherence continues, and, while these thoughts on the floating axe-head may not provide a definitive interpretation of the episode, Satterthwaite does provide other researchers with something to work with.

Second, a 1999 article in the *Journal for the Study of the Old Testament* by Nachman Levine has a number of compelling ideas.

---

[15] Moore, *God Saves*, 70.
[16] P. E. Satterthwaite, "The Elisha Narratives and the Coherence of 2 Kings 2–8," *TynBul*, 49 (1998), 19.

Paying extremely close attention to the minute details of the Hebrew text, Levine argues that

> Elisha's miracles repeat and multiply elements of the miracles of his teacher Elijah (1 Kgs 17–2 Kgs 2), from whom he requested "twice as much as your spirit" (2 Kgs 2.9). Common themes, motifs and wordplays in both narratives are used to connect, compare and contrast the two prophets and their relationship to each other and to the people of Israel to whom they minister.[17]

This vision of doubling—Levine begins his article by noting "The Midrash says Elijah did eight miracles and Elisha sixteen," and "Elisha's miracles not only double Elijah's but seem to parallel and multiply them in their themes, elements and language"—is of great interest to this present study, and a central pillar of my own investigation: to what extant is Elisha characterized as a *double agent* compared with his mentor Elijah after asking for a double portion of his spirit? A further strength of Levine's work is underlining connections, quite literally, between seemingly disparate episodes, such as this example from 2 Kings 4:25 and 4:42:

> When the son dies the lady comes from Shunem to the prophet Elisha who is in Mount Carmel (הר הכרמל). In the fourth incident the man provides the sons of the prophets with bread and parched grain: כרמל. Of course as we shall see it also refers to Elijah's miracle in Mount Carmel as well as to Elisha's becoming a prophet.[18]

If occasionally Levine's parallels strain credulity, others are fraught with possibility, as when he notices that King Ahaziah in 2 Kings 1:2 and Elisha in 2 Kings 4:10 have something in common. Both characters have a "roof chamber" (עליה), but the results could not be more different: "The king dies in his upstairs room while Elisha brings the

---

[17] N. Levine, "Twice as Much of your Spirit: Pattern, Parallel, and Paronomasia in the Miracles of Elijah and Elisha," *JSOT* 85 (1999), 46.

[18] Levine, "Twice as Much of your Spirit," 32. Cf. Cohn, *2 Kings*, 13: "One midrashic tradition interprets this double portion of spirit as expressing itself in Elisha's performance of sixteen miracles, twice the number of miracles, by its reckoning, that Elijah performs. See Louis Ginzberg, *The Legends of the Jews*, vol. IV (Philadelphia: The Jewish Publication Society, 1913, 1941), 239, and the discussion in Wolfgang Roth, *Hebrew Gospel: Cracking the Code of Mark* (Oak Park, IL: Meyer-Stone Books, 1988), 15–7." Note also Sirach 48:12: "When Elijah was enveloped in the whirlwind, Elisha was filled with his spirit. He performed twice as many signs, and marvels with every utterance of his mouth. Never in his lifetime did he tremble before any ruler, nor could anyone intimidate him at all" (NRSV).

boy back to life in his upstairs room."[19] There is ample scope to develop this point, as one can immediately sense the contrast between the king who futilely seeks healing from the god of Ekron after falling from his roof chamber and the Shunammite woman who successfully entreats the man of God who heals the lad in the roof chamber. In this book I seek to build on the foundation supplied by Levine, along with those other scholars mentioned in this section and numerous other works that will be engaged in the course of my analysis.

ELISHA BETWEEN LITERATURE AND HISTORY

From the above survey it is apparent that literary approaches are increasingly prevalent and have yielded some impressive results. The shift from a restrictive kind of historical inquiry toward a more expansive interpretive framework that allows room for literary criticism—even without eschewing the results of the former—has been well documented. On the theoretical side, a prominent scholar is Hans Frei, whose influence is nicely summarized by Tom Thatcher:

In 1974, Hans Frei observed that the biblical narratives were in a state of "eclipse." Specifically, scholars were no longer interested in the biblical narrative per se but instead focused their attention on the historical events that the Bible claimed to discuss and/or on the composition history of the books themselves. Books such as Genesis and the Gospel of Mark were thus "eclipsed" by the events behind them, hidden in the shadow of their own past and largely ignored.[20]

Led by a fecund group of scholars—to the names already listed one could add others, such as David Gunn, Phyllis Trible, Peter Miscall,

---

[19] Levine, "Twice as Much of your Spirit," 45.

[20] T. Thatcher, "Anatomies of the Fourth Gospel: Past, Present, and Future Probes," in T. Thatcher and S. D. Moore (eds), *Anatomies of Narrative Criticism: The Past, Present, and Futures of the Fourth Gospel as Literature* (Atlanta: Society of Biblical Literature, 2008), 2, referencing H. W. Frei, *The Eclipse of Biblical Narrative: A Study in Eighteenth and Nineteenth Century Hermeneutics* (New Haven: Yale University Press, 1974). In a footnote, Thatcher further comments: "In Frei's model, a 'realistic' narrative is one whose meaning lies in the holistic interaction of the elements of the story, including the characters, events, and settings. Whether the story has a reference point in the actual past or not, a realistic narrative's meaning lies in the *Gestalt* of its internal elements, not in factors outside the text itself" ("Anatomies of the Fourth Gospel," 2, n. 1).

Danna Nolan Fewell, Robert Polzin, and David Clines—new reading strategies were tested and refined, taking the analysis of biblical narrative in some productive new directions.

On the practical side this renewed focus on literary categories accrued numerous benefits, several of which are encapsulated by Manfred Oeming:

The advantages of a synchronic–literary approach result from the way in which the Bible is analyzed as literature, unburdened by the constraints of academic tradition. This approach is driven by pure enjoyment of the literary beauty of biblical texts. And it is astonishing how many biblical passages, which at first sight seem simple and somewhat dull, turn out to be complex and compositionally dense works of art.[21]

Increased popularity of literary methods in academic circles widened the scope of inquiry, and resulted in a growing diversity of approaches, with narrative criticism taking on increasing sophistication. Assuming with Peter Brooks that "narrative is one of the principal ways we organize our experience of the world," I would argue that narrative criticism in biblical studies is taking a more prominent role among interpretative methods in current scholarship.[22] In terms of definition, J. C. Robinson provides an accessible outline of what narrative criticism looks like in practice:

Narrative criticism attempts to appreciate the aesthetic nature of stories as both a literary and historical concern within the larger context of the stories or books themselves rather than isolated segments on their own. Compared to other schools of biblical criticism, narrative criticism generally places less stress on specific theological ideas, historical reference, grammar, and lexicographical matters. Instead, narrative criticism emphasizes analysis of plot, theme, motifs, characterization, style, figures of speech, symbols, repetition, etc. In cases of integrated approaches to the Bible—such as the combination of reader-response theories with narrative criticism—the result is often quite positive.[23]

---

[21] M. Oeming, *Contemporary Biblical Hermeneutics: An Introduction* trans. J. Vette (Aldershot: Ashgate, 2006), 64.

[22] Cited in M. L. Ryan, "Toward a Definition of Narrative," in D. Herman (ed.), *The Cambridge Companion to Narrative* (Cambridge: Cambridge University Press, 2007), 22; P. Brooks, *Reading for the Plot: Design and Intention in Narrative* (Cambridge, MA: Harvard University Press, 1984).

[23] J. C. Robinson, "Narrative," in Stanley E. Porter (ed.), *Dictionary of Biblical Criticism and Interpretation* (New York: Routledge, 2007), 236–7.

When Robinson mentions "integrated approaches," it strikes me as appropriate for a host of reasons, not least because my own approach to the text of 1 and 2 Kings is an eclectic one. My reading strategy in this book can be explained as follows: *I use literary analysis to study the Elisha narrative as an integral component of the Deuteronomistic History.* As I have referred to the Deuteronomistic History on a couple of occasions already, what I mean is the epic narrative compiled in the aftermath of the Babylonian invasion and destruction of Jerusalem in 586 BCE, when the temple was destroyed and a sizeable portion of the population deported into exile. The period of exile and beyond led to a massive reappraisal of Israel's history, and the books of Joshua–Kings form a long and sophisticated reflection on their experience in the land from conquest to collapse. To begin with the pioneering work of Martin Noth, the understanding of this narrative has been continually refined by subsequent scholars.[24] Others may contend that vast disagreement exists—and certainly a vigorous debate is evidenced in the scholarly literature—but there are also widespread areas of shared concern. Most would agree, for instance, with the basic structure: the Deuteronomistic History begins outside the land—with Israel located in the plains of Moab and poised to enter—and concludes with Israel once again outside the land, as the last king of Judah is seated at the table of the king of Babylon. In a compilation of articles responding to a recent book by Thomas Römer, Richard Nelson provides some helpful thoughts:

The Deuteronomistic History represented a revolutionary intellectual advance. It moved beyond the production of individual scrolls with limited horizons of temporal concern. The literary event we call the Deuteronomistic History organized such sources into a narrative history covering hundreds of

[24] Secondary literature on the Deuteronomistic History is enormous, but a sampling of recent research can be found in a collection of essays, M. Leuchter and K.-P. Adam (eds), *Soundings in Kings: Perspectives and Methods in Contemporary Scholarship* (Minneapolis: Fortress, 2010). As but one overview, note also the article of R. Coggins, "What Does 'Deuteronomistic' Mean?," in L. S. Schearing and S. L. McKenzie (eds), *Those Elusive Deuteronomists: The Phenomenon of Pan-Deuteronomism* (JSOTSup 268; Sheffield: Sheffield Academic Press, 1999), 22–35. For varying assessments of the history of scholarship and useful bibliographies with North American and European perspectives, see K. L. Noll, "Deuteronomistic History or Deuteronomic Debate? (A Thought Experiment)," *JSOT* 31/3 (2007), 311–45, and B. Halpern and A. Lemaire, "The Composition of Kings," in B. Halpern, A. Lemaire, and M. J. Adams (eds), *The Books of Kings: Sources, Composition, Historiography and Reception* (VTSup 129; Leiden: Brill, 2010), 123–53.

years of Israel's existence in the land. It presented that long stretch of time as comprising distinct eras, as measurable in a coordinated chronology, and as elucidated in terms of obedience to or violation of principles contained in an authoritative law book.[25]

The idea of a revolutionary narrative that provides an exciting literary experience is a deeply suggestive notion, and I would like to utilize and build on Nelson's comments. Assuming that the Deuteronomistic History has a high degree of literary sophistication—often an underrated feature within the debate among the eminent scholars mentioned in the previous paragraph—I would submit that there is ample scope for reading the Elisha narratives as an important component of this epic narrative. Indeed, many of the points of my analysis are informed by such questions: how is Elisha used as an agent of critique and dismantling of the northern house of Omri? How can other researchers use the analysis undertaken in this study to further our understanding of the provenance and literary workings of the Deuteronomistic History? Why is the spotlight so often fixed on Elisha, more so than any other prophetic figure in Kings in terms of scope and diversity? What is it about the personality of Elisha that elicits such conflicting reactions among some quite different but very assiduous scholars? My own method of narrative criticism and literary analysis will explore the legion of ironies and ambiguities in the text, and inquire as to their function in the developing storyline. Because I am interested in reading the Elisha material as a great work of art embedded in the larger narrative continuum of the Deuteronomistic History, I will endeavor to read sequentially as

---

[25] R. D. Nelson, "A Response to Thomas Römer, *The So-Called Deuteronomistic History*," in R. F. Person, Jr (ed.), "In Conversation with Thomas Römer, *The So-Called Deuteronomistic History: A Sociological, Historical and Literary Introduction* (London: T. & T. Clark, 2005)," *JHS* 9 (2009), article 17. In the same compilation, note also the comments of S. L. McKenzie (originally delivered in a Society of Biblical Literature session) in terms of some agreement among scholars: "We agree, first of all, that there was a Deuteronomistic History, a single running history of Israel encompassing the books of Deuteronomy—Kings. We agree that this work took its essential form in the Babylonian exile, but that its writer(s) made use of earlier sources in shaping their history at that time and that the figure of Josiah and materials from his reign were significant in that process. We agree further that there were extensive additions of a diverse nature added to the Babylonian history in the later exilic, Persian, and even Hellenistic periods. There are other points of agreement, but these are enough to show that we concur on the basic contours of the Deuteronomistic History. As we continue to discuss our differences of opinion, perhaps we do well to keep in mind the large measure to which we agree."

much as possible. Hopefully this strategy will result in a more user-friendly format, and facilitate an appreciation for the lineaments of the story in all its unfolding complexity.

CINEMATIC PREVIEW

So far I have briefly sketched some of the recent scholarship, the application of literary criticism, and the perspective of the Deuteronomistic History to the study of the Elisha material in 1 and 2 Kings. In what remains of this prologue I will present some of the key highlights and areas of analysis in the forthcoming chapters. Owing to the significance of Elijah and his shadow that is cast over many parts of the book of Kings, Chapter 1 ("The Apprentice") devotes several sections to the world of Elijah before getting to the opening material that introduces Elisha as the successor. The chapter begins with a reference to 1 Kings 16:34, a notice about Hiel of Bethel and his grievous attempts to rebuild Jericho. It is argued that Hiel's efforts—mentioned immediately after Ahab's introduction and a summary of his royal building initiatives—serve to foreground some of the prophetic activity of Elijah (and later Elisha). Elijah's early public ministry in 1 Kings 17 also is reviewed, including the first confrontation with Ahab and his announcement that rain will be withheld from the land. Elijah performs a pair of miracles in a foreign country, and, since these miracles will later be reproduced by Elisha, they are introduced in this section of Chapter 1. The rest of the chapter focuses on the appointment of Elisha and his formal entrance onto the narrative stage in 1 Kings 19:19–21. Included here is a discussion of Elisha's family, his relative affluence, and the rather cryptic opening dialogue with Elijah. The concluding section of this opening chapter also discusses the dramatic actions of Elisha, as he initially runs after Elijah, but then returns to burn his agricultural equipment and sacrifice his oxen for a communal feast. Since this kind of action may serve to foreshadow several aspects of Elisha's prophetic career, the chapter closes with some reflections on Elisha's inaugural appearance in the story.

A major portion of Chapter 2 ("Incendiary Successions") is devoted to events surrounding the passing of the prophetic torch to Elisha in 2 Kings 2. In this chapter we will interpret various facets of the transition between these two prophets, starting with the lengthy build-up that occurs mainly through travel and dialogue between the main characters, their first scene together since Elisha's investiture back in 1 Kings 19. Other issues to explore include the various places visited, especially the spatial setting of the Jordan River. At several points in 2 Kings 2 there is an appearance by a syndicate labeled "the sons of the prophets," and we will examine the identity of this group and ascertain what this collective might represent in the larger narrative. Most famously in this chapter—apart from the chariot of fire that carries up Elijah—is Elisha's bold request for a double portion of his master's spirit (פִּי שְׁנַיִם בְּרוּחֲךָ), and we will trace both how this request has been understood in the reception history of the passage and the most plausible option for this study. The chapter concludes with further discussion of Jericho's evil waters and the prophet's curse in Bethel (with the cameo appearance of those dreadful she-bears) that have been briefly introduced above.

Chapter 3 ("Music and Maternity") mainly addresses two substantial episodes: the expedition to Moab in 2 Kings 3, and the Shunammite woman's vicissitudes of fortune in 2 Kings 4. First, the joint campaign of Israel and Judah against King Mesha of Moab features Elisha the prophet as a central supporting actor. In this section of the chapter we will discuss some similarities between the invasion of Moab here and the earlier confrontation with the Arameans over Ramoth-Gilead in 1 Kings 22, noting that Jehoshaphat of Judah is involved in both skirmishes. Other issues to note involve the role of music in Elisha's prophetic activity, as well as the chilling moment of child sacrifice that abruptly ends the war. Since Elisha has been accused by some scholars of *false prophecy* in this episode, his words will be vigilantly assessed. Second, Elisha's experiences in the Israelite town of Shunem are analyzed here, including a woman's movement to motherhood in an account that resembles a type-scene of the barren wife well known from other biblical passages (e.g., Sarah and Rebekah in Genesis, Manoah's wife in Judges 13, and Hannah in 1 Samuel 1). We will also survey the role of Gehazi, Elisha's servant who makes the first of several appearances here in 2 Kings 4. Moreover, the Shunammite woman gives birth to a son, whose journey from life to death causes a crisis in the story. Mesha's son might be sacrificed in the previous chapter, but the Shunammite's son has a rather different experience. Finally, it should be noted that, sandwiched between these two larger episodes, is a short scene in 2 Kings

4:1–7 that is discussed in the middle section of this chapter. Here an anguished widow becomes the recipient of a remarkable intervention by the prophet, and we will suggest several possible ways that this scene contributes to the larger narrative.

The longest section of Chapter 4 ("Axes and Allies") is the episode of Naaman's healing in 2 Kings 5, bracketed by three short scenes highlighting the prophet's largesse. The first two short scenes both involve food, but with varying ingredients: death in the pot is followed by multiplied loaves that feed one hundred mouths. We will both canvass how these two scenes have been handled by recent interpreters, and further assay their function in the structural design of this stretch of text. After these culinary scenes there is a seismic shift to the Aramean general Naaman, a figure who no doubt has inflicted serious losses on Israel. It is this formidable character who plays a huge part in 2 Kings 5, yet the potential for something unusual to happen is signaled as early as the opening verse, where we read: "through him the LORD gave salvation (תשועה) to Aram." When the narrator reveals that Naaman suffers from leprosy, it may be supposed that Israel will be granted respite from Naaman's incursions. As it turns out, Naaman *does* visit Israel, but in search of healing rather than with hostile intent. In the course of our analysis we will concentrate particularly on three areas: Naaman's various responses and reactions, some interesting minor characters (two kings of different nations, and two Israelite servants of different genders), and the words of Elisha (as they heal a foreigner of leprosy but then shockingly afflict an Israelite with the same disease). The final section of this chapter turns to 2 Kings 6:1–8, where the sons of the prophets again surface, this time with the need to build a more spacious residence. With the prophet's help enlisted, the crisis of the scene revolves around a lost axe-head, a loss that causes a voluble complaint from the user, as it was a borrowed iron implement. As with Naaman's healing, there is a stunning reversal in the scene, causing the reader to wonder if there are further links with the previous episode in terms of verbal echoes or thematic points of continuity. It also seems that the Jordan River emerges as another example of symbolic geography in this text, and our analysis further probes this undercurrent in the story.

To this point Elisha has been a challenging character to interpret. On the one hand, he works miracles and has inside information that can only come from a supernatural source (for example, he knows about Gehazi's whereabouts in 2 Kings 5:26). But, on the other hand, he confesses that God's intentions are hidden from him in 2 Kings 4:27 (ויהוה העלים ממני ולא הגיד לי, "But the LORD has concealed from me, and has not told me"). In Chapter 5 ("Counter Intelligence") the level of complication is further enhanced through a set of episodes that, for the most part, take place in and around the northern capital of Samaria. The first episode (6:8–23) begins with the king of Aram upbraiding his senior officers, as he suspects a traitor in the midst. Informed that Elisha the prophet is somehow privy even to the king's most confidential speech, he sends a threatening host to apprehend the suspect. By means of an amazing turn of events, Elisha is the one who arrests the temporarily sightless Aramean soldiers, leading them into Samaria, where he orders that a banquet be prepared for the enemies of Israel. In this story about blindness we will analyze the insights that emerge from the prophetic alternative offered here. The second episode in this section (6:24–7:2) moves from feast to famine, as Ben-Hadad mobilizes the Aramean army and lays siege to Samaria. In a time of scarcity and desperation, the king of Israel's wrath is kindled by two cannibal mothers, and he puts the blame squarely on Elisha. Unmoved by the king's death threat, the scene comes to an end with a bold declaration from the prophet that food will be aplenty within twenty-four hours. Although Elisha is formally absent from the rest of 2 Kings 7, his prophetic word directs the action presented in the third episode studied in this chapter. There are four characters who are unlikely catalysts for a powerful reversal in this tableau, and their bumbling actions are instrumental for the fulfillment of Elisha's bold declaration in the previous section. These four characters— lepers stranded at the city gate with scant hope of survival—counter- intuitively become the means of survival for the entire city, and thus they are important for the indirect characterization of Elisha in this part of the narrative. Indeed, there is an intentionally framed repe- tition of Elisha's earlier words as 2 Kings 7 draws to a close, providing opportunity to assess the prophet's contribution to this stage of the Deuteronomistic History.

Chapter 6 ("Throne Calls") navigates some difficult narrative waters, and the reader is confronted with a number of issues that are salient for Elisha's characterization and indicate a slightly new political dynamic at work. The first episode (8:1–6) analyzed in this chapter likewise has Elisha offstage, yet he is very much the topic of conversation among the actors in this scene. Making a return to the narrative is the Shunammite woman who still has her revived son, but now has lost her land. Her advocate before the king is none other than Gehazi, he who defrauded Naaman, lied to Elisha, and is last seen at the end of 2 Kings 5 afflicted with leprosy. How can Gehazi approach the king's presence if he is leprous? This section of the chapter will assess the roles of these recycled characters and comment on their contribution to a number of thematic threads in the narrative.

When Gehazi speaks about the prophet in 2 Kings 8:4–5, it sounds as though he is evoking the memory of a departed character. However, Elisha will still be with us for a considerable time, and his final appearances in the story take on a kind of multinational urgency. Three other textual sites are visited in the rest of Chapter 6, beginning with 2 Kings 8:7–15, where Elisha ventures to Damascus. Ben-Hadad is ill, and once more Elisha is offered immense riches by a foreigner; had he accepted every gift offered during his career, Elisha would have been the wealthiest prophet in charismatic history. But the king's illness precipitates a most fateful conversation between Elisha and Hazael, and this dialogue—replete with misdirection, an awkward silence, and even a text-critical controversy—gives rise to regicide, and thus forms a crucial part of our analysis. The second textual sequence to be considered (2 Kings 9:1–3, and following) is the multifaceted affair of Jehu's anointing. The name "Jehu" has not been heard for a very long time, though his rise was forecast as far back as 1 Kings 19:16. It may have been assumed that Elijah would anoint Jehu, but that task evidently has been delegated to Elisha, who in turn instructs an unnamed son of the prophets to carry out the job. There is a notable discrepancy, however, between Elisha's instructions and what the anonymous young man actually says to Jehu. The analysis in this section of the chapter will assess whether such positions can be reconciled, and evaluate if there are any implications here for Elisha's characterization that emerge. The third episode (2 Kings 13:14–20a) does not take place until long after Jehu's purge and Athaliah's reign of terror, when Elisha is rather abruptly reintroduced in a deathly ill state. His interaction with the northern king Jehoash forms the substance of our analysis in this section, as both the king's visit and a prophetic sign with arrows contain several intriguing issues. Just as abrupt is the death notice of Elisha, and it would appear that his narrative tenure has come to an end.

Even though life has finally departed from Elisha and he has, by every estimation, exited the narrative stage, there remains a final scene in which he has a starring role (or at least what remains of him). In a short postscript ("Double Take") we will first explore the larger-than-life moment in 2 Kings 13:20–1 where Elisha's bones have the unique capacity to reanimate a corpse. This vignette provides a convenient segue to the conclusion of this book, where four areas are revisited briefly. First, there is a summary of some major literary techniques that are used in the narrative. This summary is followed, second, by a review of supporting cast members that are so vital to narrative, even though they are easily overlooked. Third, after a review of a few minor characters, there is a reiteration of the surrounding context of the Elisha story embedded in the larger narrative of the house of Omri. Fourth, there are some concluding thoughts on Elisha's characterization as his story is complete. Although this book ends with a closing consideration of these areas, it would be wise to keep them in mind as we commence our journey.

1

The Apprentice

The Elisha material occupies a prominent position between the division of the kingdom in 1 Kings 12 and the eventual demolition of Samaria recorded in 2 Kings 17. Owing to the political upheaval and ideological conflicts of this era, if one is going to embark on a careful reading of Elisha's career, then several components of background data need to be considered. Most important among these elements are some early events involving Elisha's prophetic predecessor Elijah. This chapter has three main sections, starting with a short discussion of 1 Kings 16:34. Hiel of Bethel is the subject of this verse, an often neglected but, I will submit, a vital sentence in this sector of the Deuteronomistic History. The attempt to rebuild Jericho in several respects lays out the prophetic challenge—to vitiate the royal program of the Omrides—and is placed immediately before Elijah's introduction to the narrative. The second section of this chapter assesses Elijah's beginnings as a prophet in Israel. Matters including Elijah's provenance, the confrontation with Ahab, his journey to Sidonian territory, and a pair of miraculous moments in 1 Kings 17 are featured as part of our analysis here. Since it is possible that Elisha will later "double" Elijah's miracles—or at least enhance and complicate them—some of the branches of 1 Kings 17 will need to be kept in mind as we proceed. The third section of this chapter then turns to the formal introduction of Elisha in the narrative. In the context of Elijah's flight to Horeb and mountaintop experience, Elisha is first mentioned within a divine speech that negates Elijah's resignation speech(es) and instead directs his journey to the village of Abel-meholah to anoint his prophetic successor. In 1 Kings 19:19–21 the reader is privy to Elisha's first actions and words in the story. There is a good deal happening in this scene that features Elisha's family dynamic and his initial dialogue with his mentor, and we will suggest that several aspects of his future career are foreshadowed at this stage in his presentation.

HIEL OF BETHEL

Moments before Elijah officially bursts into the narrative, there is a short unit seemingly appended to Ahab's introduction that easily can be missed. After the details about Ahab's construction of a Baal temple in Samaria and the marriage alliance with the Sidonian princess Jezebel, in 1 Kings 16:34 the reader is informed of a disastrous undertaking: "In his days Hiel of Bethel built Jericho: at the cost of Abiram his firstborn he established the foundation, and at the cost of Segub his youngest he built up the gates, according to the word of the LORD that he spoke by the hand of Joshua son of Nun." Recalling Joshua's oath uttered after the collapse of Jericho's walls, that ancient curse now finds its grim fulfillment many centuries later.[1] This sentence about Hiel's labor, it should be noted, is often dismissed by commentators as a redactional gloss or a later editorial insertion. At first blush those scholars have a point, as this notice about Hiel may seem ancillary and does not necessarily advance the action in any quantitative way; if Hiel's biography was deleted, there may be no great loss.

But, on the contrary, I would view the anecdote about Hiel of Bethel as an essential component of the introduction to the prophetic characters Elijah and Elisha, with Elijah poised to enter the storyline in the very next sentence of the narrative. In the first instance, Charles Conroy has observed a verbal link between Ahab—the formative aspects of his reign just subject to a lengthy précis in 16:29–33— and Hiel, in that both are involved in "building" (בנה).[2] The fact that

---

[1] Cf. the NRSV translation of Josh. 6:26: "Joshua then pronounced this oath, saying, 'Cursed before the LORD be anyone who tries to build this city—this Jericho! At the cost of his firstborn [בבכרו] he shall lay its foundation, and at the cost of his youngest [ובצעירו] he shall set up its gates!'" On the similar use of the preposition *beth* in 1 Kings 2:23 and 2 Sam. 23:17, see M. Cogan, *I Kings: A New Translation with Introduction and Commentary* (AB 10; New York: Doubleday, 2001), 177.

[2] C. Conroy, "Hiel between Ahab and Elijah–Elisha: 1 Kgs 16, 34 in its Immediate Literary Context," *Biblica*, 77 (1996), 212. For another assessment of "synchronically how well the verse has been crafted to link 16:29–33 on Ahab to the Elijah material beginning in 1 Kings 17," see A. G. Auld, "The Deuteronomists and the Former Prophets, or What Makes the Former Prophets Deuteronomistic?" in L. S. Schearing and S. L. McKenzie (eds), *Those Elusive Deuteronomists: The Phenomenon of Pan-Deuteronomism* (JSOTSup 268; Sheffield: Sheffield Academic Press, 1999), 116–26, at 126.

Hiel's engineering takes place *in Ahab's days* (בימיו) implies that Ahab has some direct involvement or sponsorship of Hiel's project.[3] Thus Ahab's idolatrous construction is thematically equivalent to Hiel's attempt to rebuild Jericho, and this is why several recent critics tend to connect the rebuilding of Jericho with a symbolic reversal of the conquest.[4] On this level, the report about Hiel serves to reveal a significant mandate of Elijah and Elisha, as they will be involved in counteracting multifarious building projects of the house of Omri: what these kings build, the prophetic word will deconstruct and supplant. Consequently, the places mentioned in 16:34, Bethel and Jericho, are not incidental. Ahab walks in the sins of Jeroboam, the center of whose deviant cult is Bethel. By extension, there is a concerted attempt to extend the ideological influence of Bethel to Jericho. These cities will be prominent stopping-places and centers of activity in the prophetic itinerary, so when Bethel and Jericho are foregrounded here—as the last word before the prophetic entrance—the reader is alerted to key sites in the movement of both Elijah and Elisha. When Hiel of Bethel loses his sons, we note that these deaths are not the only bereavement attached to Jericho; it is entirely possible that Hiel's sons anticipate the death of the forty-two lads of Bethel, right after Elisha heals the evil waters of Jericho and (partially) counteracts the curse of Joshua.

AHAB'S RAIN

Directly following the report of Hiel's costly endeavor, Elijah is formally introduced. The first word of the Hebrew text in 1 Kings 17:1 is a verbal construction: "and he said" (ויאמר). The spoken word of the prophet is a central element of this section, as the reader shifts from the ancient speech of Joshua to the (now) contemporary word of

---

[3] See G. Hens-Piazza, *1–2 Kings* (Nashville: Abingdon, 2006), 159: "Evidently the storyteller wants to create the impression that Jericho's reconstruction was attempted under the auspices of Ahab."

[4] e.g., P. J. Leithart, *1 & 2 Kings* (Brazos Theological Commentary on the Bible; Grand Rapids: Brazos, 2006), 120; M. A. Sweeney, "On the Literary Function of the Notice concerning Hiel's Reestablishment of Jericho in 1 Kings 16.34," in M. A. O'Brien and H. N. Wallace (eds), *Seeing Signals, Reading Signs: The Art of Exegesis.* (JSOTSup 415; Sheffield: Sheffield Academic Press, 2004), 104–15.

Elijah. Furthermore, in the opening verse of chapter 17 Elijah's provenance has raised questions among commentators, especially whether his designation should be construed as "the Tishbite from Tishbe of Gilead" (התשבי מתשבי גלעד), or "from the settlers/inhabitants of Gilead." Regardless of how one may decide to translate the difficult Hebrew, what is emphasized here, in my view, is Elijah's roots on the east of the Jordan, and thus outside the corridors of power normally connected with the house of Omri. Even if, as some commentators have suggested, a particular social category is being referred to, Elijah would still be understood as a figure removed from a more elite class. To further an insight of Hugh Pyper, Elijah's origins may foreshadow that time will be spent beyond the usual borders of Israel, as he is a figure who often breaks the boundaries of space (and time).[5]

More certain is the meaning of Elijah's name, "YHWH is my God," highlighting the struggle to come. The ideological conflict was set in motion with Ahab's building projects and foreign marriage, and is now encapsulated in Elijah's words to the king: "As the LORD lives, the God of Israel, before whom I stand, there will be neither dew nor rain these years, except by my word." One is unsure how Elijah enters Ahab's presence to deliver this word, but, like the oath of Joshua noted above, there is a tension between the prophetic utterance and the king's ambition. Because of Ahab's insistence on Baal worship, the issue of rain becomes the watershed issue of Elijah's declaration. As Marvin Sweeney explains:

> The citation of Elijah's statement concerning YHWH's vow signals the major concerns of both the immediate context and the Elijah/Elisha cycle at large—that is, opposition to the influence of Baal, the Canaanite/Phoenician god of rain, storm, and fertility, and the house of Omri, which was allied with the Phoenicians by Ahab's marriage to Jezebel. The emphasis on YHWH's withholding of rain indicates the general intent to target Baal, the deity who brought rain to the land in order to ensure its fertility and productivity.[6]

---

[5] H. S. Pyper, "The Secret of Succession: Elijah, Elisha, Jesus, and Derrida," in A. K. M. Adam (ed.), *Postmodern Interpretations of the Bible: A Reader* (St Louis: Chalice, 2001), 60–1.

[6] Sweeney, *I & II Kings*, 208–9. For a detailed study of related theological issues, see A. J. Hauser, "Yahweh versus Death: The Real Struggle in Kings 17–19," in R. Gregory and A. J. Hauser, *From Carmel to Horeb: Elijah in Crisis* (JSOTSup 85; Sheffield: Almond Press, 1990), 11–89.

No response from Ahab is recorded in the narrative, but there must be a degree of danger implied as the divine word of the LORD instructs Elijah to go east and "hide himself." Specifically, the prophet is to hide in the Wadi Cherith (נחל כרית), a site that Jerome Walsh translates as "Cut Off Creek."[7] Indeed, several of the key terms and ideas in 1 Kings 17:3–4 are also used in 1 Kings 18. For instance, in 18:4 the reader is told that Jezebel was cutting off (כרת) the prophets, while Obadiah hid 100 in a cave and sustained them (כול) with food and water. Similarly, God commands the ravens to sustain (כול) Elijah, and thus through the hiding and the miraculous supply of food from the ravens Elijah is able to avoid being cut off like many of his colleagues (assuming the simultaneity of these events). Because Elijah is protected from the drought, Walter Brueggemann suggests that Ahab's role as king might be marginalized:

In that ancient world royal responsibility for rain is not unlike contemporary presidential responsibility for the economy. The measure of an effective king is rain that produces crops. In this simple assertion the capacity to administer rain and therefore life is taken from the king. The king is made a political irrelevance, void of any critical function for society.[8]

Reminiscent of Israel after the exodus from Egypt, Elijah is divinely nourished in the wilderness courtesy of some unlikely providers, the ravens. Choon Leong Seow comments that, in the Torah, ravens are listed as unclean birds, citing Leviticus 11:15 and Deuteronomy 14:14.[9] So, on the one hand, Elijah eats remarkably well because of these birds not normally associated with such gracious hospitality. To see the ravens act in this manner is a creative expression of divine providence, further trumping Ahab's royal agenda to sponsor fertility rites. It also presages the contest with Baal, stressing God's unwavering sovereignty in times of weal or woe. On the other hand, the unclean status of the ravens perforates yet another boundary, as Elijah's engagement with these creatures indicates that God is willing

---

[7] J. T. Walsh, *1 Kings* (Berit Olam; Collegeville, MN: Liturgical Press, 1996), 228.

[8] W. Brueggemann, *1 & 2 Kings* (Macon: Smyth & Helwys, 2000), 209. On the lack of social equity and the Omrides' tilting of public policy in favor of the power elite, see H. Schulte, "The End of the Omride Dynasty: Social–Ethical Observations on the Subject of Power and Violence" (trans. C. S. Ehrlich), *Semeia*, 66 (1994), 146.

[9] C. L. Seow, "1 & 2 Kings," in *The New Interpreter's Bible*, iii (Nashville: Abingdon, 1999), 127.

to work outside the normal channels of ritual purity. This in turn anticipates Elijah's relocation to non-Israelite territory in the rest of 1 Kings 17.

OIL FUTURES

As the waters of Wadi Cherith dry up, Elijah is ordered to evacuate. Given his liminal status, it may not be surprising that the foreign village of Zarephath in Sidon is the destination, but this specific locale is not without irony. Elijah is first commanded to hide himself at Cut Off Creek, presumably to avoid the clutches of Ahab and Jezebel; now he is commanded to go to Sidonian country to hide from the royal couple, where he will *not* be found by them even in Jezebel's home territory. Indeed, during Elijah's Sidonian sojourn, the reader later finds out, Ahab was conducting a thorough search for him. According to Obadiah's testimony in 1 Kings 18:10, Ahab was relentless in his pursuit: "As the LORD your God lives, there is no nation or kingdom where my lord has not sent to seek you—and if they would say, 'He is not here,' he would make that kingdom or nation swear an oath that they had not found you." By going underground in Zarephath Elijah continues to frustrate the designs of the house of Omri, a practice that will be continued by his apprentice in due course.

Elijah's initial encounter with the widow of Zarephath in 1 Kings 17:10–16 is notable for a number of reasons, not least because these experiences are later duplicated by Elisha. But in this episode the widow is an outsider on the low end of the socio-economic ladder, gathering sticks in preparation for a last supper. In all likelihood her raiment indicates her status as a widow, thus allowing Elijah to recognize her. If so, it introduces the reader to the motif of clothing that is frequently deployed in this stretch of text. Also, the widow has something in common with the ravens: both are foraging for Elijah, although at this point she is unaware of that dimension. Despite the incredulity of the widow, the man of God's spacious utterance about the jar of flour and the cruse of oil is a striking declaration of God's power even in Baal's backyard. Still, according to Gina Hens-Piazza, "the real miracle is not only the endless supply of flour and oil. That this lowly woman finds the courage to give up her status as a victim, makes a decision to believe, and acts in the interest of life is truly extraordinary."[10] To further this observation, the widow becomes a foil for Ahab, the king who opts for a domestic policy driven by fertility rites rather than directed by the prophetic word of Elijah. The Sidonian widow, an outsider, is the beneficiary of prophetic largesse in a time of severe famine. Royal agendas and policies are subverted, therefore, through submission to the prophetic alternative, and there are hints in this episode of how the house of Omri will be countered, and how Elisha later will be involved. As I will finally argue, dismantling the Omrides will require the attention of more than one prophet, and more than one kind of prophetic personality.

Meanwhile, a single mother's crisis then precipitates a serious complaint against the prophet in the next episode of the chapter (1 Kings 17:17–24). When her son is inflicted with a serious illness whereby he stops breathing, the mother evidently forgets that she and her son would already have been dead, if not for the prophet's intervention with the oil reserves. As there is no indication to the contrary, one assumes that the famine is still on, and the household is miraculously sustained. Yet the son's grave sickness causes the mother to disregard the prophet's cruse control, even to the point that she accuses Elijah of dissembling: he has come, so she now arraigns, for death and judgment and to expose her "guilt." This kind of deprecation needs to be kept in mind, as Elisha will be similarly accused on numerous occasions. Moreover, the spatial setting of the roof chamber (עליה) may not be particularly significant in and of itself, but, since it will occur on two more occasions (2 Kings 1:2 and 2 Kings 4:10, as mentioned in the Prologue to this book), we will be invited to compare the events that take place in this same genre of spatial setting, and comment on the developing pattern.

Finally, the mother's confession—prompted by the healing of her son from the unspecified malady and Elijah's presentation of the living boy—is remarkable for her use of the term "man of God." As Robert Cohn notes, she uses this term in both verses 18 and 24, yet with a rather different utility: "At the outset she calls Elijah 'man of God' derisively; she recognizes him only as a powerful presence who has caused her son's death. At the end, however, she transforms the designation 'man of God' into a term of praise by acknowledging

---

[10] Hens-Piazza, *1–2 Kings*, 167.

Yahweh's truth in Elijah's 'mouth.'"[11] Since Elisha too will be called "man of God" many times in the forthcoming narrative, elements within this scene serve to anticipate his role in the story. As with the bereavement of Hiel of Bethel in Jericho, this episode also serves obliquely to anticipate the movements of Elijah's successor, who likewise revives a son in an upper room (with anonymous characters involved). Once Elisha is called to inherit his master's mantle, there will be more oil in the narrative future, and so the initial movement toward inheritance should now be explored.

TWIN PEAKS

In the short review of 1 Kings 17 above, we have an introduction to Elijah, whose apprentice eventually will re-enact the miracles of his mentor. The apprentice, of course, is Elisha, and we now turn to the context of his first mention in the narrative. In the aftermath of the pyrotechnic victory over the prophets of Baal on Mount Carmel, Elijah issues a warning to Ahab in the final scene of chapter 18, one that has a touch of ridicule: the king is warned to depart hastily, lest the long-awaited rains cause his chariot wheels to get stuck in the mud. Given Elijah's words, his action in 1 Kings 19:3 is unexpected. Ostensibly because of Jezebel's polytheistic threat ("So may the gods do to me, and so may they add, if I do not make your life like the life of one of them"), Elijah flees south in an agitated state. When reaching the southern town of Beersheba, Elijah "leaves his servant lad there" (וינח את־נערו שם). Those few scholars who comment on this clause view it in different ways. Mordecai Cogan writes: "Elijah was accompanied by a personal servant, as befitted a man of stature. But what was to follow was a private matter, between Elijah and his God; so he went on alone, as did Abraham and Isaac in Gen 22:5."[12] Simon DeVries takes a more metaphorical stance: "The prophet's dismissal of his servant at Beersheba, the southernmost limit of Yahweh's land, signifies that he is abandoning it altogether."[13] Utilizing both of these comments, one could add that, in the context of Elisha's introduction,

---

[11] R. L. Cohn, "The Literary Logic of 1 Kings 17–19," *JBL* 101 (1982), 336.
[12] Cogan, *I Kings*, 451.
[13] S. J. DeVries, *1 Kings* (WBC 12; Waco, TX: Word, 1985), 235.

it will be a rather different kind of subordinate who will usher Elijah back into the maelstrom of political life in the land, and beyond.

Once again sustained by divine provision, Elijah ventures deep into the wilderness of Israel's history in 1 Kings 19:4–12. Arriving at Mount Horeb—an alternate name for Sinai, the mountain of revelation—Elijah continues to complain about the destroyed altars and broken covenant at the very place where the covenant was first ratified. Elijah's death wish has been variously interpreted, but Jerome Walsh's comment is worth noting: "The narrator's psychological insight is powerful. If this were a literal request, that is, if Elijah truly wished to die, then he would have had no reason to flee from Jezebel! Elijah's words reveal something much deeper about him: his sense of hopelessness, of disillusion and despair, of the futility of any further effort."[14] Further, the reader is not quite sure how to view Elijah's grievance that he is "the only one left," especially with regards to Obadiah's work of hiding 100 prophets in caves, but God now proposes to "pass by" the prophet in the cave at Horeb. As with Moses, there are dramatic signs and a thunderous display, yet Elijah is privy to a "sound of sheer silence" (קול דממה דקה).[15] Whether or not there is variation of the type-scene of the call of the prophet here, this episode is the closest Elijah gets to a formal divine commission, especially with respect to the specific task-list he receives in the dialogue of verses 13–18:

When Elijah heard it, he wrapped his face in his mantle, and went out. He stood at the opening of the cave, and behold, a voice! He said, "What are you here for Elijah?" He said, "I have been very jealous for the Lord God of hosts, for the Israelites have abandoned your covenant, your altars they have torn down, and your prophets they have killed with the sword. I remain, I alone, and they are seeking my life, to take it." The LORD said to him, "Go, return to your journey, towards the wilderness of Damascus, and when you arrive you will anoint Hazael to be king over Aram. Jehu son of Nimshi you will anoint to be king over Israel, and Elisha son of Shaphat from Abel Meholah you will anoint to be a prophet in place of you. The one who escapes from the sword of Hazael will be put to death by Jehu, and the one who escapes from the sword of Jehu will be put to death by Elisha. I have kept in Israel seven

---

[14] Walsh, *1 Kings*, 267.
[15] See G. W. Savran, *Encountering the Divine: Theophany in Biblical Narrative* (JSOTSup 420; London: T & T Clark, 2005), 218–20.

thousand, all the knees that have not bowed to Baal, and every mouth that has not kissed him.

The first time Elisha is mentioned in the text, as numerous commentators have observed, is through the divine voice on the mountain of revelation. But Elisha is not referred to in isolation. Rather, he is one member of a group that forms a prophetic task-list, and he is designated as one of three individuals to be anointed by Elijah. The verb "anoint" (משׁח) has prompted different reactions among scholars: some are interested in the statistical anomaly (after all, no other prophet is anointed like this), while others are deeply concerned that Elijah will not actually carry out any anointing ceremony, but simply throw his mantle at Elisha. The schematics of anointing are last seen in 1 Kings 1:34 with Solomon, and this action forms an instructive parallel. The anointing of Solomon by Nathan the prophet and Zadok the priest at the Gihon spring is most significant because it nullifies the political activity of Adonijah, his principal competitor for David's throne in 1 Kings 1. In functional terms, Solomon's anointing works to override the interests of a rival. With Elisha, I am most interested in viewing his anointing within the group (two kings, one foreign and the other domestic), because this entire collective will be necessary for the work of supplanting a regime guilty of ideological coercion. Furthermore, when God says that Elisha is to be anointed as a prophet in place of Elijah (לנביא תחתיך) it is not the equivalent of some sort of corporate downsizing (where Elijah is made redundant). On the contrary, there is a new form of prophetic partnership being advocated here, whereby Elisha the apprentice will be continuing the work of his master (note the comparable use of "in your place" (תחתיך) in 1 Kings 5:19). In a strange way, Elijah's unusual order to anoint another prophet in his stead may anticipate his abrupt and unusual departure from the narrative in 2 Kings 2, a departure that will leave his successor to extend the work he has so memorably begun.

Despite what appear to be comparatively scant data, there are several details in 1 Kings 19:16 that are critical components of Elisha's characterization. By virtue of his mention alongside the two (future) kings, it is clear that Elijah's apprentice will be a prophetic catalyst for the demise of the Omride house. The two mountains—Carmel and Horeb—recently visited by Elijah will also represent parameters of Elisha's call: continue to overthrow Ahab's regime and rebuild the

covenant community. Inevitable, then, is Elisha's political involvement, as Walter Brueggemann summarizes: "The anointing of the
two kings is a maneuver whereby political coups are instigated. Of
these imperatives, the only one we know about is the anointing of
Jehu (accomplished by Elisha and not by Elijah) that brought a
bloody end to the dynasty of Omri and Ahab (2 Kgs 9:1–13). It is
not necessary," says Brueggemann, "to attribute any 'magical' significance to an anointing, but only to see it as a powerful symbolic
gesture that evokes a radical political vision and a due sense of
'sacramental' legitimation for the coup."[16] By extension, Elisha is
now drafted into a vocation with a broadened mandate, and, because
he is introduced along with the two other figures, there is an
enhanced political dimension being stressed as part of the prophetic
struggle. It could be that the meaning of Elisha's name—God saves, or
God is salvation—points to this more expansive mandate that is
signaled in the divine speech to Elijah. At the personal level the reader
is also given the name of Elisha's father and his hometown, and this
information is valuable for several reasons. In marked contrast to
Elijah, whose father is unknown, Elisha the son of Shaphat's patrilin-
eal descent is frontloaded. In John Gray's judgment, the father's
name, Shaphat, "is doubtless a hypocoristicon of Shaphaṭyahu, and
indicates the rule, or decision of Yahweh."[17] Quite plausibly, the
father's name is disclosed in order to emphasize a certain position
within the mainstream of Israelite life. Elisha, it is inferred, will be a
character with firm roots in the land, suggesting a different focus than
Elijah. In reference back to 1 Kings 17:1, Elijah is presented as a figure
located outside the corridors of the establishment, from beyond the
Jordan. With Elisha's paternity, there is not simply a personality
contrast; what is subtly underscored here is the different capacity
for which each prophet is deployed. Intimately connected is the
mention of Abel Meholah, most likely located on the west side of
the Jordan; again, the opposite of Elijah's introduction. Still, Abel
Meholah is not quite so easy to identify, and estimates vary as to its
precise location. Based on texts such as Judges 7:22 and 1 Kings 4:12
(when Solomon re-zones the traditional tribal schematics in favor of
new tax districts), the most probable area is West Manasseh in the

---

[16] Brueggemann, *1 & 2 Kings*, 237–8.
[17] Gray, *I & II Kings*, 412.

Jordan Valley.[18] The account in Judges 7 is most helpful here, the report of when the Midianites flee from Gideon as far as the border of Abel Meholah. Since Gideon next issues a rallying cry that results in the capture of the waters of the Jordan, it stands to reason that Abel Meholah is a strategically located town that "controlled the fords over the Jordan that would allow access from the Transjordan to Jezreel."[19] Elisha's place of birth furnishes another example of symbolic geography in the storyline, akin to Hiel of Bethel's rebuilding of Jericho. Given Elisha's career trajectory, at the very least it is appropriate that he hails from a place in proximity to the waters of the Jordan River.

Within the divine speech of 1 Kings 19:15–18 where Elisha is first mentioned, certainly the most difficult aspect for the interpreter is the *kill* factor: "The one who escapes from the sword of Hazael will be put to death by Jehu, and the one who escapes from the sword of Jehu will be put to death by Elisha." How should these aggressive words be understood? Two binary categories are formed: those who are killed versus those who are not killed, and from this we can extrapolate that those who bow before Baal are differentiated from those who do not. The latter category is numbered at 7,000, and also is variously interpreted, but the figure is best understood as metaphorically referring to those citizens who have withstood the pressures to follow the ideological and political path blazed by Ahab and Jezebel. Examples already seen in the narrative are Obadiah and the widow of Sidon, representatives of two radically different socio-economic spheres: one a senior advisor to the king with enough capital to keep many prophets alive and safe, the other a destitute widow at death's door.

By any measure there is a violent side to Elisha's introduction, and one that will be at odds with his actual narrative presentation.[20] Why is the reader exposed to the verb *kill*, and why bring Elisha into the orbit of Hazael and Jehu? For Uriel Simon, there is a wider purpose:

> The three swords will be wielded by persons anointed by the Lord's mandate; they are clearly His emissaries, executing His will (just like Assyria, 'rod of

---

[18] See M. J. Mulder, *1 Kings* (HCOT; Leuven: Peeters, 1998), 177–9. Cf. D. V. Edelman, "Abel-Meholah," in David Noel Freedman (ed.), *The Anchor Bible Dictionary* (New York: Doubleday, 1992), i. 11–12.

[19] Sweeney, *I & II Kings*, 92.

[20] "Elisha himself," says Richard Nelson (*First and Second Kings* (Interpretation; Atlanta: John Knox Press, 1987), 127), "is only indirectly responsible for the anointing of Jehu and Hazael's murder of his predecessor. Again, although Jehu and Hazael do plenty of killing, Elisha does not literally 'slay' anybody."

my anger' [Isa. 10:5], and Nebuchadnezzar, 'My servant' [Jer. 25:9]). The narrator does not focus on the deeds of the three swordsmen but on the fate of the remnant that each will leave behind.[21]

Still, it should be noted that Elisha has the most challenging task of the three, as the ones he is supposed to kill are the most difficult and elusive targets, who would already have escaped from the kings Hazael and Jehu, and even more so when one considers the personalities of these future kings. If we glance ahead in the story, Hazael is a fearsome leader who does not shrink from regicide, and proceeds to rip open pregnant women. For his part, Jehu is a maniacal chariot-driver who deceptively lures Baal-worshippers to their deaths and turns the place into a latrine (after piling the heads of Ahab's descendants at the gate of Jezreel, that is). For Elisha to kill the escapees from *these two* would be quite a feat, to say the least. The immediate effect of this introduction—whereby Elisha is the third member of this daunting triumvirate—is that he is presented as a rather imposing figure even before the reader has officially met him, although that is poised to change in the next episode.

FROM SWORD TO PLOWSHARE

No verbal response of Elijah to the divine speech is recorded in the narrative. He does, however, "go" on his way, and so one assumes a measure of compliance with God's instructions. It may have been thought that the first destination on his travel itinerary would be the wilderness of Damascus, and upon arriving there to anoint Hazael as king over Aram as outlined in 19:15. But, instead of Damascus, Abel Meholah is apparently Elijah's destination, since there he finds his successor, Elisha son of Shaphat. It is difficult to know whether Elijah is deviating from his divine mandate, or merely acknowledging the importance of Elisha, who is to be anointed as prophet "in place of" him. Either way, the focus of the next line is squarely on Elisha, as the reader gets a glimpse of him for the first time, and an active picture it is: "Now he was plowing with twelve pairs of oxen, and he was on the

---

[21] U. Simon, *Reading Prophetic Narratives* (Bloomington: Indiana University Press, 1997), 216.

twelfth pair" (19:19). The kinetic movement associated with Elisha here in verse 19—again, the reader's initial sight of this intriguing character, destined to wield a fearsome sword—is meaningful on at least two levels.

First, almost every recent commentator agrees that the twelve yoke of oxen indicates that Elisha is part of a wealthy family. If one was expecting Elisha to have fairly close ties to the land, such expectations are exceeded. The point of such a detail, we suppose, would be that Elisha will have to forsake a relatively affluent lifestyle for all the perils and comparative uncertainty of the prophetic vocation. Given the recent warrants for Elijah's arrest issued by both Ahab and Jezebel, not to mention the inadequate emolument, the prophetic lifestyle would certainly be less comfortable than driving the twelfth pair of oxen. If Elisha is willing to decamp from this comparative prosperity and status, it would form a favorable impression on the reader. True as this is, there is slightly more than just individuation at work in the narrative here. Granting the assumption that numerous oxen and implements point to significant wealth, this scene also foreshadows the vicissitudes of wealth and poverty that will be seen at many points during Elisha's prophetic career. Ranging from the gifts of kings to borrowed tools, wealth and poverty follow Elisha from start to finish. His advantageous background seems to anticipate how he will have different interactions with royal figures and prosperous citizens. Again, this is not so much a personality contrast with Elijah (who is pictured with only a single possession, his mantle), but rather the different role that each prophet will play in Israelite society and the surrounding nations.

Second, the number *twelve* carries a certain currency in the narrative. As the large number of oxen signify considerable resources, so many commentators view the number twelve as having some sort of symbolic association with the twelve tribes of Israel. Despite a myriad of proposals that have been put forward, the most immediate correlation with Elisha's twelve yoke of oxen is 1 Kings 18:31–2. There Elijah uses twelve stones to heal the altar that had been torn down, presumably owing to years of apostasy resulting from Ahab's policies, augmented by the vacillations of the general population. In 18:31 the association between tribes and stones is explicit: "Elijah took twelve stones, according to the number of the tribes of the sons of Jacob, to whom the word of the LORD came, saying, 'Israel will be your name.'" With Elisha's twelve pairs the reader is not given the same explicit parameters, but rather invited to make a connection: just as Elijah's twelve stones are used to (re)build the altar of Israel's covenant relationship, so Elisha's work with the twenty-four oxen will double these efforts for the nation. An early indication is provided, then, that Elisha will be a *double agent* who continues the footsteps of his predecessor. Since these events transpire during the era of the divided kingdom, the numeric symbolism works to transcend the political fragmentation wrought by the schism of 1 Kings 12. Elisha's prophetic activity has implications for every tribe—just like Elijah—and for every descendant of Jacob in both north and south.

Having located the plowing Elisha at Abel Meholah, the prophet Elijah does not formally anoint his successor, as may have been expected. Instead, "Elijah passed over to him and threw his mantle toward him" (19:19). There have been a number of different scholarly reactions to Elijah's conduct here. One group of commentators view tossing the mantle as synonymous with anointing, arguing that the most important component of prophetic investiture is the conferring of authority (accomplished by means of the mantle transfer). For another group of commentators, the verb "to throw" is troubling, and they wonder if this is not an intemperate gesture on Elijah's part. It should be noted that several of the key words here resonate with the previous episode, especially the verb "pass by/over" (עבר). In 19:11 the same verb is used for God's presence *passing by* in the theophany, as a preface to the prophet's new commission—one that includes Elisha's investiture. For Jerome Walsh, the shared language allows the reader to "infer that Elisha's encounter with Elijah is parallel to Elijah's encounter with Yahweh, and is therefore more of a prophetic empowerment that Elijah either realizes or intends."[22] Wesley Bergen sees another kind of significance of the verb "pass over" in the larger narrative of succession: "The use of עבר anticipates 2 Kgs 2.11, 14, the crossing of the Jordan, a story that more clearly symbolizes the passing of authority from one prophet to another."[23] At the same time, when Elijah throws his mantle, it must be the same garment he uses to cover his face in 19:13. It is not altogether uncommon for prophets in the Deuteronomistic History to be associated with items of clothing. Samuel is clothed in his customary robe when finally announcing the imminent death of Saul (1 Sam 28:14; cf.

---

[22] Walsh, *1 Kings*, 281.
[23] Bergen, *Elisha and the End of Prophetism*, 49.

1 Sam 15:27), and Ahijah of Shiloh tears the cloak of Jeroboam when declaring that the kingdom will be ripped from the hand of Solomon (1 Kings 11:30). In both of these instances the clothing plays a role in both recognition and signaling a transition in leadership. When Elijah throws the mantle, therefore, the reader recognizes a change in prophetic leadership with Elisha clothed in Elijah's authority.

BONFIRE OF THE AMENITIES

Taking a cue from David Kimchi, the great medieval rabbi, Uriel Simon further develops the case for a *test* in Elijah's dealings with Elisha. In other words, when Elijah throws the mantle, there is "the imposition of a trial," similar to challenging the widow of Sidon to feed him first, or asking Obadiah to summon Ahab for a meeting with the prophet.[24] Regardless of Elijah's shades of motive, if the reader understands the mantle-toss in the same way that the widow is ordered to "not fear," then Elisha must be seen to pass the test with flying colors. The instantaneous actions of *abandon* and *run* suggest an immediate compliance with the prophet's gesture ("He abandoned the oxen and ran after Elijah," 19:20). Because Elisha has to dash after him, we infer that Elijah hurled the mantle and simply kept going. Elijah is a fast mover—remember in 1 Kings 18:46 he runs ahead of Ahab's chariot all the way to Jezreel—so Elisha will most likely require tremendous energy in the days ahead.

As Elisha abandons his beasts of burden, it is notable that the same term (עזב) is used as recently as 19:14, with Elijah's complaint that the Israelites have abandoned God's covenant. Elisha's action, then, must be viewed as a positive antithesis, and a significant step toward covenant renewal. Yet his abandonment is momentarily tempered with a request, as Elisha seeks permission from the mantle-thrower: "Let me please kiss my father and mother, and then I will walk after you." In a sense this pattern has been seen before: the widow demurs before complying with Elijah's demand back in 1 Kings 17, and Obadiah recites his entire *curriculum vitae* before acquiescing to fetch Ahab in 1 Kings 18. With Elisha it is a simple farewell kiss

---

[24] Simon, *Reading Prophetic Narratives*, 222.

that reveals close family ties, much like his ties to the land, all of which he is willing to give up in an instant: the owner's son abandons familial inheritance for prophetic succession.[25]

He said to him, "Go, return! What have I done to you?" He returned from him, took the pair of oxen, sacrificed them, boiled the meat with the equipment of the oxen, gave to his people and they ate. He then arose and went after Elijah, and served him.

Elijah's response to the request for a parental embrace has confused many readers, and even a comparison of English translations reveals a subtle diversity of interpretations. For Hugh Pyper there is an oddness here: Elijah gives an answer in the form of a question.[26] For John Gray, Elijah rebukes his successor, who has not realized the weight and unconditional demands that have been thrust at him: "The sense is probably complicated here by the elliptic nature of direct speech. Probably the best sense is to take *kî* as an adversative particle, i.e., 'Go, but (remember) what I have done to you.'"[27] With enormous respect, the fact that John Gray uses the adverb "probably" on two occasions in a very short space conspires to suggest that an ambiguity exists, one that is rather difficult to resolve. I am not convinced that Elijah's question—what have I done to you?—quite so readily yields its meaning, but I am tempted to believe that Elisha's reaction reveals that he *does* understand the demands of the prophetic call despite the cryptic utterance (to go along with the enigmatic mantle-throwing). That Elisha proceeds to slaughter the oxen and use the implements to fuel the fire certainly tells me that a radical change of vocation is in his purview.

As Elisha's introductory scene draws to a close, some of the larger components—for example, the provision of a meal, interaction with parents, the presence of fire, and a sacrifice—seem symbolically to foreshadow his career. All of these elements are seen later in the story,

---

[25] Schulte ("The End of the Omride Dynasty: Social–Ethical Observations on the Subject of Power and Violence," 140) argues an alternative option—namely, that Elisha's family must have "profited from the economic changes of the period," and thus his "heeding of Elijah's call without hesitation can be attributed to his guilty conscience vis-à-vis the people who suffered under those economic realities. Even if this succession narrative is the product of a later period, Elisha's position as the scion of rich farmers must be taken into account."

[26] Pyper, "The Secret of Succession," 55.

[27] Gray, *I & II Kings*, 413.

in various guises and permutations. The communal meal also is different from Elijah's entrance back in chapter 17. Although food was present, Elijah of course required divine protection and provision to survive; here, Elisha shares his bounty, and one wonders if this indicates some changed circumstances into which Elisha will be functioning in the prophetic office. But, even though Elijah has thrown the mantle, it will be some time before he exits the narrative, and perhaps that is hinted at in the last clause about Elisha "ministering" (שרת) to the prophet. It is striking, as several commentators have observed, that the verb choice is the same as the Moses–Joshua relationship, with the latter ministering to the former (see Numbers 11:28; Joshua 1:1). Indeed, the similar language points to the possibility that Elijah is not done yet, and that Elisha will feature as an apprentice for a longer time period yet. Elijah may have left his servant lad in Beersheba when departing from the land in 1 Kings 19:3, but he has gained another one here who will rival Joshua in stature.

2

Incendiary Successions

The prophetic biographies in 1 and 2 Kings are poised to enter a new frontier in the next section of our story. Of the three figures Elijah is instructed to anoint in 1 Kings 19, Elisha is the subject who attracts the most attention. To be sure, Jehu and Hazael will emerge as strong-armed characters in their own right, but both of these political captains are eclipsed by Elisha in terms of narrative space and individuation. Elisha's prominence could be assumed from 1 Kings 19:19–21, where he is the only one of the three to be visited by the prophet. Even so, Elisha is initially pictured as an ancillary character in the commanding shadow of Elijah. Elisha's first moments of oxen-driving and unflinching response to the prophetic summons are arresting and unique: no other prophet is the recipient of quite this kind of investiture. In 2 Kings 2 Elisha gradually moves to center stage with the departure of Elijah and the uplifting events that accompany this defining moment of transition.

But, just prior to the much-anticipated succession of Elisha, 2 Kings 1 is worth a closer look for our purposes—not least because the content of the chapter has a number of pointedly similar themes and operates as a preface to the next episode. It will be argued that 2 Kings 1 and 2 showcase fiery accounts of transition, as the ill-fated career of Ahab's son Ahaziah is juxtaposed with the inheritance of Elijah's apprentice: a chaotic and sterile succession is dwarfed by a far more powerful one (with fire featured prominently in both). So, after some brief analysis of Elijah's role in the ruin of Ahaziah in 2 Kings 1, the bulk of this chapter is devoted to the story of Elijah's aeronautics and Elisha's representation. Despite a lengthy absence in the narrative, Elisha reappears in the capacity of a servant to the prophet, and by the end of 2 Kings 2 has taken full possession of his master's mantle.

FREE FALLING

Owing to the prophetic denunciation of Ahab's dynasty by Elijah in 1 Kings 20, the prospects for his son, Ahaziah, are woefully bleak. During Ahaziah's regnal introduction in 1 Kings 22:53 he is already described as walking in the ways of "his father and mother" (Ahab and Jezebel), making the previously announced judgment a grim inevitability. Coupled with the shipwreck mentioned as the first event of Ahaziah's reign (1 Kings 22:49–50), this failed maritime venture with his southern counterpart Jehoshaphat must be perceived as an ominous portent. Thus one expects the fall of Ahaziah in due course, but perhaps not so soon nor quite so literally:

Moab revolted against Israel after the death of Ahab. Then Ahaziah fell through the lattice work of his roof chamber in Samaria, and became ill. He sent messengers, and said to them, "Go, inquire of Baal Zebub god of Ekron if I will recover from this illness!" But the messenger of the LORD spoke to Elijah the Tishbite, "Arise, go up to meet the messengers of the king of Samaria and speak to them, 'Is there no God in Israel that you are going to seek Baal Zebub god of Ekron?' Now, therefore, thus says the LORD, 'The bed you are on, you will not come down from, because you *will* die!'" Then Elijah went.

The messengers returned to him, and he said to them, "What is this? You have returned." They said to him, "A man came up to meet us and said to us, 'Go, return to the king who sent you and speak to him, "Thus says the LORD: Is there no God in Israel, that you should send to inquire of Baal Zebub god of Ekron? Therefore the bed which you are on, you will not come down from it, because you *will* die."'" He spoke to them, "What was the fashion (מִשְׁפַּט) of the man who came up to meet you, and spoke these things to you?" They said to him, "A man who was an owner of hair, with a belt of leather tied around his waist." He said, "Elijah the Tishbite is he!" (2 Kings 1:1–8)

The plot configuration of the rest of the episode is not overly complicated. Ahaziah, still feeling the effects of his fall, sends troops to apprehend Elijah, who is located on top of a mountain. A pair of military companies are consumed by falling fire: the fire on the mountain looks back to the events of Mount Carmel in 1 Kings 18, and ahead to Elisha's transition into prophetic leadership in 2 Kings 2. As the third captain implores for mercy, Elijah acquiesces and consents to meet Ahaziah. The climax of the episode is the confrontation between prophet and king: as it turns out, Ahaziah is lying on his deathbed, and the prophet announces his imminent demise.

When the king dies, he is succeeded, not by a son, but instead by his brother. Ahaziah's sterility stands in metaphorical contrast to Elijah, whose successor is prominent in the next chapter.

Through the obvious humor in 2 Kings 1 a series of thematic points move into view.[1] The fall of Ahaziah is ironically underscored through his consultation of Baal Zebub, understood by most scholars as "lord of the flies;" the ill effects of the king's downward flight, he vainly hopes, will be remedied by the fly god.[2] Similarly, the king's messengers (מלאכים) are ultimately unsuccessful in seeking Baal the fly (בבעל זבוב), as they are turned back because a divine messenger (מלאך) has tipped off Elijah, whom they call a "Baal/master of hair" (בעל שער). Whether, as commentators debate, the messengers' report refers to a shaggy mantle or indicates a hirsute prophet, this newly announced characteristic of Elijah will be important for the episode involving his heir at the end of 2 Kings 2, who is mocked for a lack of hair by the youths of Bethel. The mention of hair is new information for the reader, but must be common knowledge, at least for the king. On the basis of this description, the king recognizes Elijah. Furthermore, Ahaziah is referred to as the "king of Samaria" in the divine speech of verse 3, the second (and final) time the title is ever used in the Hebrew Bible. In fact, the only other king to be referred to as such is Ahab, Ahaziah's father (1 Kings 21:1). The titular connection of these two kings of Samaria highlights the theme of succession in this stretch of text, one that is followed immediately by an account of prophetic succession in the next chapter. A note of directional contrast quickly emerges, as one dynasty tumbles (Ahab's son, Ahaziah) while prophetic succession continues. In terms of narrative architecture, the fall of the king of Samaria intentionally precedes the lift-off of Elijah. The toppled Ahaziah has no son, yet Elisha will soon cry out "my father" as his master rises from the scene in 2 Kings 2.

Ahaziah's distress about his illness triggers his inquiry of Baal Zebub. Such action, where a king consults a deity because of sickness, is not unique to 2 Kings 1. Robert Cohn locates Ahaziah's pallid inquiry within a larger pattern in Kings, classifying it as a "type-

---

[1] Note the study of C. T. Begg, "Unifying Factors in 2 Kings 1:2–17a," *JSOT* 32 (1985), 75–86.

[2] e.g., J. L. McLaughlin, "Baal Zebub," in D. N. Freedman (ed.), *Eerdmans Dictionary of the Bible* (Grand Rapids: Eerdmans, 2000), 136–7; cf. the longer discussion and possible corruption of the name in J. Day, *Yahweh and the Gods and Goddesses of Canaan* (JSOTSup 265; Sheffield: Sheffield Academic Press, 2000), 177–81.

scene" that also occurs in the reigns of Jeroboam (1 Kings 14), Ben-Hadad (2 Kings 8), and Hezekiah (2 Kings 20). The components of the type-scene are as follows: "a deathly ill king commissions his royal messengers to seek out the prophet of Yhwh and through him to inquire of Yhwh whether or not he will recover from his illness."[3] Four significant prophets in the book of Kings (Ahijah, Elijah, Elisha, and Isaiah) are involved in this category of type-scene, and in each instance the interpreter should attend to any variations in the pattern. In the case of Ahaziah there are some striking variations on the regular pattern, including the (attempted) consultation of a *foreign* deity rather than an Israelite prophet. If we consider the broader context of the Deuteronomistic History, Ahaziah's anxiety parallels Jeroboam's in 1 Kings 14. Jeroboam is concerned about his son's illness for dynastic reasons; Ahaziah (who has no son) is equally anxious about illness, but concerned for *himself*.

Yet, even as Ahaziah is virtually satirized by means of the type-scene configuration, the lineaments of Elisha's vocation are moving into view. Like his master in 2 Kings 1, Elisha is a principal agent in 2 Kings 8:7–15, a type-scene where the foreign king Ben-Hadad inquires of an Israelite prophet. So Elijah and Elisha are both involved in delivering the prophetic word to a dangerously ill monarch, and, partly because of the momentum generated in 2 Kings 1, the type-scene featuring Elisha and Ben-Hadad is decidedly more complex. As Cohn notes: "Elisha's oracle to Ben-hadad of Syria (2 Kings 8), transmitted through Hazael, results in the fulfillment of Yhwh's command given earlier to Elijah to anoint Hazael as king of Syria (1 Kgs 19:15). So," Cohn concludes, 2 Kings 8 "not only mirrors an Elijah episode, but also completes a story left unfinished at Elijah's death."[4] The announcements at Horeb, where the overthrow of the house of Omri will continue through Elijah's successor, reaches

---

[3] R. L. Cohn, "Convention and Creativity in the Book of Kings: The Case of the Dying Monarch," *CBQ* 47 (1985), 603. Other overviews and studies of the type-scene in biblical literature can be found in B. J. M. Johnson, "What Type of Son is Samson? Reading Judges 13 as a Biblical Type-Scene," *JETS* 53 (2010), 269–86; B. Britt, "Prophetic Concealment in a Biblical Type Scene," *CBQ* 64 (2002), 37–58. For an extension of the concept, see S. C. Schwartz, "From Bedroom to Courtroom: The Adultery Type-Scene and the Acts of Andrew,". in T. C. Penner and C. Vander Stichele (eds), *Mapping Gender in Ancient Religious Discourse*, 267–311 (BIS 84; Leiden: Brill, 2007), 267–311.

[4] Cohn, "Convention and Creativity in the Book of Kings," 610.

another stage in its gradual unfolding. These two prophetic careers interweave as Elisha retraces the steps of his predecessor and enlarges the work begun by Elijah.

Additionally, the illness of Ahaziah and the spatial setting of the "roof chamber" (עליה) in 2 Kings 1, as scholars are increasingly pointing out, have marked affinities with the earlier episode in 1 Kings 17:17–24. As discussed in the previous chapter, the widow of Sidon has a son who is revived in a "roof chamber" (עליה) by means of Elijah's intervention. The parallels are further evident when we recall that Ahab is killed in 1 Kings 22, and thus both women—Jezebel and Elijah's hostess in 1 Kings 17—are *widows of Sidon*. For all the similarities, a somewhat theatrical contrast emerges, as the two widows' sons have quite different experiences in the roof chamber and Elijah's involvement with their sons' illnesses: "The prophet raises the widow's son from his bed, but proclaims the death of Jezebel's son, 'by the word of YHWH.'"[5] Since Elisha will soon interact with another widow, rescuing her and her *two* sons in 2 Kings 4:1–7, these details need to be kept in mind. Even more, Elijah's interactions with the widow of Sidon and Ahaziah in 2 Kings 1 are intensified in 2 Kings 4:8–37, where Elisha *doubles* the miracles: first there is the birth of a son to a barren wife (the great woman of Shunem), and this is followed by a healing of the same son, and again a roof chamber (עליה) functions as a key spatial setting. Overall, 2 Kings 1 is a transition narrative: just before Elisha inherits the mantle of his master, there are further indications of how he will work to magnify the output of Elijah and continue the struggle against various facets of opposition—including the forces of death and economic disadvantage—resulting in further dismemberment of the house of Omri.

---

[5] Aucker, "Putting Elisha in his Place," 77–8, drawing on J. Siebert-Hommes, "The Widow of Zarephath and the Great Woman of Shunem: A Comparative Analysis of Two Stories," in B. Becking and M. Dijkstra (eds), *On Reading Prophetic Texts: Gender-Specific & Related Studies in Memory of Fokkelien van Dijk-Hemmes* (BIS 18; Brill: Leiden, 1996), 231–50, and K. A. D. Smelik, "The Literary Function of 1 Kgs 17, 8–24," in C. Brekelmans and J. Lust (eds), *Pentateuchal and Deuteronomistic Studies* (Leuven: Peeters, 1990), 239–43. Cf. J. T. Walsh, "The Elijah Cycle: A Synchronic Approach" (Ph.D. diss., University of Michigan, 1982), 134–7.

STORM RUMORS

There is a story of barren succession in 2 Kings 1 that operates as intentional preface to the next chapter, an episode of prophetic succession. Thus in a multitude of ways the fall of Ahaziah prepares for the events of 2 Kings 2, and we will see similar configurations and motifs (most visibly, fire) in this next account of succession. But Ahaziah's lack of an heir—necessitating his brother Jehoram's appointment as king—is also used for another purpose in the narrative: it momentarily suspends royal time in favor of the prophetic succession. Sandwiched in between the death of Ahaziah and the beginning of Jehoram's reign there is a suspension of the royal account, and instead the prophetic transition and inheritance of Elisha are extensively narrated.

Commentators provide several explanations as to why a suspension of royal time happens here at this point in the Deuteronomistic History. For Burke Long there is a strategic rationale, as the pausal moment in the royal story is used to capture "a momentous change in spiritual leadership: Just as Elijah represented for the DtrH an authentic voice for Yahwism in the apostasy-prone Omride northern kingdom, so Elisha will be a similarly presented prophetic power in the waning years of that same dynasty (2 Kgs 3:1–10:17). Moreover," Long concludes, "as the transition from Moses to Joshua assured continuity in Yahweh's guidance, so Elijah–Elisha, analogously portrayed, are steady voices for Jerusalemite Yahwism in a kingdom laboring under the shadow of Jeroboam and the successor Omrides."[6] For Robert Cohn, the temporary suspension of the royal storyline results in a signal deflation of monarchic pretension, and an elevation of the prophetic succession over its royal counterpart: "In the midst of, but separate from, the sequential and interlocking formulas of royal succession, this episode again sets prophetic over against royal power. If monarchy," says Cohn, "claimed to mediate a divinely given order to human time, the order represented by prophetic authority is superimposed upon it and supersedes it."[7] From these comments the reader can infer that attending to the temporal dimension of the narrative allows for an appreciation of the narrative structure: through the chronological sequencing of the episodes, there is a

---

[6] Long, *2 Kings*, 22.   [7] Cohn, *2 Kings*, 10.

diminution of Ahaziah and Jehoram, and an enhancement of the prophets Elijah and his successor, Elisha.

The suspension of royal time is not the end of the temporal complexity as 2 Kings 2 begins.[8] Even as the story stands outside the normal chronological unfolding of Kings, the opening sentence of the chapter contains its own uniqueness: "When the LORD was going to lift up Elijah in the storm to heaven, Elijah and Elisha walked from Gilgal." As will soon be clear, the first part of the chapter is replete with hearsay of Elijah's impending departure, and the narrator participates in the rumor mill by informing the reader in advance about the climactic event to come. The same term for "storm" (סערה) is used in Job 38:1, where the context is a divine theophany that brings the book of Job to its pinnacle; by analogy, one might expect a similar moment here in 2 Kings 2. Other scholars suggest there could be a polemical element at work: given that the Omrides have zealously embraced the worship of the Canaanite fertility deities, this announcement of the tempest could be seen as a reaction to the storm-god ideology.[9] The main characters are already aware that something metaphysical is imminent, as are the members of another group, the sons of the prophets:

> Elijah said to Elisha, "Stay here, please, for the LORD has sent me as far as Bethel." Elisha said, "As the LORD lives and as you live, I will not depart from you." So they went down to Bethel. And the sons of the prophets who were in Bethel came out to Elisha, and said to him, "Do you know that today the LORD is taking your master from over your head?" He said, "Yes, I know. Be silent!"

There are numerous occasions in Elijah's career where he seems agitated or intense. Given the rapacious opposition of the royal couple, Ahab and Jezebel, the prophet's brusque deportment is

---

[8] Cf. Brueggemann, *1 & 2 Kings*, 293: "It is likely that the text is intentionally placed as it is, in order to suggest that the remarkable moment of prophetic transition is so odd and so exceptional that it cannot be held in royal time or understood in royal rationality. This text is something deeply 'other' and so it is placed 'otherwise.'" In this respect, a comparison might be made with the temporal statement in 1 Kings 18:1 ("After many days the word of the LORD came to Elijah, in the third year, saying, 'Go, be visible to Ahab, and I will give rain on the face of the ground'"), where the *third year* stands outside the regnal chronology.

[9] Note the analysis and reconsiderations of H. Niehr, "'Israelite' Religion and 'Canaanite' Religion," in F. Stavrakopoulou and J. Barton (eds), *Religious Diversity in Ancient Israel and Judah* (London: T & T Clark, 2010), 23–36.

understandable. In 2 Kings 2:2–3, however, Elijah's speech accents are atypical. This is the first occasion that Elijah and Elisha are recorded together since the investiture, with Elijah in a decidedly different frame of mind (he even uses the proper name "Elisha" in verse 5). One recalls his words and actions in 1 Kings 19:19–20, where he throws the mantle, evidently walks off, and only says "Go, return! What have I done to you?" in response to Elisha's request to kiss his mother and father. During the conversations with Elisha in 2 Kings 2 Elijah is far less saturnine, and one wonders if it is because of his impending departure or for the sake of his apprentice. But, if Elijah comes across as different in the two scenes of 1 Kings 19 and 2 Kings 2, Elisha appears to be rather more consistent. In both scenes there is a tenacity about following Elijah, despite the patent risks and uncertainties. It is not altogether clear why Elijah urges his apprentice to stay behind and *not* accompany him to Bethel. For some interpreters there is a test or a rite of passage here; if so, then Elisha appears to pass this test, just like his first test in 1 Kings 19 where he is summoned to the prophetic office.[10] Elisha is willing to swear an oath—using the divine name—and this must indicate the highest level of commitment at this hour of transition. Furthermore, Elisha's thrice-repeated oath *not* to abscond from the prophet is an antipode to Ahaziah's threefold attempt to apprehend the prophet in the previous chapter.

A shadowy troupe of minor characters abruptly enter the storyline, as the "sons of the prophets" make their inaugural appearance in the Elisha narrative. Earlier in the Deuteronomistic History there are groups of prophets—on several occasions associated with Samuel himself (cf. 1 Samuel 10:5–6; 1 Samuel 19:20)—but the formal term *sons of the prophets* (בני הנביאים) is first mentioned in 1 Kings 20:35–43. That episode is weird by any standard, and begins with two members of the group, with one commanding his colleague to "strike" him. This odd request to strike the friend is refused, no doubt to the colleague's lasting regret, as a lion comes forth to attack him: he does not "strike" (נכה), and himself gets "struck" (נכה). The episode culminates with the assertive prophet—who does manage to find someone to deal the blow—using a disguise to trick Ahab into a

---

[10] e.g., Hens-Piazza, *1–2 Kings*, 234: "As part of preparations for his final departure, Elijah is testing the steadfastness of Elisha's commitment to follow in his ways, no matter how mysterious the route."

self-condemnation. Based on this episode, the reader might assume that anonymity and strange behavior will be hallmarks of this group.

Because the sons of the prophets are never defined with any real clarity in the text, the group is variously understood by scholars, and there is a wide assortment of views on how best to interpret this collective. For instance, in Wesley Bergen's survey of secondary literature on the topic, opinions on the sons of the prophets range from Richard Nelson's "hobos around stewpots" to Morton Smith's "terrorist" organization.[11] It might be wise to keep in mind that this group—however it is understood—has a remarkably short lifespan: they appear only sporadically between 1 Kings 20 and 2 Kings 9, which is not a lot of textual material. So, for 2 Kings 2, the most pressing issue is their attendance, as we wonder what they are doing in this episode. To judge from their dialogue, they already seem to understand Elisha as the next prophetic leader. From a structural vantage point, therefore, one senses the role of the sons of the prophets here. Even as the issue of kingship succession is murky, there is prophetic clarity during the "pausal moment" between the reigns within the doomed house of Omri. Ahaziah dies without a son to succeed him, whereas Elijah and his successor are surrounded by a group of "sons," a retinue of disciples who presumably will assist the resistance movement.

On a related note, one guesses it is not coincidental that this group emerges, in the first instance, from Bethel. Home to the central shrine inaugurated by Jeroboam in 1 Kings 12, Bethel must be regarded as a spiritual focal point of the northern kingdom. Elisha later visits Bethel at the end of the chapter—memorably engaging the crowd of juvenile delinquents—so it is conceivable that Bethel is configured as one of the early *conflict zones* for Elisha's leadership. Indeed, leadership is a dominant issue with the sons of the prophets, although they take care not to address Elijah, but only speak to Elisha as if he were some kind of intermediary. Such a mode of address may be a protocol of sorts, but from the manner of their speech the reader assumes that Elisha has attained a reasonably high profile despite not being mentioned since 1 Kings 19. I have translated their question in an awkwardly literal fashion—"Do you know that today the LORD is taking your

---

[11] Bergen, *Elisha and the End of Prophetism*, 57–61, citing Nelson, *First and Second Kings*, 175, and M. Smith, *Palestinian Parties and Politics that Shaped the Old Testament* (New York: Columbia University Press, 1971), 34.

master from over your head?"—in a bid to capture a humorous irony. Some commentators assert that the group means Elijah will be taken away as leader, and thus this is figurative utterance. It is hard to determine whether they mean this exactly, but, as we will see, this is quite literally what happens, as Elijah is taken from directly over Elisha's head in due course. Elisha's imperative to "be quiet" is often thought to be spoken in a hushed tone, but there is enough elasticity in the semantic range of the verb (חשׁה) to yield the sense "be inactive" (cf. the comparable uses in 1 Kings 22:3; 2 Kings 7:9). In effect, Elisha is asking them *not* to get involved. This chapter will reveal that, as a group, they are prone to interfere without necessarily knowing the whole story. Given their futile search for Elijah in a few moments, being inactive would be prudent here, and thus Elisha's cautions are entirely justified.

ALLUSIVE ITINERARY

Despite Elijah's repeated attempts to jettison his protégé, Elisha is resolute in following his master despite a route that may seem bafflingly circuitous in 2 Kings 2:4–6. At each stop, the sons of the prophets keep materializing; as a group they are repetitive with their questions but marked by a persistence that in many respects matches Elisha. Yet, in the context of the larger section of text, it nonetheless is possible that the dialogue takes place along a less arbitrary route, with a cluster of familiar place names: Gilgal, Bethel, Jericho, and ending up at the banks of the Jordan. Scholarly interpretations of this route have varied, with a quest for some sort of intricate *chiastic structure* dominating many discussions. Because Elisha will later retrace his master's steps, there have been a plethora of attempts to discern a precise correlation between the stopping-places of Elijah (then followed by Elisha) in 2 Kings 1–2. However, the chiasm does not work perfectly, despite some herculean efforts by interpreters to find a precise balance.[12] More promising, in my view, is approaching the

---

[12] On chiasm in general, see Y. T. Radday, "Chiasmus in Hebrew Biblical Narrative," in J. W. Welch (ed.), *Chiasmus in Antiquity* (Hildesheim: Gerstenberg, 1981), 50–117, and J. T. Sparks, *The Chronicler's Genealogies: Towards an Understanding of 1 Chronicles 1–9* (Academia Biblica 28; Atlanta: Society of Biblical Literature, 2008).

last journey of Elijah (that is subsequently re-travelled by Elisha) in terms of *symbolic geography*. As outlined by Victor Matthews, cultural memories become attached to certain places because of notable events, battles, monuments, theophanies, or ritual celebrations, and thus are infused with a new spatial relevance: "In this way both historical reality and the familiarity associated with significant sites play a role in the expected setting of a narrative in order to give it or its characters greater authority."[13]

The point about literary characters taking on a "greater authority" by means of spatial affiliation is particularly acute in light of the oft-observed fact that the sites of 2 Kings 2 are most prominently recalled in the Moses/Joshua era. Transition of prophetic leadership from Elijah to Elisha, so a compelling argument emerges, takes place along a deliberate patterning on some of the sites prominent in the time period of the conquest of Canaan during the transition between Moses and Joshua. Terence Fretheim has a useful summary comment here: "The succession occurs in the course of a journey through various places; though not precisely plotted, the journey seems to trace Israel's trek under Joshua backward, climaxing in a crossing of the Jordan to the east and then, crossing back, retracing that journey (see Joshua 3–8)."[14] Marvin Sweeney develops a similar observation:

With respect to Elijah and Elisha's travels in this section, note the caution of T. R. Hobbs, "2 Kings 1 and 2: Their Unity and Purpose," *SR* 13 (1984), 330: "One of the more adventurous attempts to understand the relationship between 2 Kings 1 and 2 is that of Lundbom ["Elijah's Chariot Ride," *JJS* 24 (1973), 39–50], who argues that the structure of the two chapters is chiastic, and that this chiasmus is the basis for the relationship. The chiasmus is based upon the geographical progression from Samaria, to Carmel, to Gilgal, to Bethel, to Jericho, to the Jordan, and back again. It is argued that such a device is pre-deuteronomistic, possibly from the oral stage of the stories, and is a mnemonic device to aid retention. There are several immediate problems with this," according to Hobbs, "in addition to the rather exaggerated view of chiasmus. The first and most obvious problem is that the structure as outlined does not work." For a similar chiastic caution, see M. J. Boda, "Chiasmus in Ubiquity: Symmetrical Mirages in Nehemiah 9," *JSOT* 71 (1996), 55–70.

[13] V. H. Matthews, "Back to Bethel: Geographical Reiteration in Biblical Narrative," *JBL* 128 (2009), 154.

[14] T. E. Fretheim, *First and Second Kings* (Louisville, KY: Westminster John Knox, 1999), 137. Cf. R. P. Carroll, "The Elijah–Elisha Sagas: Some Remarks on Prophetic Succession in Ancient Israel," *VT* 19 (1969), 411: "There is an obvious parallel between the actions of Elisha the successor of Elijah and the actions of Joshua the successor of Moses in the crossing of the Jordan." But Carroll quickly cautions in a footnote: "Of course this parallel can be overexaggerated. There were major differences in the various crossings, especially in the instruments used to divide the waters."

Gilgal's association with the Joshua traditions establishes the analogy between the relationship of Elijah and Elisha and that of Moses and Joshua. Joshua is the successor of Moses (Num 27:12–23; Deut 31–34), whose death and burial were not witnessed by human beings, and Joshua is closely associated with Gilgal, Jericho, and the Jordan River.[15]

Certainly the pivotal site in this chapter is the Jordan River, the terminus of the journey. When viewing the larger Deuteronomistic History, it is understandable why this spatial setting is so carefully and extensively underscored in this succession narrative. According to a recent study by Jeremy Hutton:

> In the literary logic of the DtrH, Transjordan serves as a place of exile, refuge, and incubative transformation for prospective personages of power. Throughout the History, the motif of the return from Transjordan serves as a powerful metaphor for the return (or entry) of a character into a high degree of personal authority, previously lost or nonexistent.[16]

From the perspective of Elisha's characterization, the sum total of these allusions to Joshua's succession indicate that his agenda will include a conquest of the land. It is possible that the Jordan setting represents some sort of symbolic departure from the *political zone* of the Omrides, but the manner of their crossing the river is brimming with intertextual significance, with the (twice) parted waters surely reminiscent of the exodus from Egypt and entry into the promised land under the recently transferred leadership of Joshua. Just as Joshua led the struggle against Canaanite ideology and influence, so we infer that Elisha will be a catalyst for releasing the nation from the grip of the Omrides.

OUT OF SIGHT

With a fifty-member crowd from sons of the prophets gazing intently, the chief protagonists arrive at the edge of the Jordan. The number

---

[15] Sweeney, *I & II Kings*, 272.

[16] J. M. Hutton, *The Transjordanian Palimpsest: The Overwritten Texts of Personal Exile and Transformation in the Deuteronomistic History* (BZAW 396; Berlin: Walter de Gruyter, 2009), 4. Cf. Long, *2 Kings*, 26: "The Transjordan seems less a physical place than a trope for that liminal space between the ordinariness of prophetic community and the numinous circumstances of Elijah's translation from earth."

fifty in 2 Kings 2:7 echoes the previous chapter—where fifty-member units were dispatched by the king—and works here to anticipate some further fireworks even more spectacular than the last. For the first time, there is no question posed by the guild to Elisha about impending events; perhaps they are too far away, or finally heed Elisha's request to keep quiet. Yet the following actions seem to be refracted through the visual perspective of the fifty: "And Elijah took his mantle, rolled it, struck the waters, and they were divided here and there. The two of them passed over on dry ground."[17] Unlike the earlier crossing in Joshua 3–4, no priests or ark are involved. Instead, there is an echo of Moses' action in Exodus. Elijah hurls the mantle upon the waters, though probably in a different manner from that in which he throws the same mantle at Elisha back in chapter 19 (and evidently gets it back at some point). The mantle—that symbol of prophetic succession—now comes back into play. It may have been obliquely referred to in 2 Kings 1:8, where the king's unit of fifty report their conversation with an "owner of hair." Either way, the mantle is the instrument used to part the waters whereby the two prophets are able to traverse the riverbed.

To this juncture in 2 Kings 2 the dialogue between Elijah and Elisha has been fairly repetitive, as Elijah implores his protégé to stay in various places, with the latter swearing oaths not to leave his master's side. Matters are quite different on the far side of Jordan, because in verse 9 Elijah issues an invitation to Elisha: "Ask what (שאל מה) I can do for you before I am taken away from you." Even with Elijah's history of brusque locutions and tender imperatives, this is still an unexpected request that has perplexed interpreters. To my mind there is an interesting comparison with 1 Kings 3:5, the moment when Solomon is likewise invited to ask for something. In that passage God invites Solomon: "Ask what (שאל מה) I can give you . . . ". The divine invitation to this newly minted monarch seems beneficent enough, but needs also to be interpreted by the reader as a *test* for Solomon (who has ruthlessly eliminated his brother and every other quantifiable threat to his political power). Minus the fratricide,

---

[17] On the *hapax* verb "roll" (ויגלם) note the study of J. Kaltner, who argues (based on an Arabic cognate) that "split/cut" is the preferred meaning ("What Did Elijah Do to his Mantle? The Hebrew Root *GLM*," in J. Kaltner and L. Stulman (eds), *Inspired Speech: Prophecy in the Ancient Near East: Essays in Honor of Herbert B. Huffmon* (JSOTSup 378; London: T & T Clark 2004), 225–30).

Elijah's question to Elisha also functions as something of a test, much like the testing first seen during their initial encounter at Abel Meholah back in 1 Kings 19.

Elijah's unexpected offer becomes the final test in what has been a lengthy examination period for Elisha. The latter's response—assuming that this dialogue is one more test of resolve for his fitness to succeed his master in the prophetic office—must be construed as the right answer to a strangely difficult question: "Please may a double portion of your spirit be to me." Elisha's request is thought by the majority of scholars to reflect the law of inheritance rights of a firstborn son in the book of Deuteronomy, as explained by Mark O'Brien:

> If one understands Elisha's request for a "double share of your spirit" on analogy with the primogeniture of Deut 21:17, then he is after the lion's share of Elijah's prophetic power. The Deuteronomic text refers to the eldest son's right to a double share of his father's inheritance. Elisha is therefore claiming a unique prophetic status as his right.[18]

Along these lines, one now can better appreciate the role of the other "prophetic sons" following them *in this particular episode*, as now Elisha is poised to inherit the mantle of firstborn son and heir of Elijah.

On a practical level, a reader might be tempted to think that, if indeed Elisha is going to double the miracle count of his predecessor, it stands to reason that double the spirit is a necessary prerequisite. Be that as it may, Elijah seems to grant approval to the request—assuming that his rejoinder in verse 10 ("you have shown stubbornness") is a compliment—but hastens to append an odd qualification: "If you see me being taken from you, it will be to you thus. But if not, it will not be." There could be a tacit recognition by Elijah that such a gift is not exclusively his to bestow, or there could be an echo of Numbers 27:18, a commissioning narrative where we are told that the spirit resides in Joshua ("The LORD said to Moses, 'Take Joshua son of Nun, a man in whom is the spirit (רוח), and rest your hand upon him"; cf. Deut 34:9). Furthermore, there may also be an allusion to Numbers

---

[18] M. A. O'Brien, "The Portrayal of Prophets in 2 Kings 2," *ABR* 46 (1998), 10. O'Brien also notes the option of reading "two-thirds," an interpretative move raised by several other scholars (e.g., Pyper, "The Secret of Succession," 59). However, the majority of translators and commentators prefer "double," a reading that in my view is the easiest and most sensible reading, reflected in the NRSV ("Please let me inherit a double share of your spirit" (ויהי נא פי שנים ברוחך אלי)).

11:17, where God says to Moses, "I will withdraw some of the spirit (רוח) that is on you and set it on them, and they will lift the burden of the people with you."[19] As Joshua is divinely commissioned, so Elijah's prophetic successor is appointed in what will be a spectacular commissioning ceremony. This "ceremony," however, is outside any kind of normative practice or institutional ritual, and happens in a manner that scarcely could have been anticipated. The reader knows that Elijah will be taken, but in what must rank as the most amazing departure of any character in Israel's monarchic history, the conversation between the two is interrupted with a fiery tempest (vv. 11–12):

> As they were walking along and speaking, suddenly a chariot of fire and horses of fire, and it separated the two of them, and Elijah went up in the storm to heaven! Now Elisha was seeing, and he was crying out, "My father, my father! The chariots and horsemen of Israel!" He did not see him again, and he took hold of his garments and tore them into two pieces.

In a fit of prophetic pique, Elijah implored God back in 1 Kings 19:4 to "take" him. Here in 2 Kings 2:10 God obliges in astonishing fashion: Elijah's exit from the narrative is so dramatic that it even seems to catch Elisha by surprise, as witnessed by his "crying out" participle (and followed by ripping his garments when he can longer see anything). By means of this vivid description there is no doubting that Elisha *sees* his master's departure, thus fulfilling the condition that Elijah placed on the request for a double portion. In fact, Elisha's "seeing" is stressed in the stylistic lineaments of the text, as the scene is refracted through his own visual perspective by the Hebrew particle that I have rendered "suddenly" (הנה), usually translated in the KJV as "behold" to capture that sense of compelling immediacy of a character's perception. Commentators are reminded of a similar experience in Joshua 5, when Moses' successor glimpses a celestial warrior: "When Joshua was by Jericho, he lifted up his eyes and saw: look (הנה), a man standing in front of him with a drawn sword in his hand!" Joshua's vision is a reminder that the military power of Israel—a group of former slaves recently departed from Egypt—does not primarily reside in superior logistics, sophisticated weaponry, or professionalization

---

[19] Seow, "1 & 2 Kings," 176. Cf. M. A. Christian, "Middle-Tier Levites and the Plenary Reception of Revelation," in M. Leuchter and J. M. Hutton (eds), *Levites and Priests in Biblical History and Tradition* (Atlanta: Society of Biblical Literature, 2011), 192–3.

among the rank-and-file troops. Instead, military triumph comes through the power of the God of Israel, symbolized in the vision of the captain revealed to Joshua (in the vicinity of the Jordan River upon entering the land).

By analogy, in 2 Kings 2 Elisha's vision of the chariot—even as the Omride ideology dominates the political landscape—implies that the theology of God's influence in military affairs still holds, and that to some measure Elisha will work within this sphere. The expression "My father, my father! The chariots and horsemen of Israel" occurs again in identical form in 2 Kings 13, and so this exclamation bookends the public career of Elisha. The chariot vision also foreshadows to some extent Elisha's public profile, as Joel Burnett explains:

This suggestion of a new Joshua leading a new conquest comports with the martial significance of Elisha's mission—the beginning and end of which are signaled by the slogan "the chariots of Israel and their horsemen" (2:12; 13:14) and which involves divine "chariots of fire" (2:11; 6:17), Elisha's instigation of palace coups through the anointing of generals (8:7–10:36), and Elisha's constant dealings with armies, soldiers, and war (2 Kings 3; 5; 6:8–7:20; 13:1–25), even after his own death (13:20–21)![20]

For a second time in his life Elisha receives the mantle of his master; the first time it was hurled in his general direction, and now he retrieves it after it falls from the previous owner (2:13). Elisha now uses the instrument to strike the waters of the Jordan and cross on dry ground, thus commencing his own journey in his predecessor's footsteps. Moments before the crossing he utters the question, "Where is the LORD God of Elijah, even he?" It is difficult to determine the exact audience for this question (whether for the sons of the prophets, or perhaps even himself), but it does align with Elijah's recent questions to Ahaziah ("Is it because there is no God in Israel?"), implying that Elisha's continuity of Elijah's work is already underway. Combined with parting the waters using the mantle, Elisha has emphatically—so the reader is led to believe—completed the test and assumed the role of prophetic leader in place of his lately departed master.

---

[20] Burnett, "'Going Down' to Bethel," 287. On other facets of Elijah's ascension, see C. Houtman, "Elijah," in K. van der Toorn, B. Becking, and P. W. van der Horst (eds), *Dictionary of Deities and Demons in the Bible*, (2nd edn; Leiden: Brill, 1999), 282–5.

Under the watchful eyes of the Jericho franchise of the sons of the prophets, Elisha's actions are carefully analyzed and evaluated. The group exclaims that Elijah's spirit now rests on his successor; indirectly, then, the reader is given further evidence that the request has been granted. Yet, despite the confidence of the group's assertion about the spirit (רוח) and their obsequious bowing in Elisha's presence, they nevertheless volunteer to organize a search party to locate and retrieve (a presumably alive) Elijah. In this respect their concern is similar to Obadiah's, the palace steward who bravely conceals 100 prophets in caves during Ahab's reign of terror. In 1 Kings 18:12, Obadiah complains that Elijah's movements might be unpredictable ("The spirit of the LORD will carry you off I know not where!") and as such could cause an unnecessary rift between himself and the king, his employer. With the Jericho sons of the prophets, there is a conviction that Elijah simply has been dropped off somewhere, roughly the ANE equivalent of "teleporting" in a modern science-fiction film.

The first "official" task of Elisha, consequently, has a somewhat comedic ambiance based on this belief and the subsequent dialogue with his new constituents. Even as Elisha tersely declines, they persist in asking him for permission to send the delegation "to the point of embarrassment" (2:17). The same expression is used in Judges 3:25, where the servants of Eglon king of Moab wait until the point of embarrassment: their noses can detect a most offensive odor, and they (vainly) hope that their master is "overshadowing his feet," little knowing that he has been assassinated by Ehud. What they smell, of course, is the foul refuse that has been discharged from their dead master's person. So, there is a dramatic irony at work in both of these texts, as the reader knows more than the characters. It should also be noted that the same expression will be used again in 2 Kings 8:11, so it will behoove us to revisit this matter in due course when we arrive at the Hazael episode. Meanwhile, as Elisha predicted, the search for Elijah is futile, and the fifty investigators return from their quest. For the second time in as many chapters, a contingent of *fifty* is unsuccessful in executing their task with respect to Elijah. The useless search has the overall effect of elevating Elisha onto a different plane and differentiating him from the sons of the prophets. Richard Nelson labels this group a "dramatic chorus," which to some extent is true: they do give a measure of insight into the story, but they are also a foil for Elisha's power, and their role will need to be monitored as the storyline progresses.[21]

BARE NECESSITIES

The last two scenes of this chapter (2 Kings 2:19–22; 23–5) have already been briefly surveyed in the introductory chapter of this book. As the surrounding material has now been studied in more detail, some further comments are in order about the healing of the Jericho waters and the encounter with the beasts of Bethel. Regarding the first scene, Elisha is staying in Jericho (2:18), where we have noted the residents are bedeviled with "evil" water. Elisha's formula—some salt in a new container thrown at the problem—has confounded many serious scholars, as documented by Choon Leong Seow:

Rationalistic explanations have been proffered for that situation. One theory, citing hydrological studies, suggests that geological disturbances caused a high amount of radioactive pollutants to be released into the springs of the region, yielding water that has been shown by laboratory tests to cause sterility. Another hypothesis traces the problem to certain species of fresh-water snails that have been found in excavations at Jericho; these snails are known to be carriers of a disease responsible for high infant mortality.[22]

From a rationalistic viewpoint, Elisha's saline solution makes about as much sense as Moses throwing a stick and healing the waters of Marah not long after crossing the waters in Exodus 15:22–5, a text that many interpreters believe is alluded to here. If there is such an allusion, it is notable that Elisha immediately has a different agenda in this reconquest of the land. As suggested above, Joshua sees a celestial warrior, and soon after curses the rebuilding of Jericho; now, Elisha has recently seen a celestial chariot, and heals Jericho from evil water that allows it to continue to rebuild.

The choice of salt, though, is only one facet of the scene; equally (if not more) important is the efficacy of the word of the Lord spoken through him. There is a similarity with Elijah's actions to sustain the widow of Zarephath (see 1 Kings 17:14), except that Elisha's miracle

---

[21] Nelson, *First and Second Kings*, 160.   [22] Seow, "1 & 2 Kings," 178.

is expanded to include an entire city. The widow's sustenance lasted until the end of the famine, but the narrator emphasizes that the water of Jericho remains clean "until this day" (2:22). Even in his first episode as Elijah's successor, the reader can already detect Elisha's continuity and enhancement of his master's endeavors. The structural arrangement of the episodes, which I assume is intentional, lends to the continuity, especially when considering the healing of Jericho's water with the fate of Ahaziah in the previous chapter. It is possible that the biblical writer here intends to raise the idea that Ahaziah and Jericho have something in common: no lasting dynasty. But, unlike the king, Jericho receives healing courtesy of the *prophetic son* who has just inherited the double portion of the firstborn, and now Jericho's mothers can have sons who live. This results in *houses* that continue because the waters are healed "to this day." Although a common enough phrase in the Deuteronomistic History, here it stands outside the royal chronology. Once more, prophetic succession is contrasted with the monarchic sterility of Ahaziah. Unlike the king who sought Baal Zebub, Jericho can now produce offspring because they seek the prophet Elisha, the heir of Elijah.

The final episode of the chapter (2 Kings 2:23–5), as we noted earlier, develops a further contrast between Bethel and Jericho: the waters of Jericho are healed by the prophet and bereavement ends, whereas the prophet is mocked by some Bethelites and forty-two offspring are torn up by a pair of bears that march out of the forest. There is an ironic sting to the insult, as Elisha is mocked for his head, having just lost his head, Elijah (2:3).[23] It is unclear whether those who taunt are aware of Elijah's recent departure, but of course the reader appreciates the character differentiation: Elijah was well known because of "hair" (2 Kings 1:8); now Elisha is identified for the opposite attribute. The exact age of the Bethel group has confused interpreters, as the mockers are variously described as "small young men" (נערים קטנים) and "children" (ילדים) in two successive verses. Also, the group is described as the subject of the verb "march out," most likely with hostile intent, since this same verb is then used for the violent bears marching out in the next sentence. This kind of action, though not impossible, seems more compatible with a group that is older rather than younger.

---

[23] Leithart, *1 & 2 Kings*, 176.

In my view there is a an instructive analogue in 1 Kings 12:1–15, where Solomon's son Rehoboam is faced with a crucial political decision. Either Rehoboam can listen to the counsel of those who stood before his father Solomon and acquiesce to the northern grievance, or he can heed the competing counsel of the young men who grew up with him (who infamously recommend that their friend declare his "little finger" to be thicker than his father's loins, a crass reference to male genitalia). Rehoboam begins his reign at 41 years of age according to 1 Kings 14:21, yet it is striking that those who grew up with him—and presumably the same age—are referred to as "children" (הילדים). Labeling Rehoboam's colleagues as "children" heaps derision on the immaturity and vulgarity of their counsel. With the boys of Bethel, it could be that a similar satirical use is intended. Whether or not this is the case, the analogue with 1 Kings 12 certainly makes the conduct of the Bethel group more ideologically charged, as though their taunt has a political dimension as much as a personal insult.

A central issue that emerges from this scene and should not be overlooked is the fate of Bethel that to some degree is foreshadowed. After Jerusalem, Bethel is the most frequently mentioned Israelite city, and, as a spiritual center of the Omride regime, it is not surprising that the site is subject to scrutiny here.[24] As we recall, this is not the first occasion of bereavement in the vicinity of Bethel, where ferocious creatures have a habit of turning up for judgment: in 1 Kings 13:24 a lion attacks the man of God from Judah when there is a conflict over *respect* for the prophetic word. Furthermore, this is not the last bereavement that will affect Bethel. The same verb "tear open" (בקע) used for the bears is later used of the ravenous Hazael in

---

[24] On the statistics, see Matthews, "Back to Bethel," 156; on Bethel as a site of cultural memory, see R. Hendel, "Cultural Memory," in R. Hendel (ed.), *Reading Genesis: Ten Methods* (New York: Cambridge University Press, 2010), 28–46. Also note Burnett's ("'Going Down' to Bethel," 297) layered argument about the age of the Bethel group and possible connection with the cultic center of Bethel: "In sum, those who suffer Elisha's curse and die in 2 Kings 2 are not children but a group of young adult males connected with the royal sanctuary of Bethel, who offer reproach rather than recognition of Elisha's mission as Yahweh's prophet and who call for the prophet to worship at Bethel. Like Jehu's purge, the cursing and slaying of the נערים קטנים [small lads] are part of the conquest Elisha brings. Though Bethel itself still stands (as it will after Jehu), 2 Kings 2 shows that, unlike Jericho, Bethel remains a city and sanctuary under curse, doomed for destruction—destruction that will finally occur with the DH's second-greatest king, Josiah."

2 Kings 8:12, when Elisha forecasts that pregnant women in Israel will be "torn open."[25] Like Hiel of Bethel, who also lost sons not so long ago, others will follow. More specifically, the forty-two casualties in Bethel will be matched by forty-two more deaths within the Omride circle in 2 Kings 10:14. Elisha's actions against the group, therefore, should be viewed as one component within the larger context of a protracted struggle that emanates from the cultic activity of Bethel and elsewhere under the aegis of royal sponsorship. That Elisha then proceeds to Carmel and on to Samaria as the chapter ends (2:25) amplifies the scope of the ideological battle, lately contested by Elijah and now poised to continue by this agent who has received the inheritance of a double portion of his master's spirit.

---

[25] Mead, "'Elisha Will Kill'? The Deuteronomistic Rhetoric of Life and Death in the Theology of the Elisha Narratives," 113.

3

Music and Maternity

The narrative of Elisha's succession in 2 Kings 2 is marked by some singular shades of dialogue and an arresting sequence of action. The unexpected request for a double portion of prophetic inheritance is countered with a strange condition: Elijah assures his apprentice that, if he sees him being taken, the request will be accommodated. So when Elisha glimpses the heavenly transport—a fiery chariot more spectacular than any belonging to an earthly potentate—he takes possession of the fallen mantle and officially crosses into his own unique contribution to Israel's political and religious life. The three scenes that follow the moments of succession in 2 Kings 2 include Elisha's interaction with the sons of the prophets, healing the waters of Jericho, and uttering a curse on the jeering crowd from Bethel. Different combinations of these kinds of activity, especially prophetic leadership and the distribution of water or food, continue in the days ahead, with developments and detours along the way that are hardly predictable. The episodes of crisis and controversy at the outset of Elisha's career, it should be stated, are not abated in the next phases of the story.

In this next chapter of our study we analyze the disparate events of 2 Kings 3 and 4, including Elisha's diverse roles in both international affairs and domestic tribulations. In this set of scenes the reader is privy to acts of environmental destruction, a prophetic word with musical accompaniment, and the untimely death of a young man who had earlier enjoyed a miraculous birth. Among the matters to consider in our analysis are two characters who play recurring roles in the larger storyline: the king of Israel and the Shunammite woman. After the demise of the ill-fated Ahaziah, Jehoram assumes the throne of Israel, and his time in office falls under the purview of Elisha's prophetic career. The woman of Shunem is never named in the story, but her attitude toward the prophet is contrasted with the king, though they both direct complaints toward Elisha. Furthermore, both Jehoram's campaign against the Moabites and the Shunammite woman's episode with her son have intertextual connections with episodes in 1 Kings: the war with Moab has affinities with Ahab's battle against Ramoth-Gilead, while the Shunammite woman's experience of death and revival has clear connections with Elijah's experiences with the widow in Zarephath of Sidon. 2 Kings 3 and 4 offers ample material further to consider the idea of Elisha as a *double agent* who replicates and enhances Elijah's work.

CAMPAIGN TRIAL

The rise and fall of the northern house of Omri receives considerable attention in the book of Kings.[1] From a literary perspective, some of the more memorable characters in northern royalty stem from the Omrides. Although the founder of the dynasty, Omri, is only briefly sketched in 1 Kings 16:21–8, figures such as Ahab and Jezebel are portrayed as more complex figures. Jehoram (also referred to by the short form Joram in some translations) continues this trend of literary characterization among the Omrides in 2 Kings 3 and following, where he takes the stage after only being briefly introduced as successor by default because of his brother Ahaziah's lack of a son. Jehoram's twelve-year reign will span a substantial part of Elisha's career, and, from his opening exchange with the prophet in 2 Kings 3 until his assassination at the hands of Jehu in 2 Kings 9, he remains an intriguing entity.[2] Owing to a regnal introduction that is fraught with ambivalence (2 Kings 3:1–3), Jehoram quickly emerges as a conflicted character in the narrative. On the one hand, there is the qualification that he is slightly less iniquitous than his parents because he removes

---

[1] For a historical overview, see L. L. Grabbe, "The Kingdom of Israel from Omri to the Fall of Samaria: If We Had Only the Bible . . . ," in L. L. Grabbe (ed.), *Ahab Agonistes: The Rise and Fall of the Omri Dynasty* (LHBOTS 421/ESHM 6; New York and London: T & T Clark, 2007), 54–99.

[2] J. T. Walsh ("The Organization of 2 Kings 3–11," *CBQ* 72 (2010), 240) notes the anonymity that soon follows Jehoram: "Although 2 Kings 3 opens with the standard regnal formula for Jehoram of Israel (3:1–3), the Israelite king's name quickly disappears from the text."

the "Baal pillar" (מצבת הבעל), but, on the other hand, he does not turn aside from the sins of Jeroboam son of Nebat. The sense of ambivalence conveyed in Jehoram's introduction, as we will soon see, also comes across in his interactions with Elisha both in 2 Kings 3 and later in the story.

The first major event of Jehoram's reign picks up a thread from earlier in the account, the rebellion of Mesha king of Moab that is mentioned in 2 Kings 1:1. Any further report on the nature of Moabite insurrection is then held in abeyance, as Ahaziah's fall and his efforts to seek Baal Zebub are given narrative priority. Even if there is a slight dislocation in 2 Kings 1:1, it is possible that the mention of Moab's rebellion becomes a symbolic commentary on Ahaziah's rebellious move to consult a foreign deity.[3] In the present context of 2 Kings 3 Jehoram's sights are directed at the Moabite rebellion, given that his brother Ahaziah was distracted with his own issues. Enlisted in the campaign is the southern king of Judah, Jehoshaphat. His resurfacing catches the reader off guard because his son is reported as succeeding him in 1 Kings 22:50, but of course this is not the first time Jehoshaphat has been a military ally of the north.[4] Earlier in 1 Kings 22:1–5 Jehoshaphat is recruited for Ahab's campaign against Ramoth-Gilead, where he utters the same line of solidarity that is now parroted here in 2 Kings 3 ("my people are your people, my horses are your horses"). Jehoshaphat barely survives that conflict, especially because Ahab forced him to wear his royal robes while he (Ahab) went to battle in a disguise; had Jehoshaphat not "cried out" and revealed his identity in 1 Kings 22:32, he may well have been critically wounded by the Aramean cavalry.

---

[3] The "Moabite Stone" (or "Mesha Stele") provides an invaluable historical resource; for useful overviews of the inscription and its relation to the battle recounted in 2 Kings 3, see C. A. Rollston, *Writing and Literacy in the World of Ancient Israel: Epigraphic Evidence from the Iron Age* (Atlanta: Society of Biblical Literature, 2010), 53–5, and K. A. D. Smelik, *Writings from Ancient Israel: A Handbook of Historical and Religious Documents* (Edinburgh: T & T Clark, 1991), 29–40. See also P. D. Stern, "Of Kings and Moabites: History and Theology in 2 Kings 3 and the Mesha Inscription," *HUCA* 64 (1993), 1–14.

[4] On the chronological issues surrounding Jehoshaphat, and the ancillary problem of Edomite kingship (1 Kings 22:47), see J. R. Bartlett, "The 'United' Campaign against Moab in 2 Kgs 3.4–27," in J. F. A. Sawyer and D. J. A. Clines (eds), *Midian, Moab and Edom: The History and Archaeology of Late Bronze and Iron Age Jordan and North West Arabia* (JSOTSup 24; Sheffield: JSOT Press, 1983), 135–46.

The alliance with the Omrides has been a snare for Jehoshaphat, and the Moabite campaign provides yet another kind of entrapment: the water crisis. Ahab's career was plagued with dryness, and now Jehoram's circumambulation through the desert results in a similar kind of drastic experience. Walter Brueggemann reflects on a larger thematic issue:

> The territory east of the Jordan is notoriously arid. It appears that Jehoram's excessively eager military mobilization was poorly planned. Perhaps the narrative is reminiscent of the drought that Elijah had announced and then ended (1 Kgs 17:1; 18:45), reminding that the Omride dynasty is endlessly vexed by drought and is not good at water management.[5]

Furthermore, it is the king of Israel's existential complaint ("Alas, for the LORD has summoned these three kings to give them into the hand of Moab") in 2 Kings 3:10 that prompts Jehoshaphat to show initiative rather than acquiescence. Jehoshaphat's question ("Is there not a prophet of the LORD here, that we might seek the LORD from him?") is similar to his query in 1 Kings 22:7, but there are some crucial differences in context. Earlier Jehoshaphat requested that a prophet be sought *before* embarking on the campaign against Ramoth-Gilead, whereas here in the desert he asks for prophetic counsel as a result of extenuating circumstances. Whether Jehoshaphat is finally prompted by the water crisis or Jehoram's gasp of despair, his question becomes the means for the prophet Elisha to enter the fray.

PROPHETIC TUNES

It may be assumed that Jehoshaphat's inquiry about a prophet is directed to his northern counterpart, but it is not the king of Israel who responds. Instead, an anonymous courtier supplies a response in 2 Kings 3:11 that contains some interesting data: "One of the servants of the king of Israel spoke up, and said, 'Here is Elisha son of Shaphat, who poured water on the hands of Elijah.'" The exact image of *pouring water* as a sign of servitude is not particularly common in the Hebrew Bible, and certainly has not been used in describing the Elijah–Elisha relationship to this point. More importantly here it

---

[5] Brueggemann, *1 & 2 Kings*, 308.

communicates to the reader that news of Elisha's succession has moved beyond the prophetic circles to the point that it can be referred to by members of the royal entourage. Even so, there is an undeniable irony in describing Elisha as "one who pours water" in the midst of a life-threatening water crisis. It is impossible to determine whether the servant is being intentionally critical of the king, implying that the water crisis is due to the mismanagement of the campaign or the deficient attitude of the Omrides toward Elijah and Elisha. The servant, irrespective of any intention, provides some indirect characterization of Elisha that is augmented by Jehoshaphat's agreement in 3:12: "There is the word of the LORD with him." News of Elisha has spread to the point that he is known in the royal circles of Judah as well, and his experience with water no doubt would prove convenient in such dehydrated circumstances.

The servant's testimony and Jehoshaphat's endorsement are persuasive enough, such that the three kings "went down to him" (וירדו אליו). Commentators debate whether this verb means that Elisha accompanies the troops on the campaign, or if instead the kings send a delegation to fetch him.[6] Based on the servant's description, Elisha is "here" (פֹּה), meaning at hand or nearby; since all three kings go down (the verb is plural), it is doubtful that they travel very far. In my judgment this description implies that Elisha has ventured into the desert with the troops and the royal entourage, seemingly anticipating the very situation that has now developed: a water crisis that prompts the need for a prophetic word. The question arises, though, as to whether or not King Jehoram is aware of Elisha's presence; if so, why would he utter a cry of despair instead of consulting the prophet? Like his (lately departed) brother Ahaziah, there is a hesitancy to seek out the prophetic word.

This scene presents the first royal encounter in Elisha's career, and there are both differences and continuities with Elijah's previous work. Elijah was hard to find and frustrated Ahab, who looked high and low for him (but ends the drought in 1 Kings 18). Now Elisha is seemingly at hand and accessible, and likewise has a solution for the water shortage in 2 Kings 3. A further comparison emerges with Micaiah in 1 Kings 22, the prophet who was sarcastic and

---

[6] e.g., E. Gass, "Topographical Considerations in 2 Kings 3," *JBL* 128 (2009), 67: "How is it that Elisha was around just when the allied kings were looking for a prophet of YHWH?"

confrontational with the king of Israel (see particularly 1 Kings 22:15–18). Elisha, we note, has a similar kind of engagement with Jehoram in the next scene (vv. 13–15a). No formalities are included; instead, Elisha launches into a theological trial of sorts, with accusations pointed squarely at Jehoram:

Elisha said to the king of Israel, "What could be with me and you? Go to the prophets of your father and the prophets of your mother!" The king of Israel said to him, "No, for the LORD has called these three kings to give them into the hand of Moab." Elisha said, "As the LORD of hosts lives, whom I stand before, were it not that I regard Jehoshaphat king of Judah, I would neither acknowledge nor look at you. Now then, bring me a musician."

There is a measure of tension between Elisha's bold remarks and the narrator's earlier evaluation of Jehoram in 3:2–3. On the one hand, the king of Israel is assessed as better than his parents Ahab and Jezebel, principally on the basis of his removal of the Baal pillar (מצבת הבעל). This compliment, on the other hand, is tempered in light of the later divulgence of 2 Kings 10:27, when the Baal pillar is removed (again) during Jehu's purge and the Baal temple renovated into a lavatory. It is assumed that at some point during Jehoram's reign the pillar reappears, hence the legitimacy of Elisha's derogatory reference. For his part, Jehoram does not dispute the prophet's charge, nor does he respond to the issue of consulting "the prophets of his mother and father." Instead, he simply repeats his utterance about God's handing over the three kings to a death sentence in the wilderness. Numerous commentators draw comparisons between this episode of a water shortage and similar traditions of Israel's grumbling in the Pentateuch.[7] If so, then Jehoram's murmuring will be countered by the words of Elisha, who emerges as the Mosaic figure in the chapter. Even more acutely, the Micaiah comparison is particularly germane here. In terms of posture before the king of Israel, Micaiah does not cower in Ahab's presence, nor does Elisha appear to tremor before Jehoram. Micaiah's word in 1 Kings 22:17–23, moreover, is stratified and complex, and also works *counter* to the king's best interest, so Elisha's word in 2 Kings 3:16–19 might be similarly configured.

Some unique contours of Elisha's character have already been proffered (the episode with the bears ripping apart forty-two

---

[7] Water is not turned to blood in 2 Kings 3, but the Moabite mistake could act as something of a parody of the Exodus account.

Bethelites readily comes to mind), and calling for a minstrel in verse 15 also puts this scene in its own key. In 1 Kings 22 Micaiah evidently speaks his prophetic word without any musical accompaniment, a fact that would not be startling in itself, except that Elisha does so here in 2 Kings 3. Because no music is associated with Elijah, the call for the minstrel here is an unforeseen development. Still, for prophetic activity to be connected with music is not entirely unheard of in Israel's recent history (see 1 Samuel 10:5); thus Elisha's request is not altogether novel, but it is curious that he is interested in reviving the fashion. Commentators offer a score of suggestions as to the role and purpose of the music here, although none is overly convincing, and the call for a minstrel ultimately has an elusive strain.[8] The reader might be tempted, therefore, to interpret the music as a throwback to an earlier era, a reminder of antecedent traditions displaced by the innovations of Jeroboam and the Omrides. The delivery of the prophetic word in this scene is categorically discordant from the word sought by Ahaziah in 2 Kings 1, and such differentiation may be part of the purpose for the music here.

WATER COLORS

Elisha's request for musical accompaniment may sound strange to the ears of some scholars, but it is not questioned by any of the kings nor any member of the royal retinues. The music is effective: as the minstrel plays, "the hand of the LORD" comes upon Elisha. Back in 1 Kings 18:46 the hand of the LORD also comes upon Elijah, allowing him to outrun Ahab's chariot ahead of the much-needed rain that had been recently forecast by God (rather than Baal). The events of 2 Kings 3 take place on foreign soil in the context of war, but the water scarcity is similar. Furthermore, Elijah makes (עשה) a trench around the altar (2 Kings 18.32) to hold water preceding the miraculous fire,

---

[8] For the idea that the harpist is part of a larger ruse, see J. C. Long, "Elisha's Deceptive Prophecy in 2 Kings 3: A Response to Raymond Westbrook," *JBL* 126 (2007), 171; cf. R. Westbrook, "Elisha's True Prophecy in 2 Kings 3," *JBL* 124 (2005), 530–2; J. C. Long, Jr, and M. Sneed, "'Yahweh Has Given These Three Kings into the Hand of Moab': A Socio-Literary Reading of 2 Kings 3," in J. Kaltner and L. Stulman (eds), *Inspired Speech: Prophecy in the Ancient Near East. Essays in Honor of Herbert B. Huffmon* (JSOTSup 378; London: T&T Clark, 2004), 253–75.

and now Elisha's word about making (עשׂה) ditches precedes the supply of miraculous water. It is argued by some that the music puts Elisha in a trance-like state, and the syntax of the direct speech in verse 16 certainly sounds as though the words are emitted from a visionary state: "Make this valley, pools, pools." After this the utterance becomes more conventional—replete with the "thus says the LORD" formula—and is twofold in scope. First, the valley will be filled with water, and none will die of thirst. Second, as though this were a trifling matter, Moab will be given into hand of the allied forces.

A number of interpreters are disturbed by the environmental disaster that is forecast along with the rain: not only will Moab be handed over to the coalition of kings, but "good trees" will be cut down, springs of water polluted, and the land marred with stones (2 Kings 3:19). It is not merely an ecological conscience that discomfits such interpreters—though for such sentiments in an era of rampant industrial pollution one might be forgiven—but because Deuteronomy 20:19 is thought to prohibit much of this kind of ecocidal frenzy: "If you besiege a city for many days, making war against it in order to seize it, you must not ruin its trees by thrusting an axe against it. From it you can eat, but not cut down. Is a tree of the field a human being to go before you in a siege?"[9] It should be pointed out, however, that, since there is no prolonged siege in this context, it is debatable whether this stricture applies in the present case. Yet the most controversial aspect is not the destruction of land, but rather the accusation of false prophecy that is made by some interpreters toward Elisha. Complication arises at the end of the episode, as the prediction in verses 18–19 ("Moab will be given into your hand, and you will strike every fortified city and choice town") is alleged to be problematic.

Preceding any charges of false prophecy that might be leveled, in the very next scene (vv. 20–4) there are two items that flow from Elisha's inescapably *true* word, beginning with the water: "In the morning, when the gift (מנחה) would be offered up, behold, water was coming from the way of Edom, and the land was filled with

---

[9] Note the detailed survey of J. L. Wright, "Warfare and Wanton Destruction: A Reexamination of Deuteronomy 20:19–20 in Relation to Ancient Siegecraft," *JBL* 127 (2008), 423–58. Fretheim (*First and Second Kings*, 143) wonders if the outbreak of great wrath in 2 Kings 3:27 is related to the "environmental degradation" in the campaign.

water!" Any attempt rationalistically to explain the sudden appearance of water is mitigated by the chronological notice that connects the supply of water with the time of sacrifice. But what is unstated in the chronological note is: who does the offering and where is it offered? In the absence of any other qualification, I must assume the Jerusalem temple to be the place of sacrifice, and thus representing a rebuke to the Omrides, who eschew the cultic centrality of Jerusalem in favor of Jeroboam's installations. The appearance of the water, in terms of the narrative, stands outside *royal time*, much like the account of Elisha's succession in the previous chapter. Moreover the connection in verse 20 between the morning offering and the divine source of water parallels Elijah's endeavors on Mt Carmel in 1 Kings 18:36, when he prays for the people "at the time the gift (מנחה) was offered up," preceding the divine fire that consumes the sacrifice. Elijah's actions on Mt Carmel bring an end to a drought, and Elisha's prophetic word results in the supply of water in the Moabite desert.

As events unfold, the water also is instrumental in securing victory over Moab, as predicted in the second part of Elisha's prophetic oracle. After the appearance of water, the narrative perspective immediately shifts to the Moabite point of view. The multitude of Moabite troops view the liquid in the valley, but their rationalistic interpretation is not correct: they see the red color and conclude, "This is blood! The kings have surely attacked themselves, and each man has struck his companion! Now to the plunder, O Moab!" Within the annals of Israel's history there are some great miscalculations. One example is King Saul in 1 Samuel 18:25–7, where he sets a dowry of 100 Philistine foreskins, reckoning that David will fall by the hand of the same Philistines (who no doubt would object to such gratuitous surgery). Saul's hopes are dashed when David returns with 200 foreskins, and Saul is thus left with twice the unenviable cache of grisly trophies. In the same vein as Saul's miscalculation (but with graver consequences), the Moabites' "impulsive reasoning" paves the way for their defeat in verse 24.[10] Jehoram has insufficient confidence in Elisha (the one who used to pour water on Elijah's hands), whereas the Moabites are overconfident that the valley is full of blood (rather than divinely supplied water), and guilty of what C. F. Keil once

---

[10] Cohn, *2 Kings*, 23.

labeled as an "optical delusion."[11] The Moabites move forward to plunder what they think is a decimated camp, but are soundly defeated by the rehydrated coalition forces.

STONEWALLED

In the context of the campaign, the materializing water has a dual utility: saving the troops and defeating the Moabites. When surveying Elisha's career, it also could be said that he *doubles* his earlier water miracle in Jericho, in that the parched army is sustained by the same water that is subsequently used to deceive the Moabites. Not only are the allied forces victorious in the battle, but in accordance with the prophetic word the good trees are chopped down and the springs of water stopped up. All the Moabite cities are torn down, with the exception of Kir Hareseth. But even this ancient capital appears doomed when verse 25 describes its stone walls as "surrounded by the slingers, and they struck it."[12] Most critics agree that, if the story ended with the pelting of Kir Hareseth, the impression left on the reader would be: a victory for the Omride king Jehoram, whose imperiled campaign is rescued by the prophetic word of Elisha. But the final moments of the chapter (vv. 26–7) are brimming with reversals, starting with the king of Moab's strange string of actions. With his back against the wall, Mesha and 700 swordsmen make a final attempt to repel the Edomites. The details are difficult to decipher, but the defensive actions of the Moabite king are not enough, leading to his last act of desperation: "Then he took his son—the first born, who was to reign in his place—and offered him up as a burnt offering on the wall. There was great wrath on Israel. They pulled away from him, and returned to the land."

The episode's appalling denouement has aroused heated discussion in the secondary literature, as it includes human sacrifice, the ambiguity of "great wrath," and the withdrawal of Israel's troops prior to

---

[11] C. F. Keil, *I & II Kings, I & II Chronicles* (Commentary on the Old Testament, 10 vols), ed. C. F. Keil and F. Delitzsch (Peabody, MA: Hendrickson, 1996) (originally published 1866–91), 216.

[12] On the location of the city, see B. C. Jones, "In Search of Kir Hareseth: A Case Study in site Identification," *JSOT* 52 (1991), 3–24.

the total defeat of Mesha.[13] Of these elements, the departure from Kir Hareseth especially merits our consideration: according to some interpreters, Israel's military withdrawal nullifies Elisha's word, opening him to the charge of false prophecy.[14] Even if he cannot be formally charged with false prophecy, for Wesley Bergen the closing verse "acts as a wrecking ball, knocking down the image of Elisha."[15] Though I appreciate Bergen's honesty, the wrecking-ball image seems as destructive as the coalition army's clear-cutting of every good tree in Moab. Indeed, Marvin Sweeney has a view that is antithetical to Bergen, and sees no case for false prophecy in the closing moments of 2 Kings 3. Sweeney provides a more sanguine reading, and in his interpretation Elisha is not culpable:

The reference to anger must be read as 'upon' ('*al*) Israel, that is, Israel became angry at the sight of Mesha's sacrifice of his son, and consequently withdrew from Kir Hareseth. Israel/Jehoram—and not YHWH—would be responsible for the failure to achieve victory over the Moabites. The scenario provides a parallel to the wilderness tradition—for example, the Israelite spies refused to accept YHWH's guarantees of victory and suffered as a result (Num 14).[16]

My approach to 2 Kings 3:27 inclines in a different direction, as I consider this closing line of the chapter to make several *thematic* contributions to the overall storyline, starting with the configuration of King Mesha of Moab. Mesha's sacrifice is not the only reference to cultic practice in this chapter: his grim offering on the wall is intended to contrast "the time of sacrifice" back in verse 20, when Elisha's miracle of the water takes place. What needs to be taken into account, and has not been adequately considered by interpreters, is the significance of this final verse within the larger theme of *succession* that has been witnessed in 2 Kings 1–3. When Mesha sacrifices his first-born son and heir to the throne, it forms a bitter contrast to Elisha's prophetic succession. Consequently, Elisha's succession to the prophetic office is bracketed by flawed succession narratives of both

---

[13] e.g., S. Morschauser, "A 'Diagnostic' Note on the 'Great Wrath upon Israel' in 2 Kings 3:27," *JBL* 129 (2010), 299–302.

[14] A number of views are canvassed in R. B. Chisholm, Jr, "Israel's Retreat and the Failure of Prophecy in 2 Kings 3," *Biblica*, 92 (2011), 71–80. Among others, Chisholm cites L.-S. Tiemeyer, "Prophecy as a Way of Cancelling Prophecy—The Strategic Uses of Foreknowledge," *ZAW* 117 (2005), 329–50.

[15] Bergen, *Elisha and the End of Prophetism*, 82.

[16] Sweeney, *I & II Kings*, 284.

Israelite and Moabite royalty: first Ahaziah's fall (without an heir) in 2 Kings 1, then Mesha of Moab (who sacrifices his heir) in 2 Kings 3. Far from any charge of false prophecy at the end of 2 Kings 3, there is a vindication of prophetic succession and a corresponding eclipse of kingship. On a related note, the withdrawal of the Israelite army does not reflect badly on Elisha; rather, it is a negative conclusion that reflects on Jehoram's leadership. Burke Long suggests that the strange combination of victory tainted by "great wrath" corresponds to the "mixed evaluation" of Jehoram at the beginning of the chapter.[17] The various kings in 2 Kings 3—whether Israelite, Judahite, Edomite, or Moabite—either capitulate, cannot supply water for their troops, or fail to finish the attack on a city, and, in Mesha's case, is guilty of destroying his own heir and successor. All of these features stand in marked contrast with Elisha, and are preparatory for the next scenes in the narrative where the prophet is the central character. The overall point of the ending in 2 Kings 3:27, therefore, cannot lie in some permutation of unfulfilled prophecy or deceptive act on Elisha's part. Rather, the ambiguous ending returns the focus to the king of Israel, whose utterance of categorical despair and initial reluctance to consult the prophet causes this campaign to end badly, much like his own career will end badly in due course. Ahaziah distanced himself from the prophetic word in favor of some other program, and felt the bitter consequences. His brother Jehoram is now on course for a similar experience. As for Elisha, presumably many Israelite lives are spared because of his involvement in the Moabite campaign, much like the Jericho spring in the previous chapter, and much like the widow's sons in the next segment.

CREDIT SQUEEZE

When the army retreats from Moab and returns home, by all estimation so does Elisha. Although not specified in the text, the next scene (2 Kings 4:1–7) must take place within Israelite territory, as the reader is transferred from the international stage to the domestic arena for Elisha's next sequence of action. Like the previous episode, this scene

---

[17] Long, *2 Kings*, 46; cf. Aucker, "Putting Elisha in his Place," 106–7.

features a severe crisis, albeit one where only a single family is affected. The wife of a member of "the sons of the prophets" directs an appeal to Elisha, and several commentators note that the usual recipient of such an appeal is God or the king. There is an ironic contrast between the woman who implores the prophet and King Jehoram in 2 Kings 3, who exhales a cry of despair instead of seeking a word from Elisha. The unnamed woman's impassioned speech provides a number of background details: "Your servant my husband died, and *you* know (ואתה ידעת) that your servant feared the LORD, but the creditor is coming to take my two boys for himself as slaves!" From these words it emerges that the woman is a widow, and the syntax of the utterance (using the second-person pronoun for emphasis) seems to presuppose some familiarity. Elisha may have been acquainted with the (deceased) husband, and hence the wife has the necessary access to gain an audience and plead with the prophet.

Interpreters often observe that the set of circumstances found in this scene—a widow in dire need, rescued by a prophet—have some obvious similarities with Elijah's adventures recounted in 1 Kings 17:8–16 in Zarephath of Sidon.[18] The parallels between the two stories lead G. H. Jones to conclude "that the Elijah tradition borrowed from the Elisha stories, in order to make the master seem greater than the disciple."[19] A relationship between these two episodes is undeniably the case, but I would argue the opposite of Jones: namely, the similarities are intended to illustrate that Elisha reproduces and amplifies his master's work. Rather than the master outshining the disciple, it is the other way around in 2 Kings 4:1–7, where the reader immediately notices a doubling, as the widow in this scene has twice the number of sons as the widow of Sidon in 1 Kings 17. Moreover, as the scene in 2 Kings 4 unfolds, we also notice a functional doubling of Elisha's miracle, since the widow is able both to satisfy her creditor *and* to live on the remainder.

Neither the identity of the creditor nor the reasons for the economic distress are fleshed out in the story. The majority of exegetes point to texts such as Exodus 21 to understand the widow's crisis. For

[18] e.g., J. Keinänen, *Traditions in Collision: A Literary and Redaction-Critical Study on the Elijah Narratives 1 Kings 17–19* (Helsinki: The Finnish Exegetical Society; Göttingen: Vandenhoeck & Ruprecht, 2001), 20–7.

[19] Mead, "'Elisha Will Kill'? The Deuteronomistic Rhetoric of Life and Death in the Theology of the Elisha Narratives," 165, citing Jones, *1 and 2 Kings*, 402.

example, Cogan and Tadmor explain the background as follows: "Biblical law regulated the seizure of wives and children for nonpayment of debts; see Exod 21:7; cf. Amos 2:6, Isa 50:1. These 'salable' persons were to be freed in the jubilee year, according to Lev 25:39–42, or could be released by a special decree, as in Neh 5."[20] There are comparatively fewer reactions, however, to the creditor as a character in this scene, albeit one who never makes a formal appearance on the stage.[21] Is the creditor presented as having a legitimate case against the widow, or is the creditor exploitative, with a ferocity that evokes a measure of sympathy for the family? Again, the creditor is an anonymous character in this story, but Michael Fishbane notes that Jewish tradition labels him as none other than Jehoram son of Ahab, king of Israel.[22]

Floating the idea that the creditor in 2 Kings 4:1 is King Jehoram will no doubt be regarded as a fanciful claim that few modern scholars would take seriously, but I would suggest that from a literary perspective there might be some value here. Not that Jehoram is the creditor, but it is possible that the creditor is configured as a *cipher* for the king in this scene. Such a notion gains currency when it is taken into account that the widow appeals to the prophet for help rather than the king, implying she has a better chance at receiving justice from a prophetic representative rather than from royalty. Omride kings, as Brian Aucker reminds us, have a poor track record in providing foodstuffs for their subjects, and in some cases seize the assets of their citizens (for example, the affair of Naboth's vineyard in 1 Kings 21).[23] Furthermore, there are a number of verbal links with the preceding episode in Moab, where Jehoram appears in a negative

---

[20] M. Cogan and H. Tadmor, *II Kings: A New Translation with Introduction and Commentary* (AB 11; New York: Doubleday, 1988), 56. Cf. Nelson, *First and Second Kings*, 171: "Slavery for debt was part of the Hebrew legal system (Exod. 21:7), and the oppressive economic conditions that brought it about are reflected in Amos 2:6; 8:6; Micah 2:9. Verse 2 makes the widow's need even more apparent, but paradoxically the one little thing left to her will prove to be her salvation."

[21] Mead ("'Elisha Will Kill'? The Deuteronomistic Rhetoric of Life and Death in the Theology of the Elisha Narratives," 167–8) provides a short but helpful survey of some commentators and compiles a list of those scholars who assert that the creditor is within his rights, and others who believe the creditor is presented as harsh or unmerciful.

[22] M. Fishbane, *Haftarot: The Traditional Hebrew Text with the New JPS Translation* (Philadelphia: Jewish Publication Society, 2002), 19.

[23] Aucker, "Putting Elisha in his Place," 116. Cf. Mead, "'Elisha Will Kill'? The Deuteronomistic Rhetoric of Life and Death in the Theology of the Elisha Narratives,"

light.[24] The repetition of terms such as "pour" (יצק), "fill" (מלא), and "withdraw" (נסע) align the two stories to draw heightened attention to Jehoram's unwillingness to consult the prophet during the water crisis, as opposed to the widow who pours out oil until the supply of jars ceases. The widow's sons remain in her house and have a future, much like the residents of Jericho no longer plagued by evil water that causes bereavement. For the first time in his career, Elisha is given the title "man of God." Having earlier inherited the mantle of his master, now Elisha is bestowed with the same honorific, leading us to suspect that he will continue his master's work in the next phase of the story.

THE BENEFACTRESS

During the events of 1 Kings 17:8–24, the troubles of the Sidonian widow of Zarephath do not end with Elijah's provisions of oil and flour. Of course, Elijah's intervention allows the widow and her son to survive the famine, but, when that same son is subsequently struck with a serious illness, Elijah has to intervene again and rescue him from death in the roof chamber (עליה) where he has been lodging. As just observed in 2 Kings 4:1–7, Elisha similarly rescues a distressed widow with a supply of oil that satisfies her insistent creditor, and therefore he is pictured as following the example of his predecessor. This trend of Elisha's replication of Elijah's deeds continues in the long episode of 2 Kings 4:8–37, but with some colorful variation. In this story it will not be one (or both) of the widow's two sons who are imperiled. Instead, there is a new character in the drama, the "great

169: "Parker has noted that most biblical petitionary narratives, marked by 'cries' from the needy, are addressed to the king. In the woman's turning to the prophet instead of the king, Parker and others see a subtle challenge to the king's ineffective handling of such economic problems," citing S. B. Parker, *Stories in Scripture and Inscriptions: Comparative Studies on Narratives in Northwest Semitic Inscriptions and the Hebrew Bible* (New York: Oxford University Press, 1997), 19–35.

[24] Satterthwaite, "The Elisha Narratives and the Coherence of 2 Kings 2–8," 12, wonders "if some analogy is here suggested with the immediately preceding narrative: there, too, YHWH has miraculously *filled* pools of water, and thus delivered Israel; and the latter stages of the war against Moab might be described as a case where YHWH's *blessing finally stopped*, and stopped, on that occasion leaving his people well short of final deliverance." Similar links are posited by Y. Shemesh, "Elisha and the Miraculous Jug of Oil (2 Kgs 4:1–7)," *JHS* 8 (2008), 1–18.

woman" of Shunem, who is located on the opposite end of the socio-economic scale as the two widows in the previous episodes.

Elijah's movements were unpredictable and usually proved elusive, as evidenced when Obadiah testifies that there is "no nation or kingdom" where Ahab did not search for him (1 Kings 18:10). Elisha, however, has a much more established itinerary, even though the text does not elaborate his actual activities during these peregrinations. The great woman of Shunem, who will not be named at any point in the story, regularly hosts the prophet on his travels "whenever he was passing through." Her insistence is conveyed through the verb "strong" (חזק), as she must urge Elisha to accept the offer of hospitality. At the same time, it seems to me that this verb *strong* becomes a metonymic image for her character in this episode, as her forcefulness is manifested in several different ways during this lengthy episode. To be sure, the prophet is not the only man she is "strong" with, as she convinces her husband (likewise unnamed) to build a roof chamber (עליה) for Elisha. This type of spatial setting has been seen before, both in Elijah's healing of the widow's son in Zarephath and Ahaziah's fall in 2 Kings 1. Owing to these previous usages, the reader might well suspect that an ominous injury will occur at some point here in the northern locale of Shunem.

But, before anything remotely ominous takes place, there is a stretch of dialogue that begins with Elisha and his servant lad, Gehazi, in the relative comfort of the roof chamber provided by the great woman. This is Gehazi's first appearance in the story, and he receives no formal introduction of any kind, but he plays an active role in the next few episodes of the story; not unlike the great woman of Shunem, he will undergo his own vicissitudes of fortune. Meanwhile, in this particular scene Gehazi's role is to mediate the conversation between the woman and Elisha, a strange protocol to say the least (though one that the woman will break later in the episode, in v. 27). Out of gratitude for the woman's efforts, Elisha offers to speak on her behalf to the king or general of the military, and, if his words are taken at face value, it must indicate his considerable level of influence. Even though he basically insults the king in the previous chapter (see 3:14), here he claims to be able to lobby on her behalf. The identity of the Israelite general is unknown, but, given that Elisha recently provided water for his troops in the desert of Moab, it is fair to imagine that any request from the prophet would be favorably received. Despite Elisha's offer, the Shunammite woman is sufficiently well placed and politically secure enough to decline the gesture, suggesting that her motives for offering hospitality to the man of God are not self-serving or directed toward a more utilitarian motive.

The woman not only declares that she has no need for prophetic intervention of any kind, but with that she departs the roof chamber. It is Gehazi—in response to Elisha's further inquiry about doing something for the Shunammite—who volunteers the information that the woman is childless with an "old" husband. The combination of age and sterility sets the stage for what scholars usually label the *type-scene of the barren wife*, a familiar pattern established in Genesis with Sarah, Rebekah, and Rachel, and continuing with Samson's mother and Hannah in the Deuteronomistic History.[25] A unique variation in this version of the conventional type-scene here in 2 Kings 4 is the Shunammite woman's plea "Don't lie (כזב) to your maidservant," an utterance that elicits no response from Elisha. Several commentators draw a comparison with the words of Sarah in Genesis 18:12, where she says, "After I'm worn out, will I have this pleasure? *And* my husband is old!"[26] Like Sarah, against the odds the woman indeed gives birth just as Elisha forecast (4:17), no doubt heightening her respect for the holiness of her guest. Danna Fewell also notes a possible connection between Sarah's son Isaac, and the boy born to the Shunammite, perhaps implying that this child faces a steep challenge in the days ahead.[27]

It is notable that *children in crisis* form a common thread in a number of episodes early in Elisha's career, ranging from the boys of Bethel to the (deceased) heir of the king of Moab. This theme continues in the next sequence (vv. 18–19), where some narrative acceleration moves the Shunammite's miraculous son into

---

[25] On type-scenes in general, see Alter, *The Art of Biblical Narrative*, 47–62, and, on this particular kind, "How Convention Helps Us Read: The Case of the Bible's Annunciation Type-Scene," *Prooftexts*, 3 (1983), 115–30. Alter has a negative view of Elisha in the type-scene of 2 Kings 4, whereas M. Roncace ("Elisha and the Woman of Shunem: 2 Kings 4.8–37 and 8.1–6 Read in Conjunction," *JSOT* 91 (2000), 115) argues that 2 Kings 4 does not "fit the pattern." By contrast, I would maintain that it does fit the pattern, and add that the boy is far from irrelevant, as he is used as a typological representation of how property is restored after "exile" (see the discussion below in the sequel episode of 2 Kings 8:1–6).

[26] e.g., Brueggemann, *1 & 2 Kings*, 322.

[27] D. N. Fewell, "The Gift: World Alteration and Obligation in 2 Kings 4:8–37," in S. M. Olyan and R. C. Culley (eds), *A Wise and Discerning Mind: Essays in Honor of Burke O. Long* (Providence, RI: Brown Judaic Studies, 2000), 109–23, at 119.

adolescence: "The child grew up, and one day he went out to his father, among the harvesters. He said to his father, 'My head! My head!'" Scholars often speculate on the precise nature of the malady, but the symptoms are serious enough that within a short time he dies on his mother's knees. This mortal news is hidden from the aged husband by the mother herself, who only asks permission to journey to Elisha, who, as it turns out, is at Mt Carmel:

So she went, and came to the man of God, to Mt Carmel. When the man of God saw her from afar, he said to Gehazi his lad, "Look, this Shunammite! Please run to meet her, and say to her, 'Is there peace to you, peace to your husband, peace to the child?'" She said, "Peace." Then she came to the man of God, to the mountain, and she took hold of his feet. Gehazi drew near to drive her away, but the man of God said, "Refrain from her, for her soul is bitter, but the LORD has concealed it from me, and not told me." She said, "Did I request a son from my lord? Didn't I say, 'Don't mislead me'?" (vv. 25–8)

Compared with the preceding dialogue, there are some strange moments in this conversation on Mt Carmel, where in 1 Kings 18 Elijah was victorious over the prophets of Baal: first, Elisha says that he has not been divinely apprised of the situation, and, second, the woman refers bitterly to her earlier desire not to be given false hope about having a son. The woman's words of pathos, though, at least have an antecedent in the text, as she indeed pleaded with the prophet not to "lie" to her in verse 16. Elisha's comment about divine *secrecy*, however, has no other referent and is difficult to interpret. This divine concealment does not prevent the prophet from trying, and, recognizing the desperation, he first sends Gehazi ahead. Gehazi, it should be pointed out, does not leave for Shunem empty-handed, but carries with him the "staff" of Elisha, an instrument that has not been mentioned in connection with the prophet until now. Despite Gehazi's pains, "there is no voice, no attentiveness." The child of the type-scene lies in Elisha's bed, and, although there is a narrative ellipsis, the reader recalls that the bed is located in the roof chamber of the house. As this is the same spatial setting where Elijah successfully interceded back in 1 Kings 17, so now Elisha stretches himself out until the lad's flesh became warm.[28] The denouement is much less chilling than the previous episode with an imperiled child of Moab: after the

---

[28] For a cultural reading of the healing procedure, see S. Lasine, "Matters of Life and Death: The Story of Elijah and the Widow's Son in Comparative Perspective," *BibInt*, 12 (2004), 117–44.

Shunammite's lad has sneezed "seven times," he opens his eyes, and in short order he is back with his mother, though she is not recorded as saying a word upon departing the room.[29]

Reviewing the whole of this lengthy episode, we can conclude that 2 Kings 4:8–37 makes a substantial contribution to Elisha's unfolding characterization in this stretch of the Deuteronomistic History. Placed as it is after the Moabite campaign, the subject matter appears quite different on the surface. But similar themes and literary tropes provide ample connection between the two stories, most notably the idea of prophetic intervention in times of crisis. Three supporting actors—the aged husband, Gehazi, and above all the great woman of Shunem—each plays a role in illuminating a different facet of Elisha's profile in this account. As Wesley Bergen summarizes:

> This story is also the first one in the Elisha corpus that presents a character other than Elisha who is portrayed with definite complexity. While the Shunammite woman remains unnamed, readers can certainly piece together a rather complex picture of this person based on her various interactions with Elisha, Gehazi and her husband.[30]

The husband, for his part, is in the dark about the lad's fate, and so parallels Elisha, who likewise declares that God has hidden from him the reason for the woman's journey. Gehazi, for his part, makes his first narrative appearance but comes away with a mixed grade. He is compliant enough and does Elisha's bidding when asked, but carries Elisha's staff without efficacy. Some commentators have suggested that Gehazi is a foil for the prophet, but to my mind there is something else going on here: it could foreshadow the *lack of a successor*, and the double portion previously inherited by Elisha will not be passed on. Gehazi makes a memorable appearance in the next chapter of 2 Kings, where he certainly will not be carrying the staff of his master. We should also note that, in 4:27, the mother, in the moment of emergency, virtually ignores Gehazi. There might be a slightly comical element here as Gehazi's security perimeter is breached, but bear in mind that this is not his (nor Elisha's) last involvement with the Shunammite.

---

[29] According to Levine's calculations ("Twice as Much of your Spirit," 31), the seven sneezes correspond to the seventh miracle of Elisha.

[30] Bergen, *Elisha and the End of Prophetism*, 88.

The great woman of Shunem is a dynamic figure in 2 Kings 4, and at every turn her speech and actions influence the developing characterization of Elisha: she is referred to as *a great woman* and proceeds to become a great and complex actor in the drama. Recent scholarship has invested a good deal of energy, and rightly so, to the Shunammite, although some of the conclusions of such studies merit further appraisal. For instance, in an illuminating study of this story, Mary Shields concludes that "the woman's status is elevated at the expense of that of Elisha," and that the prophet's lack of knowledge reflects a deep flaw.[31] I certainly agree that the great woman of Shunem is a nuanced character, but her literary complexity is not achieved by means of a deflation of the prophet. Instead, the Shunammite is used as a foil for the king of Israel as she opts for prophetic consultation in a time of crisis. Situated in the north, the great woman resists seeking other deities and so furthers the diminution of northern royalty seen in the past few episodes. As for Elisha's lack of knowledge, it is possible that this scene represents a prophetic test or challenge.[32] The positive resolution of this episode—placed after the Moabite debacle and the rescue of the distressed widow's two sons—implies that the challenge has been met. The roof chamber (עליה), built for Elisha at the woman's insistence, is once again a site where life triumphs over death.

---

[31] M. E. Shields, "Subverting a Man of God, Elevating a Woman: Role and Power Reversals in 2 Kings 4," *JSOT* 58 (1993), 65; cf. D. Jobling, "A Bettered Woman: Elisha and the Shunammite in the Deuteronomic Work," in F. Black, R. Boer and E. Runions (eds), *The Labour of Reading: Desire, Alienation and Biblical Interpretation*. (Semeia Studies 36; Atlanta: Scholars Press, 1999), 177–92. Note also A. Kalmanofsky, "Women of God: Maternal Grief and Religious Response in 1 Kings 17 and 2 Kings 4," *JSOT* 36 (2011), 55–74.

[32] See Y. Amit, "A Prophet Tested: Elisha, the Great Woman of Shunem, and the Story's Double Message," *BibInt*, 11 (2003), 279–94, though I would debate her conclusion.

4

Axes and Allies

"Since ancient times," writes Dennis Olson in a useful essay on recent trends in literary and rhetorical approaches to biblical material,

Interpreters have recognized the Bible's capacity as literature to delight, disturb, challenge, teach, move, or transform readers and hearers. The various methods under the broad umbrella of literary and rhetorical criticism seek to analyze in detail the cluster of words, literary forms, styles, tropes, and strategies embedded within biblical texts that work together to provoke such a wide range of reactions in audiences.[1]

In those portions of the book of Kings we have studied so far there are a rich variety of literary techniques that are used to create a vivid reading experience. Of central concern to this study is the figure of Elisha, sketched with an imaginative vitality yet still remaining elusive, as witnessed by the differing reactions among interpreters that have been sampled so far. By any measure the reader has travelled a considerable distance, starting with the image of Elisha plowing the field with twelve yoke of oxen, and most recently restoring the Shunammite's son to life. Along the way there has been continuity with Elijah's work, but also some expansion as we have seen Elisha's prophetic mandate take several new directions. Furthermore, over the course of Elisha's itinerary there have been a number of characters used as *royal foils* in the narrative, and such figures will continue to appear in the next installment of the story.

Four events provide the subjects for our analysis in this chapter. The first two (2 Kings 4:38–41 and 42–4) deal with feeding: healing a

---

[1] D. T. Olson, "Literary and Rhetorical Criticism," in T. B. Dozeman (ed.), *Methods for Exodus*, (Methods in Biblical Interpretation; Cambridge: Cambridge University Press, 2010), 13–54, at 13.

poisonous pot of stew is followed by providing food for a multitude from a modest amount. In these two anecdotes we will pay attention to the inevitable comparisons with the earlier healing of the Jericho spring in 2:19–22, and also how Elisha is pictured as a provider. These short accounts are followed by the long episode of 2 Kings 5, where the Aramean presence is reasserted in the storyline after a hiatus of sorts, as the Arameans have not featured since 1 Kings 22. Prominent here is Naaman, the commander of the Aramean military, whose story is fraught with reversals and unexpected actions, as this figure who surely inflicted much misery now seeks healing from the Israelite prophet. Along with the Aramean and Israelite kings, Elisha's servant lad (נער) Gehazi plays a memorable role in this episode, and is the conduit for a number of thematic connections and disjunctions with the preceding account with the Shunammite. In that episode Elisha tells Gehazi that God has hidden a crucial matter from him (2 Kings 4:27), but in this episode he knows exactly what Gehazi does (2 Kings 5:26). Perhaps the most easily overlooked character in this entire stretch of 2 Kings is an unnamed servant girl (נערה), and, though her role is small, she continues the pattern of pockets of faithfulness in the northern extremities. The fourth episode considered in this chapter is the brief story of the floating axehead in 2 Kings 6:1–8, and we will assess the contribution of this story to both Elisha's unfolding characterization and some of the broader movements in the narrative.

FAMINE AND FEAST

Taking stock of Elisha's career so far, it is notable that the prophet frequently is involved in situations where food or provisions are required by some desperate petitioner. Commentators have often gestured toward an ideological dimension of this narrative, and, indeed, it is not difficult to hear the polemical accents directed toward fertility cults as Elisha works to counteract famine and death. But more than just the ideology of the Omrides is under critique here, as we also sense that the Omrides as royal figures are incrementally undermined in the narrative. The association of Elisha with food and provisions underscores the notion that God's prophet supplies Israel with what the Omride kings are unable to provide their constituents.

A residual effect of Elisha's association with food, in my view, provides a clue to the larger structural design of his career. The organization of 2 Kings 2–10 has often puzzled interpreters, as Wesley Bergen admits: "One of the continuing difficulties for readers is relating the picture these stories paint of Elisha as head of small prophetic communities with the contrasting picture of Elisha as international power broker in regular contact with the king. Whether this contrast leads to confusion or complexity is largely up to the reader."[2] By means of this fluidity—whereby the prophet engages with the great leaders and the average citizens—a critique of Omride kingship is unfurled in the text. During this narrative segment, Elisha is God's representative who meets the needs of the constituents even as the wayward kings are confounded.

The first episode in 2 Kings 4:38–41 begins with both spatial and temporal indicators, as presumably Elisha carries on his prophetic itinerary: "Elisha returned to Gilgal, and there was a famine in the land." Gilgal is previously mentioned as a place on the travels of Elijah and Elisha in 2 Kings 1; in this present context it is the site of a prophetic community, but one that must be hard pressed during a time of famine. Several commentators venture a comparison to the drought in the days of Elijah (1 Kings 17), where the absence of rain is directly linked to the policies of Ahab. Although there is no comparable attribution here in Gilgal, the reader may well infer that judgment against Israel's kings is hovering in the background. Even so, famine is not the only threat to the prophetic community in this episode: there is also "death in the pot" (מות בסיר) because of a toxic herb placed in the cauldron by one of the members. Some creative attempts have been made to identify the poisonous plant, though others downplay the matter and refer to the questionable herb as merely a "laxative."[3]

---

[2] Bergen, *Elisha and the End of Prophetism*, 104; cf. Aucker, "Putting Elisha in his Place," 113: "Stories in which Elisha moves amidst the common folk are distinguished from those in which he is involved in the great political events of the day." Note also Brueggemann, *1 & 2 Kings*, 326: "I have no interest in championing the historicity of the narratives that surely seem to us implausible. We ought, however, at least to struggle with the intention of the text. I suggest that in these stories—and more largely the corpus of stories of Elijah and Elisha—an argument is being made that there is an alternative world of reality beyond royal control and royal reason. Our problem with these stories, characteristically, is that we are wont to 'explain' them in terms of royal reason, which quickly renders them incredible."

[3] e.g., A. F. Chiffolo and R. W. Hesse, Jr, *Cooking with the Bible: Biblical Food, Feasts, and Lore* (Westport, CT: Greenwood Press, 2006), 119–20.

The situation in Gilgal seems rather more serious than a nasty case of fecal evacuation, however, as indicated by the group's use of the verb "cry out" (צעק). As we recall, this is the same verb used by the distressed widow in 2 Kings 4:1, and earlier it was noted that such an appeal is typically directed to God or the king.[4] Once again, though, the prophet Elisha is the one to whom the appellants "cry out," further indicating the high status of Elisha (or at least one who meets the needs of the population, ostensibly the king's responsibility). Less predictable is the mechanism deployed by Elisha: he orders "flour" (קמח) and proceeds to throw it into the cauldron. Like the aforementioned laxative, there is no shortage of rationalistic interpretations by scholars regarding the healing properties of the flour. More compelling is the immediate connection with the salt thrown into the Jericho spring. In 2 Kings 2:19–21 the water brings death, and here there is death in the pot, but a prophetic directive counters the lethal material in both Jericho and Gilgal. There also are some acute connections between the deadly soup and the deadly illness in the previous episode, as James Mead observes: "Against the immediate background of the Shunammite's story, where life was restored to a child physically dead, [the reader is given] the impression here that *even before death can harm*, Elisha has the power to hold it back."[5] Almost the opposite situation is encountered when considering the second episode of 2 Kings 4:42–4. Instead of famine and death, there are the first fruits of a new harvest. The problem is not poisonous stew during a food crisis, but rather the limited provisions available for the people:

A man came from Baal Shalishah, and brought to the man of God the first fruits of bread, twenty loaves of barley, and produce of his harvest. He said, "Give to the people, that they may eat." His servant said, "What, I am to set this before one hundred men?" He said, "Give to the people that they may eat, for thus says the Lord: 'Eating, and leaving over.'" So he gave it out before the people. They ate, and there was some left over, according to the word of the Lord.

---

[4] See J. K. Bruckner, *Implied Law in the Abraham Narrative: A Literary and Theological Analysis* (JSOTSup 335; London: Sheffield Academic Press, 2001), 79–80, noting the work of R. N. Boyce, *The Cry to God in the Old Testament* (SBLDS 103; Atlanta: Scholars Press, 1988).

[5] Mead, "'Elisha Will Kill'? The Deuteronomistic Rhetoric of Life and Death in the Theology of the Elisha Narratives," 173.

Straightaway the reader notices a change in the temporal setting, as the famine of the previous episode must be over since the farmer brings a gift of first fruits. In this term some hear cultic overtones, or sense the idea that the farmer is attempting to purchase a prophetic favor.[6] Instead, I would understand the farmer's gift as akin to the hospitality extended by the great woman of Shunem, an action devoid of any self-seeking motive. But most important for this study is the exchange between Elisha—who I assume is speaking in verse 42—and his unnamed servant lad, who speaks in the next line. It is possible, as some interpreters think, that the servant is Gehazi, yet if such were the case it is odd why this detail would be omitted. Consequently, there is heightened attention on these words of skepticism because of the anonymity of the speaker (though, by virtue of the role, it is a figure pictured as close to Elisha). So why is this voice of skepticism preserved in the episode—where the prophet feeds a multitude—and what is its purpose in the larger storyline?

The servant lad's utterance of incredulity is certainly not the last such word that will be directed toward the prophet during his career, but it is notable because it is spoken by a perceived *insider* who doubts Elisha's capacity to influence the situation. In my opinion the servant's query parallels the royal disbelief seen earlier (in 2 Kings 3:10–13 with the emphatic questions of Jehoram, who likewise is skeptical) and that later occurs in 2 Kings 7:2. As a result, the narrative continues the Omride critique, even though the king makes no formal appearance in this episode. By keeping the voice anonymous (though attributed to a servant), it allows the reader some flexibility in connecting the earlier voice of despair from the king with the leery utterance of Elisha's unnamed servant here. Of course the servant could be Gehazi, and if that is the case then it prepares the reader for Gehazi's conduct in 2 Kings 5:19–27, in terms of both his counter-initiative against the prophet and his independent agenda. Both stories, incidentally, deal with gifts and gift management, so the

---

[6] This episode forms the background for the New Testament account of Jesus using 5 loaves and 2 fish to feed 5,000 people (with 12 baskets left over) in Matt.14:13–21 (cf. Mark 6:32–44; Luke 9:10–17; John 6:1–13; and the comparable story in Matt. 15:29–39). On various comparisons with the gospel narratives, see T. L. Brodie, *The Crucial Bridge: The Elijah–Elisha Narrative as an Interpretive Synthesis of Genesis–Kings and a Literary Model for the Gospels* (Collegeville, MN: Liturgical Press, 2000). Note also the tabulation of P. Guillaume, "Miracles Miraculously Repeated: Gospel Miracles as Duplication of Elijah–Elisha's," *BN* 98 (1999), 21–3.

servant's role needs to be considered. 2 Kings 4:42–4 provides yet
another instance of how the prophetic word eschews skepticism, and,
along similar lines as the Moabite campaign (despite the king's lack of
confidence), there is enough sustenance for an entire group.

THE PRISONER

The pair of episodes at the end of 2 Kings 4 serve to amplify Elisha's
profile, and continue the larger royal critique in the narrative. In the
next story—the long episode in 2 Kings 5—there are some new facets
of the prophet's characterization that add to a growing complexity.
The events of this chapter take place on a slightly different stage, and
Elisha interacts with a range of figures, including a foreign military
commander, and the king of Israel in a manner quite unlike anything
seen to this point. International conflict has already featured in
Elisha's career, most dramatically in the Moabite campaign that
included several layers of threat. Two new characters come to the
forefront at the beginning of the chapter: Naaman the Aramean
general, and an unnamed Israelite servant girl captured by raiding
Arameans. The latter character will give a further indication of the
circulation of Elisha's fame. Earlier a servant of the king of Israel
knew all about Elisha (see 2 Kings 3:11), and likewise in this story
there is another *servant* voice that is informed of Elisha's capacity as a
transformative agent both within and beyond the borders of Israel.
For an audience acquainted with the crisis of Jerusalem's collapse in
586 BCE and the trauma of exile, 2 Kings 5—like the story of feeding a
multitude we have just read—provides ample fodder for reflection.

By far the most colorful Aramean in recent Israelite history is Ben-
Hadad, especially in 1 Kings 20:16–20, where he is confidently getting
drunk at high noon, only to be routed by Ahab's makeshift forces led
by the assistants to the provincial administrators. For all of Ben-
Hadad's interesting exploits, he remains a relatively flat character in
the story, and in literary terms he is quickly eclipsed by Naaman,
whose *vita* is given a substantial exposition as 2 Kings 5 opens:
"Naaman, commander of the army of the king of Aram, was a great
man before his master and highly honored, because by him the LORD
had given salvation to Aram. The man was a mighty warrior, a leper."
Whether or not Naaman's high standing with his master stems from

his military victories or his status as a mighty warrior is a minor matter; more jarring is the juxtaposition of Naaman's exalted status with the last item in verse 1 referring to his leprous (מצרע) condition. Another issue is whether an early Israelite audience would be inclined toward sympathy for someone who has this malady, or rejoice in the affliction of an Aramean military leader who has no doubt caused suffering. But this is a secondary question because it comes in the midst of a sensational theological declaration: namely, that Naaman is merely an agent of the God of Israel *who has given* him victory over Israel.

Numerous scholars agree that the narrator's comment about Naaman as God's instrument of salvation for Aram at Israel's expense is the kind of statement that expands the boundaries of divine sovereignty and provides different perspective in the story. There is less agreement, though, on the nature of Naaman's ailment, as commentators have carried on a vigorous dermatological debate. On the one hand, it is conceded by all sides that the Hebrew term usually translated as leprosy (מצרע) can refer to a variety of skin diseases.[7] But, on the other hand, the highest frequency of the term "leper" does involve social removal of some kind, rendering that person ceremonially unclean and having a stigma attached.[8] Examples of this type would include Miriam in Numbers 12:10, or David's curse on Joab's descendants in 2 Samuel 3:29, both containing a pariah element. So the issue in 2 Kings 5 revolves around socialization, and the degree to which Naaman is disbarred from normal public interaction. He seems to engage in conversation with the king, but the narrative conveys the idea that his leprosy is serious. What is not stated is whether Naaman was inflicted with this condition during his victories over Israel, or if this disease is a more recent acquisition. Yet his leprous condition has to be considered debilitating enough for him to take the rather humbling steps that he does in this story.

It must be an embarrassing experience for this mighty warrior to be brought low and branded a leper. This affliction, though, triggers the

---

[7] According to R. D. Nelson (*First and Second Kings*, 177): "The Old Testament classified a wide variety of skin diseases under the heading of leprosy. Naaman's was one of the more minor types which created no barrier to social intercourse." Cf. J. K. Kim, "Reading and Retelling Naaman's Story (2 Kings 5)," *JSOT* 30/1 (2005), 53; J. A. Montgomery and H. S. Gehman, *A Critical and Exegetical Commentary on the Books of Kings* (ICC; Edinburgh: T & T Clark, 1951), 373–4.

[8] Note the discussion in Sweeney, *1 & 2 Kings*, 298.

occasion for a new character to be introduced and speak up, and an unlikely figure by any measure: "Now Aram had sent out raiding parties, and they brought back from the land of Israel a little girl, and she was serving before the wife of Naaman. She said to her matron, 'Oh, that my lord were before the prophet who is in Samaria, then he would remove his leprosy from him!'" Since Naaman is captain of the host for Aram's king, responsibility for raiding parties presumably lies within his portfolio. Even if he is not the one who ultimately sanctions the activities of such marauders, at the very least he personally profits from their exploits, as a captive Israelite from some unspecified incursion ends up in his house. Within the early readership of the Deuteronomistic History, there surely are those who can relate this story of an Israelite maiden being (violently) taken from her homeland and forced into servitude. Astonishing, therefore, are the little girl's words of compassion for her captor; few would begrudge her for harboring bitterness toward the Arameans, and Naaman in particular.

Instead of gloating over Naaman's malady, the little Israelite girl points to an avenue of rehabilitation. Through her words the reader is further acquainted with the fame of Elisha and his capacity as an emissary of healing. The girl's words also clash with the voice of skepticism from an unnamed servant who expresses doubt about the quantity of food (2 Kings 4:43). There are no reservations, so it seems, as the girl presents "the prophet who is in Samaria" as a viable option for a *foreign* general's skin ailment. Reference to Samaria has struck some interpreters as an odd geographical reference, although the text does mention that Elisha "returned" there in 2 Kings 2:25. Samaria is associated as the seat of the Omride kings, so, unless the girl is mistaken or generalizing, it is surprising to find Elisha there in light of his recent hostility with Jehoram the king of northern Israel during the Moabite campaign. I assume that the king in this episode is Jehoram, and that it is also Jehoram whom Elisha offers to address on the Shunammite's behalf (2 Kings 4:13). Fittingly, Elisha will soon voice an alternative option to the king in this episode (just as he announces a solution to the water problem in the Moabite story), once more supplying something that the king cannot provide.

STATELY HISTRIONICS

Equally surprising as the little girl's words is the fact that the words are believed by the powerful Aramean general, to the point that Naaman brings the matter directly to the king. Naaman's standing is sufficient (or his leprosy is mild enough) that he gains an audience with his monarch, who likewise takes the girl's word (mediated by his general) on trust. So, armed with a royal letter and a trainload of gifts fit for a king, Naaman begins his journey to Israel. The sizeable gift should be kept in mind, as it provides quite a temptation for an Israelite character later in the episode. Meanwhile, some commentators have noted two quirks within the king of Aram's letter: first, there is no mention of a prophet, and, second, the letter implies that the king of Israel is the one who will heal Naaman ("that you may remove his leprosy from him"). Possibly an irony is at work here, as noticed by Aucker: "Jehoram's brother Ahaziah sought Baal-zebub for healing (2 Kgs 1) and now the king of Aram seeks healing for his servant Naaman from Jehoram. The royal figures in each case (Ahaziah; Benhadad on behalf of Naaman) seek healing from an inappropriate source (Baal-zebub; Jehoram)."[9] It is difficult to know if the king of Aram is simply following a typical protocol in his missive (and assumes that prophets are under the auspices of the king's court), or if he simply does not understand the situation and thinks that Jehoram is the healer, or that the prophet is under his control.

But of more immediate interest to me is the reaction of Israel's king (v. 7) upon receiving the letter: "When the king of Israel read the letter, he tore his clothes, and said, 'Am I God, to make people dead or alive, that this one is sending to me to remove a man's leprosy? But surely know and see that he is looking to quarrel with me!'" If the king of Aram can be accused of misreading the situation in his letter, so Israel's king misreads that same letter when it arrives. Because of the hostility between the nations, some apprehension or suspicion of an ulterior motive is perhaps understandable, and in his view the gift is not what it seems (along the lines of the infamous Trojan Horse). Somehow Elisha hears about the king's hysteria and once more intervenes by sending a message to the king, in this case arguably preventing the escalation of an international conflict: "Why would

---

[9] Aucker, "Putting Elisha in his Place," 126.

you tear your clothes? Let him come to me, that he may know that there is a prophet in Israel." The king's rage is offset by the prophet's alternative, one that is *counter-intuitive* as it involves compassion on an obvious adversary. In this respect, therefore, Elisha's reaction parallels that of the captured Israelite girl.

Elisha responds to the report of the king's discomposure by saying "let him come to me," and it must be said that the king accedes to the prophet's word. No further dialogue is provided in the narrative, but Naaman must have been given the address, and in due course—without further dialogue or description, and for all we know the king of Israel still may have doubts about the motives for the Aramean state visit—the military commander arrives at a new spatial setting: the house of Elisha. This spatial designation may just be a generality, but, as the little girl earlier exclaimed, there most certainly is a prophet in Samaria (whose house also features in 2 Kings 6:32). As with many modern celebrities, Naaman arrives at Elisha's house accompanied by a considerable entourage. This escort includes horses and chariots, the very war machinery that conceivably has caused no end of grief for many an Israelite. Some interpreters have suggested that this show of horses and chariots is a flex of muscles on Naaman's part and an attempt to influence the prophet. But there is no initial meeting between the two parties, as Elisha sends a "messenger" (מלאך) to Naaman, and the text does not specify if the messenger is deployed because of the social implications of leprosy, or if it is a custom that is previously seen in the transaction with the Shunammite woman in chapter 4. Regardless, the instruction from Elisha to the military commander ("Go and wash seven times in the Jordan, and your flesh will be restored to you, and be pure") is not complicated. The reader is here reminded of other instructions such as throwing salt in the spring or the flour in the cauldron, and through the number "seven" this moment connects with previous events in the story such as the "seven times" Elijah's servant is sent to look for clouds that portend the arrival of the long-needed rain (1 Kings 18:43–4), and the "seven sneezes" of the Shunammite's son signaling his restoration to life (2 Kings 4:35).

The relative ordinariness of Elisha's instruction may not be overly surprising to the reader when compared with other prophetic activities seen thus far in the story, but for Naaman it is infuriating, triggering great wrath in the great man. Naaman's histrionic reaction is not unlike that of Israel's king, continuing the pattern of *misunderstanding* displayed by the powerful figures in this episode. By means of an interior monologue Naaman discloses his own mindset in verses 11–12, as he reckoned the prophet would personally come forth and enact a dramatic miracle rather than sending a messenger with instructions to dip seven times in the Jordan. He makes a derogatory contrast between the rivers of Damascus and the waters of Israel, though he may be bluffing here; more likely, the real reason for his anger is either the absence of a dramatic miracle (as he admits) or that he is not used to taking orders, especially an order that seems so strange (as he does not admit). Having made the journey to Samaria, why does he not heed Elisha's directive much as he was willing to listen to the little girl? In showing such reluctance to heed the prophetic word, Naaman is not alone, but has plenty of company in the Omride kings.

As Naaman turns away in a tantrum because of the prophet's command for a sevenfold ablution in the Jordan, his histrionics mimic that of the Israelite king upon receiving the Aramean letter earlier in the story. But, just as Elisha's word countered the king's anger, so there is another voice that counters the wrath of Naaman (5:13). The source of an unexpected and creative counter-move that births a new plot movement is Naaman's servants, surely Arameans themselves. The role of Naaman's servants—acting as arbiters of good sense and encouraging their master to attend to the prophet's words—is similar to the role of the Israelite servant in the Moabite campaign (see 3:11), where a positive word was spoken about Elisha from the Israelite camp. In the view of Rick Dale Moore, Naaman's servants ask a question gently designed to unmask the commander's pretenses: "The question beautifully penetrates to the heart of Naaman's hang-up. Aimed at pointing up the reasonableness of Elisha's request, the question unwittingly, it seems, accomplishes much more." Moore concludes: "It exposes Naaman's obsession with greatness. The thrust of the servants' logic is that something small is easier to perform than something great."[10]

Listening to the words of the little Israelite girl first sets Naaman on the path to Samaria in search of healing, and now he listens to the words of his servants and follows Elisha's directive. Several scholars understand that the verbal sequence "he went down [וירד] and

---

[10] Moore, *God Saves*, 76.

immersed" is not only a physical act, but equally a "lowering" of the great man into obedience to the Israelite prophet. The result is that, without any explicit attribution to God (though the narrator is careful to say "according to the word of the man of God"), Naaman is cleansed of his leprosy and his flesh becomes "like a little lad." This description of Naaman's healing and the reference to a little lad (נער קטן) closely corresponds to the earlier description of the little girl (נערה קטנה), implying that Naaman now symbolically resembles the girl who testified about prophetic efficacy. Indeed, when considering his forth-coming confession (vv. 15–18), it could be said that Naaman's phys-ical healing is the outward display of a spiritual transformation, as witnessed by his remarkable dialogue with Elisha in the next scene.[11]

The unnamed Israelite girl expressed to Naaman's wife, "O, that my lord would be before the prophet"; after the cleansing wash, Naaman does come "before" the prophet, just as the girl had desired. Naaman's posture is augmented by a verbal repetition: in verse 14 his flesh is restored (וישב), and then he returns (וישב) to the man of God in verse 15. The substantial gift brought from Aram to Israel with Naa-man's retinue ("ten talents of silver, six thousand shekels of gold, and ten sets of garments") and held in abeyance now comes back into play, as the fresh-fleshed commander urges Elisha to receive his material "blessing." Emphatically refused by the prophet, Naaman's riches will again surface in the next installment of the story as the object of considerable interest for a certain character in the story. Meanwhile, Naaman's confession creates a neat symmetry in the narrative: "Elisha had come forward to heal Naaman in order that Naaman might 'know that there is a prophet in Israel'; now we hear Naaman's confession that 'there is no other god in all the earth except in Israel.'"[12] This affirmation places Naaman is some elite company—alongside figures such as Ruth and Rahab—foreigners who acknow-ledge the supremacy of Israel's God.

Naaman's confession is soon accompanied by a new self-designation, as he classifies himself as Elisha's "servant." Five times in a short span Naaman uses this epithet, underscoring a new status.[13] Use of the title "your servant" in verse 17 forms the preface to a request for a load of soil in order to present sacrifices exclusively to the LORD. Previously

[11] See R. L. Cohn, "Form and Perspective in 2 Kings V," *VT* 31 (1983), 171–84.
[12] Seow, "1 & 2 Kings," 195.
[13] Moore, *God Saves*, 78.

Naaman has denigrated the waters of Israel; now he politely requests some dirt.[14] The mention of sacrifice leads to another ritual issue raised by Naaman: his need periodically to venture into the house of Rimmon in his vocational capacity of right-hand man to the king (literally, the one whose arm the king leans on). Because he seeks forgiveness in advance, I assume that Naaman will retain his post, but with a "transformation of allegiance."[15] Some would argue that it is nothing short of amazing that the small Israelite girl, a captive and a servant, has so influenced international events, to the point that her words set in motion a grand visit of state that culminate in the confession of the commander. At the outset of the narrative the reader is told of raiding parties entering the land of Israel for malfeasant ends; yet now, on account of the captured girl's testimony, the most powerful Aramean warrior enters for healing and prepares to depart taking no prisoners, only a couple of mule loads of *land* (that is, some dirt) from Israel.

REGAL PLUNDER

Naaman is loquacious in his requests for dirt and advance forgiveness for having to enter the house of Rimmon with the Aramean king. His long speech contrasts with the brevity of Elisha's reply, "Go in peace." I certainly agree with those commentators who affirm that Elisha's words are not a curt dismissal nor some sort of appeasement, but rather a recognition of the legitimacy of Naaman's words of confession. The episode could have concluded at this point, and it would have ranked as one of the happier moments in the Deuteronomistic History. But, abruptly, a familiar-enough character re-enters the storyline, and, from the reader's point of view, will destabilize the episode and bring a more somber denouement. Gehazi may have been the unnamed servant or messenger of Elisha earlier in this scene or at the feast of 4:43, but such ambiguities cannot be resolved. Undeniably, Gehazi was an active participant in the story of the birth and restoration of the Shunammite's son; although his attempts

[14] Cohn, "Form and Perspective in 2 Kings V," 178.
[15] Mead, "'Elisha Will Kill'? The Deuteronomistic Rhetoric of Life and Death in the Theology of the Elisha Narratives," 205.

to revive the dead son were not effective, at the very least he is established as a fast runner. As Gehazi re-emerges here in 2 Kings 5, he will again be pictured as an aggressive runner, albeit with a darker finish line. In 4:26 Gehazi is directed by Elisha to run (רוץ) and ask the Shunammite if there is peace (הֲשָׁלוֹם); now he takes his own counsel and resolves to run (רוץ) and take something from Naaman, who will likewise ask if there is peace (הֲשָׁלוֹם).

Gehazi's decision to run after Naaman is communicated by means of a soliloquy: in the absence of an obvious interlocutor, it is natural to assume that Gehazi is talking to himself. In a survey of inner speech in biblical narrative Maren Niehoff provides some insight:

> The soliloquy has been regarded as the most refined narrative depiction of a literary character's self-awareness. This claim can be justified by considering the following facts: Primarily, the soliloquizing figure is portrayed as formulating his or her thoughts in his or her own words, thus clearly defining or conceptualizing what might otherwise be unconscious feelings or dormant emotions.

Niehoff further remarks, and this is particularly applicable to 2 Kings 5, "the soliloquy presents the figure as a divided self, where one part of the character is debating with another . . . It thus emerges that the ability to talk to oneself presupposes a highly complex character who has a strong sense of his or her individuality."[16] Gehazi's soliloquy provides another example of the often unheralded narrative sophistication of this material, and at the same time makes Gehazi a more complex character. His self-talk has a curious dovetail with Naaman's earlier complaint, in that both characters are unhappy with what Elisha *has not* done: Naaman was upset Elisha did not come forth and wave his hand, while Gehazi complains that Elisha was too soft on Naaman, and could have acquired some precious goods. Naaman changes course by listening to his servants, whereas Gehazi listens only to his divided self (to appropriate Niehoff's category), somewhat analogous to Gollum in Tolkien's *Lord of the Rings*.

The oath of Gehazi ("As the LORD lives, I will surely run after him and I will take something from him") has some affinities with Elisha's oath about refusing to take anything from Naaman. But there is a

---

[16] M. Niehoff, "Do Biblical Characters Talk to Themselves? Narrative Modes of Representing Inner Speech in Early Biblical Fiction," *JBL* 111 (1992), 577. Niehoff's article is cited in Kim, "Reading and Retelling Naaman's Story (2 Kings 5)," 56.

telling omission: Elisha included the phrase "As the LORD lives *whom I stand before*," but Gehazi does not, setting further distance between the two characters.[17] Commentators have varying views on Gehazi's motives, ranging from outright greed to xenophobic tendencies. If we bear in mind that Naaman and the Arameans have caused considerable damage in Israel, it could be that Gehazi represents a popular viewpoint: hostility toward the oppressors. When Naaman arrives in Samaria, he brings an extensive caravan of material goods, begging the question as to how such goods were acquired. In all likelihood, these possessions have been removed from Israel among other places, and the reader has already been informed how Aramean raiders stole the little girl (who eventually serves Naaman's wife) from Israelite territory. Elisha's refusal to accept a blessing from Naaman, therefore, is probably based on multiple grounds. Gehazi's reaction is quite different, and he cannot resist the opportunity to plunder the plunderer. Several recent interpreters also argue that Gehazi's actions here resemble that of a corrupt king. To be sure, the use of the verb "take" in Gehazi's inner deliberation (v. 20) is reminiscent of Samuel's warning of what kings will do (1 Samuel 8:11–18), a speech that has a high concentration of the verb "to take." The notion of Gehazi as a stand-in for royalty here—much like the unidentified creditor of 4:1–7 acted as a cipher for the Omrides—is given further consideration below, because, like the king of Israel, Gehazi soon will feel the sting of a prophetic invective.

Meanwhile, Naaman notices Gehazi running toward him, yet it most likely does not occur to him to question the motives of the servant, especially the servant of the prophet who was the instrument of healing. Naaman's question to Gehazi ("Is there peace?") echoes Elisha's dismissal, and is the same question that Gehazi was earlier instructed to ask the Shunammite. Any nervousness on Naaman's part is quickly assuaged by Gehazi through a convincing ruse. Gehazi takes advantage of his *insider* position to exploit the *outsider*, and uses a form of pious language that is probably calculated to appeal to the

---

[17] Moore, *God Saves*, 80–1. The various connections between the scenes of this chapter militate against the notion that different sources have been amalgamated, a redactional argument that has been defused by Gerhard von Rad: "This end to the story has no real independence," says von Rad pointing to the integration of the Gehazi scenes in the larger episode, "it is only the unedifying counterpart to the story of Naaman." See G. von Rad, "Naaman: A Critical Retelling," in *God at Work in Israel* (Nashville: Abingdon Press, 1980), 54.

new-found faith of Naaman in order to further his scheme. It is hard to deny that there is a certain genius in his plan: Gehazi comes up with a plausible exigency as to why Elisha would now be willing to take Naaman's gifts after just swearing an oath (using the divine name) to the contrary. Naaman is unlikely to question something done in the name of Elisha, suggesting that, during Naaman's confession, Gehazi is furtively lurking in the background. Gehazi is obviously a convincing actor, and his tale about some needy members of the company of the prophets is persuasive enough to secure double the requested amount of silver at Naaman's urging, and this must be an unexpected boon. Naaman the Aramean brings home two mule loads of Israelite dirt, and Gehazi the Israelite brings home two servant loads of Aramean gifts.

Gehazi hides his newly acquired cache in a house at a peculiar location, as "the hill" or "Ophel" (העפל) is a site often associated with Jerusalem royalty. Some scholars reason that there must be a similar place in Samaria; for example, John Gray notes that the term Ophel "means etymologically a 'tumour' or 'swelling' (e.g. 1 Sam. 5.6), so that it might conceivably denote a hill or mound. Here, however, the definite article suggests some feature more specific than a hill, hence we suggest that it was the citadel of Samaria, crowned by the inner wall and palace of Omri and Ahab."[18] By transferring his plunder to the Ophel or "the citadel" (so NRSV), Gehazi is further configured as a royal surrogate in this episode. Of course, he should have just stayed there, because, after the two servants have departed, Gehazi then presents himself to his master in what can only be described as an uncomfortable confrontation. The awkward syntax underscores the situation: Elisha asks "From where, Gehazi," who evasively replies, "Your servant did not go anywhere" (אנה ואנה). In the previous chapter Elisha stated that God had "hidden" from him the reason for the Shunammite's distress (2 Kings 4:27). Gehazi's actions, by every indication, have not been so opaque: "Did not my heart go when a man turned from his chariot to meet you?" Commentators have debated the meaning of Elisha's words here, as some argue that the prophet simply knows the tendencies of his servant, whereas others suggest that the spirit of prophecy would provide such knowledge of Gehazi's activities (and the specificities of the Naaman's dismounting

---

[18] Gray, *I & II Kings*, 510.

from the chariot). Both positions have some merit, but when one considers that Naaman's gifts are not the only items that Gehazi acquires—Naaman's leprosy will soon be transferred to him at Elisha's word—the prophet's supernatural perception cannot be discounted. There are other instances to come of Elisha's unique insight and foreknowledge, so this penetrating gaze directed at Gehazi anticipates several other scenes in the next chapters of Kings.

But before any penalty is imposed on Gehazi, Elisha unveils one of the longest and most complex speeches in his career (vv. 26-7), beginning with an expansive question: "Was it a time to take silver, to take clothes, olive trees, vineyards, flocks and cattle, male and female servants?" Gehazi is recorded as accepting clothes and silver from Naaman, but scholars puzzle over the other items in Elisha's inventory. A recent line of interpretation suggests that Elisha is providing a catalogue of royal plunder, as Robert Cohn explains: "These items likely constitute a formulaic list, for they are included in the possessions which a despotic king can be expected to take from the people, according to Samuel's warning (1 Sam. viii 14–17). Here they associate Gehazi's crime with the worst excesses of royal corruption."[19] Such an argument is compelling, as it is consistent with the recent tenor of the Elisha story and enhances the critique of kingship. Like the Omride kings, Gehazi disregards the prophetic word in favor of some other agenda. In this case he suffers immediate consequences, as the penalty of *leprosy* is now imposed on him. When he departs from Elisha's presence, Gehazi's skin is "like the snow," inviting a comparison with Numbers 12:10, where Miriam is divinely inflicted with the same condition as Gehazi.[20] A common feature in both stories is underlings (Miriam and Gehazi) registering complaints against their superiors (Moses and Elisha).

A key difference in the leprosy of 2 Kings 5:27, however, is that Gehazi is not the only one infected. Elisha's word of judgment spreads throughout Gehazi's line: "the leprosy of Naaman will cling to you and your descendants forever." The severity of the punishment is along different lines from the bears of Bethel in 2 Kings 2:23–5. In that episode the lads (נערים) were ripped apart; here the lad Gehazi (נער) remains intact, but with a congenital skin disease that serves as a

---

[19] Cohn, "Form and Perspective in 2 Kings V," 182. Cf. Moore, *God Saves*, 83; Aucker, "Putting Elisha in his Place," 129–34.

[20] See Cogan and Tadmor, *II Kings*, 66.

living example. For Gehazi, the punishment of leprosy is connected to the plunder at the heart of Elisha's inquiry. D. P. O'Brien hears Elisha's question in more national terms: "Elisha's use of the rhetorical question is an attempt to highlight to Gehazi (and to the exilic reader) that the conversion of the gentile, Naaman, to Yahwism did not signify the time of Yahweh's favour upon Israel, but, ironically, should be interpreted as an indictment against Israel. Certainly," concludes O'Brien, "most scholars concur that Naaman's confession of faith of v. 15 is intended as a deliberate foil to the general faithlessness of the Israelites and their kings in that age."[21] In my opinion, the dynastic component of Gehazi's leprosy foreshadows the judgment to fall on corrupt kings who eschew prophetic counsel.

UPWARD MOBILITY

After Gehazi's snowfall, in the next episode of 2 Kings 6:1–7 the company of the prophets resurfaces in the narrative. The Naaman story is long and interwoven, whereas this episode—like the two scenes at the end of chapter four—is short with a fairly simple plot. The prophets want to build a larger residence, and Elisha is urged to go along with them. A crisis ensues, as a borrowed axe-head is lost in the river, but Elisha intervenes and "the iron did swim" (as the KJV memorably translates). The challenge here, as with most other episodes in 2 Kings 3–8, is the question of structural design, and whether (as some assert) the scene with the floating iron is randomly placed or if (as others argue) there is intentionality in the scene's sequencing. As there are a number of connections or similarities with other texts in the Elisha cycle, the reader can sense some intentionality at work. The centerpiece—swimming iron—is odd, but no more so than healing the Jericho spring, producing water in the desert, or restoring the dead to life. "To make iron float to the surface," Terence Fretheim dryly remarks, "is not your usual daily event. The common options for interpretation have been three (or some combination thereof): to interpret literally, to dismiss as impossible, or to understand as

---

[21] D. P. O'Brien, "'Is this the Time to Accept...?' (2 Kings V 26B): Simply Moralizing (LXX) or an Ominous Foreboding of Yahweh's Rejection of Israel (MT)?" *VT* 46 (1996), 456–7.

symbolic narrative."[22] This last line of inquiry is particularly promising, especially because of the cluster of allusions to the exodus/conquest narratives that are evoked in 2 Kings 6:1–7.

The episode begins with a collective utterance from the company of the prophets, seeking permission from Elisha to expand their premises: "Behold, please, the place where we are living before you is too restricting for us. Please let us go to the Jordan, so each man can take a beam from there, that we might make a place for ourselves to live." Needing a bigger space is quite a development in the storyline, as not so long ago (e.g., 1 Kings 18:4) prophets needed to be hidden in caves, barely able to survive. Even Elijah was a hunted fugitive. The need for expanded living quarters—with Elisha moving freely in the land—implies that the Omride grip has been loosened, ushering in a new phase where the company of the prophets are more upwardly mobile than at previous points in Kings. It must be no accident, therefore, that various tropes of the conquest narratives can be glimpsed here, as Philip Satterthwaite suggests: "The action the 'sons of the prophets' propose, building a place to dwell near the Jordan, evokes memories of the conquest under Joshua. It seems to be a deliberate gesture: now that Elisha's followers are growing in numbers, they may start to 'take possession' of the land, starting from the Jordan."[23] The previous story of Naaman featured the same Jordan River as a prominent spatial setting and the site of healing; perhaps the Jordan River setting in 2 Kings 6:1–7 indicates a movement toward restoration of the prophetic word in Israel's national life. Moreover, Naaman asks Elisha's permission on the matters of soil and advance forgiveness, and likewise the company of the prophets ask his permission to build as well as go along with them (or at least one member urges him to come). Perhaps the group is still fearful of the Omrides, with Elisha's presence sufficient to ward off any pernicious royal influences. As is clear from the rest of the scene in verses 4–7, Elisha's accompaniment proves vital:

He went with them, and they came to the Jordan and cut down the trees. As one of them was felling a beam, the iron fell into the water. He cried out, and said, "Oh my master, but it was borrowed!" The man of God said, "Where did it fall?" So he showed him the place. He cut off some wood, threw it there,

---

[22] Fretheim, *First and Second Kings*, 156.
[23] Satterthwaite, "The Elisha Narratives and the Coherence of 2 Kings 2–8," 18.

and the iron floated. He said, "Raise it up to yourself." And he sent forth his hand and took it.

The conquest motifs continue with the house construction in the second part of the episode: "Israel comes from Egypt with spoils to build the tabernacle, and similarly the sons of the prophets, liberated from the Omride kingdom, build a house, an alternative to the various houses and shrines that the Omrides built."[24] Yet crisis quickly ensues, and the project appears threatened by the loss of a borrowed tool. It is tempting to think that Gehazi's money would be appreciated by the member of the prophetic guild right now. Scholars note that the same verb "borrow" (שׁאל) occurs in 2 Kings 4:3, where the widow is instructed by Elisha to borrow vessels from her neighbors.[25] Similar to the widow, our "borrower" in this episode has a substantial risk of running afoul of a creditor, since it is his responsibility to return the expensive iron implement to the owner (Exodus 22:13–14).[26] Fear of incurring a substantial debt with no ready means of repayment is probably why the borrower issues a "cry of distress" (צעק), again the same cry as the widow in 4:1. As is now predictable, the borrower addresses his cry for help to the prophet Elisha rather than to the king.

In response to the cry of distress, Elisha asks a strange question, wanting to know the location of where the iron fell. Obviously the prophet's "heart" does not go with the axe-head as it goes with Gehazi. When he is shown the spot where the axe dropped in the river, Elisha adopts his customary mode of throwing an object at the problem, like the salt and the flour in other episodes. Tossing a stick in the water, as in those other cases, proves effective as the iron swims (to the relief of the anxious borrower, one surmises). There have been many scholarly attempts at a rationalistic explanation—"it has been suggested that Elisha poked about in the water with a stick until he managed to push his stick through the socket in the axe-head prepared for the shaft"[27]—none of which is particularly convincing. It is worth noting, though, that, when Elisha invites the borrower to "raise

---

[24] Leithart, *1 & 2 Kings*, 199.

[25] e.g., Mead, "'Elisha Will Kill'? The Deuteronomistic Rhetoric of Life and Death in the Theology of the Elisha Narratives," 178.

[26] Sweeney, *I & II Kings*, 301.

[27] J. Robinson, *The Second Book of Kings* (CBC; Cambridge and New York: Cambridge University Press, 1976), 57.

up" (רום) the buoyant metal, a verb form is used that is not common in the Hebrew Bible. Brian Aucker notes that in Genesis–Kings there are only two other places where the *hiphil* imperative aspect ("raise up") of this verb is used: in Exodus 14:16 and Joshua 4:5. Both of these cases are "important crossing points," as the people of Israel are passing through the Red Sea (Exodus) and the Jordan River (Joshua) respectively.[28] On a more modest scale, even the last lines of this scene continue the exodus/conquest imagery, and the reader is reminded that the Omride house will soon be submerged by the floodwaters of judgment.

[28] Aucker, "Putting Elisha in his Place," 164.

5

Counter Intelligence

Over the course of his career thus far Elisha has been a player on the international stage alternating with lower-key domestic matters. In the next phase of the story there is a return to great affairs of state, as conflict with the Arameans reaches critical heights. There are two main parts in this chapter: in part one (2 Kings 6:8–23) the prophet is under siege, and in part two (6:24–7:20) the city of Samaria is under siege. In part one the Arameans and the king of Aram's court are prominent, whereas in part two the Israelites and the king of Israel's court are prominent. In both parts a king is angry and attempts to apprehend Elisha, and in both parts there is remarkable deliverance that concludes with a feast *sponsored* by the enemy. Even though Elisha was generous to Naaman, the Aramean threat reaches a tipping point in this section of text, yet this crisis becomes the means whereby the prophet is captivatingly characterized. Moreover, the king of Israel has a more active role in these episodes. In 2 Kings 3 he is mainly featured in dialogue, and is a foil for Elisha. In 2 Kings 4 he is present only in more subtle ways, as the "creditor" can be understood as a cipher for the king. There is no formal appearance of the king in the Shunammite episode, but the woman gives birth to a son (one who presumably will inherit the family property) in contrast to the sterility of the Omride dynasty. In 2 Kings 5 the king of Israel plays a minor role, as Elisha hears about his angry reaction to Naaman's letter of introduction. The engagement between Elisha and the king of Israel is more attenuated in this next installment of the story, where the king's vacillations are central elements of the plot.

"In these narratives," notes Robert LaBarbera, "kings, officials, and soldiers are without effect in every military situation, despite all their horses and chariots. Instead, Yahweh brings victory to Israel through the actions of non-military personnel and the word of the man of

God, Elisha."[1] Over the course of my analysis I will emphasize how
the two parts of this section cohere, and how new hues of individuality are apparent in Elisha's profile as conflict with the Arameans in 2
Kings 6–7 escalates. For instance, the prophet has a *trickster* side that
is more obvious in this section, and his royal rebukes are more
elaborate than at any previous time.[2] When compared with earlier
scenes in Elisha's life, there are some intriguing variations. For instance, during the Moabite crisis he calls for a minstrel to deliver his
oracle; in the next episodes there will be no musical accompaniment,
but the prophetic word will be loud and clear. Further, in the Shunammite episode Elisha claims that God hides the matter from him,
but in the next scene he is a *mind-reader*, even infiltrating the inner
thoughts of a foreign monarch.[3] These factors do not make Elisha
easier to interpret, but certainly make him more lively. Combined with
some stylish literary devices in 2 Kings 6:8–7:23—ranging from important word-plays to the use of suspense and temporal dislocation—
it creates an entertaining reading experience.

ARRESTED DEVELOPMENT

Despite the recent healing of Naaman, commander of the Aramean
armed forces, animosity between Israel and Aram apparently has not
abated. The king of Israel earlier feared (2 Kings 5:7) that his Aramean counterpart was "seeking an occasion" and picking a quarrel.
The king of Israel had good reason for such a fear, as the syntax of 6:8

---

[1] R. LaBarbera, "The Man of War and the Man of God: Social Satire in 2 Kings 6:8–7:20," *CBQ* 46 (1984), 637–8.

[2] e.g., S. Niditch, "Samson as Culture Hero, Trickster, and Bandit: The Empower-ment of the Weak," *CBQ* 52 (1985), 608–24. For a related interpretation of the trickster motif and main characters in the book of Daniel, see D. M. Valeta, "Poly-glossia and Parody: Language in Daniel 1–6," in R. Boer (ed.), *Bakhtin and Genre Theory in Biblical Studies* (Semeia Studies; Atlanta: Society of Biblical Literature, 2007), 91–108, at 100: "Their resistance takes the form of the trickster hero, which Scott defines as one that makes his way through a treacherous environment of enemies not by strength but by wit and cunning (162). This resistance is covert and invisible to the king and yet is powerfully subversive and indicative of the true relationship between the king and his subjects," drawing on J. C. Scott, *Domination and the Arts of Resistance: Hidden Transcripts* (New Haven: Yale University Press, 1990).

[3] Moore, *God Saves*, 87.

makes it sound like the "battling" has been happening for a while, and that numerous "occasions" have been sought: "Now the king of Aram was battling against Israel." It can be assumed that these scenes take place after the Naaman healing, but there is no specific timeframe for this episode, and commentators have long attempted to slot this account into a historical chronology. However, the rest of 6:8 makes both time and space even more elusive, as the king of Aram counseled his servants, saying, "At such and such a place (פלני אלמני) I will camp." For vagueness, it is hard to beat the Hebrew phrase "such and such," an expression used elsewhere to signal a deliberate obfuscation (e.g., 1 Samuel 21:2). Given the sensitivity of the martial context, Brian Aucker cautions: "In view of the importance of the information it is unlikely that such an abstract statement would occur in an interchange between a king and his advisors."[4] By extension, one could infer that such a phrase is used in the story to stress both the *covert* nature of the operations, and to highlight the extraordinary knowledge of Elisha, as exhibited in verses 9–10: "Then the man of God sent to the king of Israel, saying, 'Be on guard from passing by this place, for there Aram is descending.' So the king of Israel sent to the place which the man of God told him. He warned him, and he was on guard not once or twice."

Top secret codes and sophisticated encryption have long been staples of wartime communications. Elisha's decipherment here, though, has to rank higher than even that of the *Enigma* machine of the Second World War. Military intelligence on this scale of reliability—as the king of Israel is provided with advanced warning time after time—would surely be the envy of many of a modern superpower. Still, it should be noted that some scholars rationally suggest that Elisha procures the logistical data from an informant. For instance, Bergen discusses Norman Gottwald's "belief in a prophetic underground that would provide Elisha with information."[5] In response, one might demur that Elisha's extraordinary perception here is perhaps only slightly more impressive than swimming iron, transferring the leprosy of Naaman to Gehazi, or responding to the bald insult with a curse resulting in she-bears marching out

---

[4] Aucker, "Putting Elisha in his Place," 147.
[5] Bergen, *Elisha and the End of Prophetism*, 128, citing N. K. Gottwald, *All the Kingdoms of the Earth: Israelite Prophecy and International Relations in the Ancient Near East* (New York: Harper & Row, 1964), 75.

from the forest. Israel's king could provide a helpful perspective on Elisha's inside information, but no royal reaction is provided in the text (whether good or ill). Because of the recent tensions—Elisha's remarks to the king usually are sarcastic, or some sort of rebuke—the king's silence is understandable. During the water crisis in the Moabite desert (3:13), Elisha delivers what amounts to a taunt: "Go to the prophets of your father and the prophets of your mother!" Here in 2 Kings it is unlikely that the king calls on these prophets for a second opinion when Elisha provides the strategic information on Aramean troop movements.

As useful as the advanced warnings are for the king of Israel, another king is deeply annoyed by these continual frustrations: "Thus the heart of the king of Aram was storming over this matter, and he called to his servants, and said, 'Will you not tell me who from among us is for the king of Israel?'" The comedic side of biblical narrative is often an underappreciated commodity, but even the most melancholic reader or somber scholar would have to smile at this tableau. At the risk of getting hyper-theoretical when no theory is needed, I would assay that the humor proceeds from *dramatic irony*—that is, from the knowledge gap in the story: the reader is aware of factors outside the purview of the foreign king.[6] But the comic side of this story is quite serious, as the knowledge gap is an integral element of the plot. Another level of dramatic irony will soon be apparent, as in the next scene Elisha knows considerably more than any character (or the reader, for that matter). Meanwhile, any talk of humor is hardly applicable to the king of Aram, who is storming (סער) with rage. It should be noted that the nominal form of this root (סערה) occurs in 2 Kings 2:1 to describe the "storm" that ushers Elijah to heaven. In light of the forthcoming appearance of chariots of fire later in this episode, such a verb choice is not accidental. The king's wrath is kindled because the army's whereabouts are continually anticipated; in contrast to Norman Gottwald, the king of

---

[6] For an overview of irony, note the study of C. J. Sharp, *Irony and Meaning in the Hebrew Bible* (Bloomington: Indiana University Press, 2009). See also the essay of Y. Zakovitch, "Humor and Theology or the Successful Failure of Israelite Intelligence: A Literary-Folkloric Approach to Joshua 2," in Susan Niditch (ed.), *Text and Tradition: The Hebrew Bible and Folklore* (Atlanta: Scholars Press, 1990), 75–98, and the collection of studies in A. Brenner and Y. T. Radday (eds), *On Humour and the Comic in the Hebrew Bible* (JSOTSup 92; Sheffield: Almond Press, 1990).

Aram does not hypothesize an underground prophetic network, but instead reckons there is a double-crosser within his own ranks!

For the king of Aram, this is not his first miscalculation with respect to Elisha. In the previous chapter, he wrote a letter to his Israelite counterpart but made no mention of the prophet. By all accounts he similarly overlooks the prophet here in chapter 6, perhaps surprising in the wake of Naaman's leprous adventure (assuming the king is aware of the healing). The king's first impulse is that a traitor is in the midst, though, for LaBarbera, "it is not clear whether he actually suspects spies or is only venting his frustration through irony."[7] One of the servants (אחד מעבדיו) responds to the king in verse 12, but it is doubtful that the servant appreciates any shades of irony in the royal speech. Furious kings, after all, have a habit of damaging their employees, and, when the servant speaks up, fear is probably the key motivator. According to the servant's penetrating words, there is no mole in the Aramean situation room: "No, my lord the king, rather Elisha the prophet who is in Israel tells the king of Israel the words that you speak in your bedroom."

Rank-and-file Arameans are rapidly emerging as a fairly sensible group. In 2 Kings 5, for example, Naaman is disappointed with Elisha's instructions, and the entire journey to Samaria is jeopardized. However, his servants' urge him (5:13) to reconsider, and Naaman heeds their counsel by submitting to the prophetic directive. The servant here in chapter 6 does not offer advice as much as information, but likewise is taken seriously by his superior. Still, some crucial facts are left unstated: the servant asserts that Elisha even knows the king's words in his bedroom, but it is unclear how the servant knows about Elisha's knowledge *and* subsequent warnings to the Israelite king. I am reminded of an unnamed servant in Saul's court who equally offers crucial information at an important juncture in the story. In 1 Samuel 16 Saul is tormented by an evil spirit from God, and is in dire need of music therapy. In due course (16:18), one of the young men imparts some vital statistics: "Behold, I have seen a son of Jesse from Bethlehem. He is a skillful player, a mighty warrior, a man of battle, a discerning speaker, good-looking, and the LORD is with him." The servant's words are instrumental for plot (as through his speech David enters the court as a musician) and character (as the

---

[7] LaBarbera, "The Man of War and the Man of God: Social Satire in 2 Kings 6:8–7:20," 640.

qualities mentioned by the servant are incrementally revealed in the storyline). In the same way, the Aramean servant's words in 2 Kings 6:12 continue the plot, and provide indirect characterization of Elisha. The servant resembles the little girl from the previous chapter, who certainly understood the power of the prophet in Samaria.

The king does not question his servant's communiqué about Elisha, and straightaway issues an arrest order: "Go, find out where he is, that I might send and take him" (6:13a). There is no passage of time recorded, but in the second half of the verse a report comes to the king from an anonymous source: "Behold, in Dothan." Over the course of his career Elisha has traversed many kilometers and visited numerous locales. The reader has recently been told that Elisha had a house in Samaria (cf. v. 32), and, because he kindly restored the lost axe-head, presumably he would be welcome to stay by the Jordan River with the sons of the prophets. Dothan has not been mentioned before, and, indeed, this is the first mention of the town in the Deuteronomistic History, and so the reader is unsure of Elisha's reason for being there. According to the calculations of the fourth-century historian Eusebius of Caesarea, Dothan was north of Samaria and located a distance of twelve Roman miles away.[8] This brings Elisha closer to Aramean territory, and so most plausibly he is in Dothan in order to foil Aramean raids into Israel. The object of Aramean raids, we infer from the story of the little captive Israelite girl, is plunder. Now, however, the Aramean raiders have a different object in mind.

THE BLIND SIDE

Armed with the location of Elisha, the king of Aram moves toward the arrest, and, for the second time in as many chapters, a huge Aramean host is sent to Elisha. There are no half-measures when the Arameans enter Israel: Naaman came with a hefty entourage and chariots, and now the king sends horses, chariots, and a great army. Although the Aramean host is quite a spectacle, commentators point out a certain disproportion: apprehending a single prophet requires

---

[8] Keil, *I & II Kings, I & II Chronicles*, 325. Cf. Gen. 37:17.

the king to expend considerable resources and gather a fearsome military force. Expensive as these efforts are, they do raise a simple question: given Elisha's recent track record of predicting Aramean movements, does the king expect that Elisha will be easy to arrest? This question may explain why the king opts for a nocturnal arrival into Dothan. As Choon Leong Seow notes: "despite the fact that Elisha had previously known of the king's secret plans through his extrasensory powers, the Arameans think it would make a difference for them to approach under the cover of darkness."[9] On a different level, the ambiance of *night* in verse 14 foreshadows the coming darkness that will soon envelop the army.[10]

If Elisha is aware of the Aramean presence in Dothan, he does not appear agitated; in fact, there is a change in narrative perspective between verses 14 and 15, as the point of view shifts from the picture of the vast army to a solitary servant in Dothan—labeled the minister (משׁרת) of the man of God. The first glimpse of the surrounding army will be refracted through this (unnamed) servant's perspective. While some commentators suggest that Gehazi is the servant, others disagree because of Gehazi's leprosy. One recalls Elisha's unnamed assistant(s) in 2 Kings 4:38 and 43, but no other details are provided. The reader may not be given the servant's identity here, but we are given his actions: he rises in the early morning, merely out of habit, in complete innocence. The sense of innocence is then exploited, as the syntax of verse 15 captures both the servant's surprise and the intimidation factor that was surely the intention of the Aramean king: "Look, an army surrounding the city: horses and chariots!" The scale of the invading force triggers the servant's reaction, "Alas my master (אהה אדני), what can we do!" This is not the first time such an interjection has been uttered in Elisha's career. In 2 Kings 3:10 the king of Israel reacts with the same "Alas" (אהה) when faced with disaster in the Moabite desert. Even closer is the response of the axe-borrower in the previous episode, who says "Alas my master

---

[9] Seow, "1 & 2 Kings," 201. Cf. C. Dorn, "The Ways of God in the World: The Drama of 2 Kings 6:8–23," in J. H. Ellens and J. T. Greene (eds), *Probing the Frontiers of Biblical Studies* (Princeton Theological Monograph Series 111; Eugene, OR.: Pickwick, 2009), 9–20, 11: "The irony here can hardly escape the reader. The king plots the capture of one who already knows his every move! However, the king somehow vainly imagines that he can overcome the clairvoyant powers of his opponent by sending a detachment of soldiers under the covers of darkness."

[10] Cf. Aucker, "Putting Elisha in his Place," 156.

(אהה אדני)" in a cry of despair over the lost implement. The servant in Dothan likewise expresses a sense of helplessness and resignation, as though he is acquiescing to the inevitability of capture by this formidable assembly of chariots and soldiers.

Elisha's response to his servant begins with "Do not fear," a common prophetic utterance but the only occasion where it is used by Elisha. It is possible that Elisha begins with this reassurance because a notably high percentage of his servants (or assistants) are lacking in basic faith; despite spending time in the presence of this dominant prophetic personality, the servants tend not to absorb much confidence. This particular servant is told not to fear because "many more are with us than with them." The servant may well be baffled by this locution, and inquire as to the precise identity of the "many more." It is helpful, therefore, that Elisha does not wait for a response but instead prays for illumination: "O LORD, please open his eyes, that he might see." The prayer is immediately answered, and again the servant's visual perspective is refracted: previously he saw only the Aramean horses and chariots, but now God opens his eyes, "and he saw, and look, the mountain was filled with horses and chariots of fire encircling Elisha!" Nachman Levine draws a connection between this episode and 2 Kings 2, where Elisha witnesses his master transported to heaven in a similar vehicle.[11] The same chariots of fire are now surrounding Elisha, and, according to Christopher Dorn, such accompaniment anticipates a favorable outcome for the Israelite prophet.[12] It is uncertain whether this celestial entourage *always* encircles Elisha (and the reader is privy only now, like the servant), or whether the supernatural host is assembled ad hoc for this occasion. In terms of the servant, the Aramean army may have been intimidating, but the revelation of this other army must alleviate his alarm. As scary as the Aramean host may be, most servants would take chariots of fire over any earthly alternative. For the reader, Elisha's encirclement by this army adds a new dimension to his

---

[11] Levine, "Twice as Much of your Spirit," 41.

[12] Dorn, "The Ways of God in the World," 12. For the view that the fiery cavalry is a "dead end" because there is no follow-up, see A. Rofé, "Elisha at Dothan (2 Kgs 6:8–23): Historico-Literary Criticism Sustained by the Midrash," in R. Chazan, W. W. Hallo, and L. H. Schiffman (eds), *Ki Baruch Hu: Ancient Near Eastern, Biblical, and Judaic Studies in Honor of Baruch A. Levine* (Winona Lake: Eisenbrauns, 1999), 345–53, at 348.

characterization, and the odds must be in favor of the fiery horses obliterating the Aramean opponents.

In light of the flaming army that surrounds Elisha, the reader might reasonably expect military engagement, but that is not how the next scene unfolds. Not privy to the same vision as Elisha's servant, the Aramean army moves for the arrest of the suspect: "They came down toward him, and Elisha prayed to the LORD, and said, 'Please strike this nation with sudden blindness,' and they were struck with sudden blindness (סנורים) according to the word of Elisha." There is a binary moment here: the servant has just received uncanny insight because of Elisha's prayer; now the prophet prays for blindness to engulf the Arameans. It should be noted that the most common term for blindness (עור) is not used in Elisha's prayer, but instead there is a different term that I am translating as *sudden blindness* (סנורים). This rare phenomenon—a more narrow and technical category of temporary sightlessness—has been seen only once before, in Genesis 19:11 "where the men of Sodom are struck 'blind' while attempting to enter Lot's house for the purpose of assaulting his guests. But their 'blindness' does not deter them from pursuing their goal. It only makes it impossible for them to find the door."[13] In Genesis 19 the sudden blindness allows Lot to escape the fanatical mob, and, here, the sudden blindness also stifles the extravagant attempt to arrest the prophet Elisha by the armed forces of Aram. Still, what is Elisha now going to do with this blind group of soldiers?

CATCH AND RELEASE

The legendary film-maker Alfred Hitchcock is credited with saying: "There is no terror in a bang, only in the anticipation of it."[14] Hitchcock was a master of generating suspense, and he realized that a sense of anticipation (or the capacity for surprise) is what viewers enjoy—and still do when viewing one of those classic movies. In 2 Kings 6 there is a quality of surprise that exceeds even the golden age of

---

[13] LaBarbera, "The Man of War and the Man of God: Social Satire in 2 Kings 6:8–7:20," 643.

[14] Cited in R. Gilmour, "Suspense and Anticipation in 1 Samuel 9:1–14," *JHS* 9 (2009), 2.

cinema, stemming from Elisha's words and actions. To the recently blinded military, Elisha says: "This is not the way, nor is this the city! Walk after me, and I will bring you to the man who you are seeking." In reality, Elisha is *misleading* the Arameans on a twelve-mile journey—if we trust the cartography of Eusebius—ending up in Israel's capital ("He brought them to Samaria," v. 19). The soldiers came to take Elisha captive, but now have become captives themselves. It is not immediately clear why Samaria is Elisha's destination, assuming he is not simply trying to rile the Arameans with a long and obviously inconvenient march. Elisha's plan—and anyone who is encircled by blazing horses and chariots of fire must have a plan—is to continue his ongoing dialogue with the Omride king, probably with a rebuke or a memorable action designed to remind the king that there is a prophet in Israel. Elisha leading a group of blinded Arameans into the city of Samaria certainly would be a sight for the king to behold.

The king of Israel's reaction to the arrival of the captive soldiers is given only *after* Elisha has prayed; in Dothan Elisha prayed for sudden blindness, now in 6:20 he prays that the same Aramean eyes be opened. In both cases the prayer is answered, and the soldiers—who must have marched into Dothan with great confidence—are now completely on the defensive, and their perspective is refracted: "the LORD opened their eyes, and they saw, and behold, in the midst of Samaria!" If there was a sense of confusion with the onset of blindness, that confusion must now give way to panic as the full-orbed soldiers realize they are incarcerated in Samaria. With his adversaries at a disadvantage, the king must sense his chance as he turns to Elisha and seemingly asks his permission: "Should I strike? I will strike, my father!" Scholars have pointed out some difficulties with syntax of the king's utterance (האכה אכה אבי), yet some interpreters suggest that the very awkwardness is intentional. Burke Long, for instance, comments that the words are "tumbling redundantly with excitement."[15] If the king is anticipating that a Hitchcock bomb will soon be detonated, such euphoria might explain why he temporarily abandons conventional grammar. It might also explain why he uses the unexpected "my father" in reference to Elisha. "My father" is used by Elisha himself when witnessing the chariot carrying off his master in

---

[15] Long, *2 Kings*, 87. Cf. G. A. Rendsburg, "Confused Language as a Deliberate Literary Device in Biblical Hebrew Narrative," *JHS* 2 (1999), 1–20.

2 Kings 2:12, and again when Naaman's servants speak to their commander and persuade him to heed Elisha's directive (5:13). Has the king of Israel's lucidity been swept away in the giddiness of the moment, or is he sincerely acknowledging the prophet's authority? Regardless of the king's disposition, Elisha is characterized as the figure in charge.

Awkward as the king's utterance may be, if the Arameans hear it, they could hardly miss the lethal intent: the verb "strike" is used twice, and sounds decidedly dangerous. The likelihood of their impending demise is increased when we consider a proposal of Walter Brueggemann, who draws a parallel with an earlier episode in 1 Kings 20:31–43. In that scene, the captured Aramean king is spared by Ahab, but then Ahab is severely chastised by a member of the sons of the prophets for extending clemency.[16] Consequently, the Aramean soldiers here in Samaria have every reason to expect the worst. Any expectation of death, though, is not realized. Elisha has a habit of posing rhetorical questions and giving directions to the king of Israel, and the present moment is no exception: "You will not strike. Who did you capture with your sword or your bow, that you can strike? Set food and water before them, that they may eat and drink, and then go to their lord."

Elisha's proposal of a feast, as one can immediately perceive, now illuminates the reason for the sudden blindness. As LaBarbera puts it: "In Genesis the men of Sodom were struck with confused vision (סנורים) because they intended to violate the ancient law of hospitality. Here, in what may be an intentional irony, the Arameans have been struck in the same way so that hospitality might now be given to them."[17] Another reason can also be offered, as in my view the feast is not so much for the benefit of the Arameans—though they probably have never been more relieved to attend a banquet—but rather for the king of Israel. When the king sets the table and pays the bill for the feast, he is indeed reminded of the necessity of heeding the prophetic voice. It is to the king's credit that he complies with Elisha's directive and gives the feast. The Arameans are then dismissed, and the end result in 6:23 scarcely could have been predicted: "So the raiding parties of Aram did not again enter into the land of Israel." Elisha initially frustrates the king of Aram, and ends up countering the king

---

[16] Brueggemann, *1 & 2 Kings*, 347–8.
[17] LaBarbera, "The Man of War and the Man of God: Social Satire in 2 Kings 6:8–7:20," 644.

of Israel as well: "Thus the character of Elisha emerges in contrast to that of the two kings: one malevolent king sends men to capture and perhaps kill a prophet; this same prophet now sends those men away unharmed from a second malevolent king who sees them vulnerable and wants to kill them."[18] For the second time in as many chapters, a sizeable Aramean contingent is sent home in peace: first Naaman and his entourage, and now this unit of soldiers at the conclusion of the feast. It would be advisable for the citizens of Samaria to eat as much as they can during this time, for there soon will be a food crisis that plunges the city into extreme measures.

UNDER SIEGE

Israel's king had the Aramean soldiers, as one interpreter puts it, like fish in a barrel.[19] The king is ready to shoot, but Elisha commands that the fish be released. This seems like a good move at the time, especially since the scene ends with notice of a cessation of hostilities, and raiding parties no longer terrorized the countryside. However, there is an abrupt change in 2 Kings 6:24: "After this (ויהי אחרי־כן), Ben Hadad king of Aram assembled all his troops. He went up and besieged Samaria." The incursions of the raiding parties may have ended, but they are replaced with a large-scale invasion led by the king. Identification of the Aramean king as Ben-Hadad has led some scholars to posit a different source or tradition for this episode in 6:24–7:20, while others view the king's presence as indication of full-blown assault. But the main controversy among scholars is how to reconcile verses 23 and 24, as a cessation of hostility gives way to a massive offensive. Wesley Bergen is particularly troubled by this development, arguing that the Hebrew phrase "After this" (ויהי אחרי־כן) undermines the reader's confidence in the prophet: "Thus, in three short words the credibility of Elisha collapses."[20] Conversely, one may point out that the siege of Samaria—under the direct command by Ben-Hadad—palpably differs in scale from a raiding party making a foray into Israelite territory. In the previous episode

---

[18] Dorn, "The Ways of God in the World," 16.
[19] Leithart, *1 & 2 Kings*, 202.
[20] Bergen, *Elisha and the End of Prophetism*, 136.

Elisha is located in Dothan in order to frustrate such smaller initiatives, as I suggested above. The more substantial issue for Elisha's characterization, to my mind, is that the king of Israel will soon be angry with Elisha, who commanded the king to release the captives in the previous episode. When the siege brings famine, the king questions that quality of mercy.

During a period of prolonged siege, normal agricultural activities come to a standstill, so Jacob Wright explains, causing economic hardship and scarcity of resources.[21] Such deprivation is evident in verse 25: "There was a great famine in Samaria, and behold, they were besieging it until a donkey's head was eighty silver pieces, and a quarter of one kab of dove's dung was five silver pieces." Not so long before, Samaria was the venue for a copious feast; now the best item on the menu is donkey brain, not the first menu choice for most restaurant connoisseurs, it must be said. There is no consensus among scholars for the exact use of dove's dung (if that is the best translation), but one guess is that it is a source of fuel for burning (perhaps to warm up the expensive meal). As if that description is not morbid enough, the next scene (vv. 26–31) paints an even more frightening picture:

> The king of Israel was passing by on the wall, and a woman cried out to him, saying, "Save, my lord the king!" He said, "If the LORD does not save you, from where will I save you – from the threshing floor or from the wine vat?" The king said to her, "What is with you?" She said, "This woman said to me, 'Give up your son that we may eat him today, and my son we will eat tomorrow.' So we boiled my son and we ate him. Then I said to her on the next day, 'Give up your son that we may eat him,' but she had hidden her son." When the king heard the words of woman, he tore his clothes, as he was crossing by on the wall. The people looked, and behold, sackcloth was on his flesh, on the inside! Then he said, "Thus may God do to me and even more if the head of Elisha son of Shaphat remains on him today!"

It has been suggested that the king is walking on the city wall to survey the devastation caused by the Aramean siege, and it is during this inspection that he is implored by the unnamed woman.[22] The verb "cry out" (צעק) has been heard before, only of late it was used with respect to Elisha rather than the king. In this instance, though,

---

[21] Wright, "Warfare and Wanton Destruction," 648.
[22] Seow, "1 & 2 Kings," 204.

the cry for justice is particularly repulsive, as the cannibal mother argues that her colleague has not honored their deal. In this respect, scholars draw attention to parallels between this scene and Solomon's judgment in the case of the two harlots.[23] Of more immediate import for this study is the king's oath about Elisha's (hairless) head. A decapitating irony emerges: the king is angered at the speech of the cannibal mother, but now swears an oath that Elisha *son of Shaphat* will be yet another dead son in Samaria. The king referred to Elisha as "my father" in the previous scene, but, if the king has his way, donkeys will not be the only headless creatures in Samaria. At the end of chapter 3 there was a child sacrifice on the wall in Moab, but now the king of Israel is on the wall calling for a prophetic execution. It is possible that the king blames Elisha for not acting earlier, but most likely he is angry that Elisha released the soldiers who are besieging the city—causing a famine where they once feasted on Elisha's order (and against the king's instinct). The king should exercise caution, because it never works to make a remark about Elisha's head, as forty-two former residents of Bethel can testify.

Distinguished guests have visited Elisha's house before, as in 2 Kings 5:9 we recall Naaman's considerable entourage: horses, chariots, and enough wealth to induce Gehazi to concoct a story about needy prophets. Elisha has other visitors on this more austere occasion, as he is sitting with "the elders" (v. 32). This marks the first appearance of the elders in the storyline so far, perhaps pointing to emerging factions as the siege wears on. If the elders are siding with Elisha, it also indicates the king's increasing alienation; in a moment he will be attended by a senior official who is also *hostile* to the prophet, so we get the impression that the politics of Samaria are increasingly partisan. The posture of "sitting" implies a council meeting, and Sweeney believes the elders are seeking a divine word from the prophet.[24] The reader notices the king is not invited to the meeting, but he too is about to pay a visit to Elisha's busy house.

---

[23] e.g., S. Lasine, "Jehoram and the Cannibal Mothers (2 Kings 6.24–33): Solomon's Judgment in an Inverted World," *JSOT* 50 (1991), 27–53. Note also H. S. Pyper, "Judging the Wisdom of Solomon: The Two-Way Effect of Intertextuality," *JSOT* 59 (1993), 25–36; S. Lasine, "The Ups and Downs of Monarchical Justice: Solomon and Jehoram in an Intertextual World," *JSOT* 59 (1993), 37–53; L. Lanner, "Cannibal Mothers and Me: A Mother's Reading of 2 Kings 6.24–7.20," *JSOT* 85 (1999), 107–16; G. Hens-Piazza, *Nameless, Blameless, and without Shame: Two Cannibal Mothers before a King* (Interfaces; Collegeville, MN: Liturgical Press/Michael Glazier, 2003).

[24] Sweeney, *1 & 2 Kings*, 311.

SHUT THE DOOR

The Hebrew syntax of 2 Kings 6:32 is difficult, but the sense is that the king dispatches a messenger ahead of him, and follows close behind (the NRSV changes the order for a smoother translation). A key point is that Elisha reads the situation with the same prescience as in the previous episode, and he addresses the elders *prior to* the arrival of the messenger: "Do you see that this son of a murderer has been sent to remove my head? Look, when the messenger arrives, close the door and squeeze him with the door. Is not the sound of his master's feet behind him?" Not only is the king denied an invitation to the assembly, but Elisha makes a concerted attempt even to refuse entry. Despite the severity of the famine and the death threat, there is a slapstick element here: "The scene is thoroughly comical. Elisha calls on a bunch of old men to hold the door shut as the message from the king is delivered."[25] Over the course of Elisha's last few scenes some classic ploys of the *trickster* can be observed, although this scholarly construct can be overused and subject to varying applications.[26] For my purposes, the following definition is useful: "Trickster stories are frequently characterized by the outrageous, the miraculous, and the comic, as well as turning the tables on the rich and powerful."[27] If the trickster figure is understood as a subversive agent with connections in both the material and spiritual realms, then Elisha's outwitting the king and knowing *ahead of time* that the king's messenger will arrive can be interpreted within this framework. Elijah, we recall, was not characterized in this manner, so Elisha is uniquely profiled here. In this respect Elisha is closer to the prophet Micaiah in 1 Kings 22:15–23,

---

[25] Seow, "1 & 2 Kings," 205. For the opposite view, see Bergen (*Elisha and the End of Prophetism*, 142): "The picture of a group of elders hastily barring the door against the intrusion of the king and his messenger hardly stands as a great demonstration of YHWH's power."

[26] See J. C. Exum, *Tragedy and Biblical Narrative: Arrows of the Almighty* (Cambridge: Cambridge University Press, 1992), 38. Exum (p. 162) cites the work of B. Babcock-Abrahams ("'A Tolerated Margin of Mess': The Trickster and his Tales Reconsidered," *Journal of the Folklore Institute*, 11 (1975), 147–86), who cautions: "it would perhaps be better to call both this type of tale and persona by the literary term 'picaresque' which combines with the notion of trickery and roguish behavior the idea of the uncertain or hostile attitude of an individual to existing society and an involvement in narrative focused on movement, within and beyond that society" (p. 159).

[27] F. Landy, Review of "D. A. Nicholas, *The Trickster Revisited: Deception as a Motif in the Pentateuch*," *CBQ* 73 (2011), 133.

whose sarcastic exchange with Ahab forms a prelude to his heavenly vision.[28]

On cue, the anticipated messenger arrives, even as Elisha is still talking with the elders. The direct speech in verse 33 is difficult, as there is no speaker explicitly marked for the direct speech: "He was yet speaking with them, and behold, the messenger was coming down to him! He said, 'Behold, this evil is from the LORD! Why should I hope for the LORD any longer?'" Some translators assume that the messenger speaks this line (the NRSV emends the text to read "king"), while others infer from the context that it must be the king. Regardless of the actual speaker, the sentiments expressed are surely those of the king, and hence one should interpret the words as the king's utterance. The frequency with which the king invokes the divine name is forming a pattern: back in 2 Kings 3 he claims that God has given the three kings into the hands of Moab, and in chapter 5 he is angry with the Aramean king for insinuating that he has power over life and death. In this chapter, the king's earlier speech to the distressed mother (6:27) declares that only God can save; even if he is being sarcastic, it proves true in the storyline. Here in verse 33 the statement is that evil (as well as good) is under the aegis of divine sovereignty, yet the king's solution is to abandon hope (or waiting, יחל) and murder the prophet. The despair of this line, in the context of lack of food, parallels the despair of the desert when there was a lack of water. In chapter 3 Elisha delivers a stunning oracle about *both* a miracle of water and an elimination of the enemy's threat. A similar oracle is declared here (7:1), as the prophet predicts a dramatic reversal: "Hear the word of the LORD! Thus says the LORD: at this time tomorrow a measure of flour will go for a shekel, and two measures of barley for a shekel at the gate of Samaria."

The specificity of this oracle even includes the exact prices of these desperately needed commodities in the city. Given the inflated costs of the donkey's head, such a colossal deflation would be the envy of many a modern economy. Elisha does not call for a musician here, but, then, there is an oath on his head, so the exigency of the moment might necessitate some haste. One also notices the surplus

---

[28] For other implications of this exchange between king and prophet, see K. Bodner, "The Locutions of 1 Kings 22:28: A New Proposal," *JBL* 122 (2003), 533–43.

of architectural terms in this stretch of the episode: from the wall, to the house, to the closed door. Moore suggests there is a gradual constriction, to provide a sense of the prophet's entrapment, as though he personally is captive: "a siege within a siege."[29] Notably, Elisha's oracle speaks about an open gate, and the reader also hears about an open window, albeit from the negative voice of the king's adjutant.

Instead of celebrating the forthcoming provision—and, in view of the Moabite water, Elisha has earned the benefit of the doubt—the king's senior bureaucrat caustically expresses disbelief: "Behold, the LORD is about to make windows in heaven! How can this thing be?" The description of the speaker—"the king's adjutant, upon whose arm the king was leaning (שׁען)"—creates a vocational parallel with Naaman (5:18), the one upon whose arm the king of Aram leans (שׁען). By means of this description, a contrast emerges between these two high-ranking royal officers. Naaman, the outsider, makes a profession of faith; in fact, Naaman's vocational description comes *in the midst of* his lengthy confession. The Israelite insider, by antithesis, makes a profession of incredulity even while the skeptical king is leaning on his arm. As for Elisha's response, further similarities can be observed with Micaiah in 1 Kings 22. Like Elisha, in 1 Kings 22 Micaiah is surrounded by a chorus of pro-Ahab voices, and he responds to Zedekiah's rebuke (22:25) with a wager: "Behold, you will see in the day when you go into an inner room to hide!" Micaiah, we recall, is physically slapped by Zedekiah just before he delivers the wager. Elisha is verbally slapped, but then snaps back with a wager of his own to the royal consigliore: "Behold, you are about to see it, but from it you will not eat!" As the last word of this scene in the prophet's house, the reader notices that Elisha's head is still attached, despite the ferocity of the king's oath.

TWILIGHT ZONE

For the first time since the translation of Elijah, Elisha is not the main character in an episode. While he may not be formally present in

---

[29] Moore, *God Saves*, 99.

2 Kings 7:3–20, nonetheless the next scenes are all about the fulfillment of his (unlikely) prophetic word about the *gate* of Samaria being
a place for bargain prices. As the first scene opens, the reader is taken,
of all places, to the same city *gate* where four unnamed lepers are not
sounding altogether buoyant. Being part of a city under siege is one
thing, but being a leper who depends on handouts is even worse, and
it is doubtful whether the average resident of Samaria is tossing out
donkey leftovers to the likes of these four chaps. More importantly,
recent scholars point out a quadratic wordplay, as the Hebrew term
"four" (ארבע) bears a striking resemblance to "window" (ארבה).[30]
A major function of wordplay in Hebrew narrative is to signal a
reversal of fortune, so through wordplay on *window* and *four* the
reader senses a momentous change in the story.[31] The king's adjutant
was skeptical about the windows, but these four lepers will be the first
to witness a radical change in fortune. The most recent (unhealed)
leper is Gehazi, who himself accumulates a serious amount of Aramean silver by fraudulent means. The four lepers, without any swind-
ling, will themselves discover an even bigger Aramean cache in due
course.

The four lepers are sitting at the "door" of the gate, and the NRSV
assumes from the context of the verse that the group is outside the
city. If so, we sense their desperation: if the mothers inside the city
are reduced to cannibalism, what are the options of these four on the
wrong side of the wall? But, whereas the mothers decided to consume
their offspring, these four lepers undertake a lengthy conversation
("each man said to his friend") that results in a quite different
resolution: "What, are we just sitting here until we die? If we say,
'Let's enter the city,' then the famine is in the city, and we will die
there. If we sit here, we will die. So now, come and let's surrender to
the camp of Aram; if they let us live, we will live, and if they kill us,
we'll die." If there were comic elements in earlier scenes, then such
moments are equaled by the corporate speech of the four lepers. In
retrospect, the humor increases when the reader discovers that these

---

[30] e.g., LaBarbera, "The Man of War and the Man of God: Social Satire in 2 Kings
6:8–7:20," 648.

[31] W. G. E. Watson, *Classical Hebrew Poetry* (Sheffield: JSOT Press, 1986), 246.
Note my discussion of the key wordplay in 1 Kings 11, where the prophet Ahijah rips
the coat (שלמה) of Jeroboam symbolizing the ripping apart of Solomon's (שלמה)
kingdom, in K. Bodner, *Jeroboam's Royal Drama* (Oxford: Oxford University Press,
2012), 52.

four (ארבע) will be the first to see that the window (ארבה) has already been opened.

> Then they arose at twilight to go to the camp of Aram. They came to the edge of the camp of Aram, but behold, no man was there—because the Lord had caused the camp of Aram to hear the sound of chariots, the sound of horses, and the sound of a great army, such that each man said to his brother, "Behold, the king of Israel has hired against us the kings of the Hittites and the kings of Egypt to come out against us!" So they arose and fled at twilight, abandoned their tents, horses, donkeys, and the camp just as it was, and fled for their lives. (vv. 5–7)

No reason is stated as to why the four lepers choose the cover of impending darkness to venture toward the Aramean camp. Nonetheless, the reader is reminded that the Arameans also chose the cover of darkness to journey to Dothan (6:13) for Elisha's arrest; both scenes feature surprising reversals and unanticipated horses and chariots. I assume the group of four wait until evening for their march of surrender so that they can slip away unseen. Even if they are lepers, there still might be some repercussions for desertion. More specifically, when they leave "at twilight," there is a sense of *simultaneity* established in the episode.[32] At twilight (נשׁף) the lepers arise after debating ("each man said to his friend," ויאמרו איש אל־רעהו) whether to abandon Samaria, while at the same time ("twilight," נשׁף) the Arameans were deciding to abandon their camp ("each man said to his brother," ויאמרו איש אל־אחיו). The verb "arise" (קום) is used for the action of both parties: when the lepers arise to begin their surrender, the Arameans arise to depart in haste. In the case of the Arameans, God causes them to hear the sounds of horses, chariots, and a great army; in chapter 6 the presence of horses and chariots of fire ensure the safety of Elisha in Dothan, and now the same sound rescues the city of Samaria and operates to fulfill Elisha's word. There may be an echo here to Elijah's contest on Mt Carmel, as Walter Brueggemann opines: "The threefold 'voice' matches the threefold negation of 1 Kings 18:29. While Baal, in that contest, has no 'voice,' Yahweh

---

[32] For an overview, see S. Talmon, "The Presentation of Synchroneity and Simultaneity in Biblical Narrative," in J. Heinemann and S. Werses (eds), *Studies in Hebrew Narrative Art throughout the Ages* (Scripta hierosolymitana 27; Jerusalem: Magnes Press, 1978), 9–26.

sounds in many effective voices."[33] Misleading the opposition has happened before in Elisha's career, as back in 2 Kings 3:23 the Moabites see the reflection of the water and erroneously conclude that Israel and the Israelite allies have slaughtered themselves. In both instances, the misperceptions of the opposing army coincide with Elisha's oracle about the resolution of a life-threatening crisis.

Because of the narrative sequencing, the reader is aware of the empty camp before the lepers, and, for all they know, they are walking onto the sharp end of a bayonet. Consequently, one can easily imagine their surprise when no Arameans are around; instead, the tables are seemingly set for dinner. Several commentators have noted an odd picture here—namely, the abandoned horses and donkeys. When the Arameans were fleeing at the sound of the great army, it stands to reason that horses would have assisted in the speed of their flight. The sense of confusion, then, is amplified by these idle animals. But the lepers are probably not asking the same questions as those commentators, because they are busy eating and drinking the Aramean victuals, and hiding gold, silver, and clothes—reminiscent of Gehazi in 2 Kings 5:24 stashing Aramean silver and clothes taken from Naaman the Aramean. It is unclear *where* the four lepers are concealing these treasures, but there must be quite a surplus as they rummage from tent to tent. In the midst of this spree they pause (v. 9), and for the second time in the episode have a conference: "What we are doing is not right! Today is a day of good news, but we are keeping silent. If we wait until the light of morning, we may encounter guilt. So now, come, let's go that we may tell the king's house." The lepers' corporate conscience, it must be said, is initially pricked by a fear of judgment, and in this sense the guilt must be related to a social violation or hoarding (perhaps a foil to the mother who hid her offspring from her companion, out of an unwillingness to share). On this score, Moore understands a contrast in the narrative, as

---

[33] Brueggemann, *1 & 2 Kings*, 359. On the possible polemical thrust here (and the "window" of 6:33 in Baal mythology), see Mead, "'Elisha Will Kill'? The Deuteronomistic Rhetoric of Life and Death in the Theology of the Elisha Narratives," 160; cf. the larger study of L. Bronner, *The Stories of Elijah and Elisha as Polemics against Baal Worship* (Leiden: Brill, 1968).

the lepers' co-operation and benevolence are in contrast with the social upheaval in the city. While those within the city are making decisions to devour each other, both figuratively (6.31) and literally (6.29), the four lepers outside the city act to save themselves and then the city with decisions which arise in each case out of mutually supportive dialogue.[34]

The lepers recognize that the abandoned camp is "good news"; the term for good news and its related verb are variously used to describe the birth of a child (Jer. 20:15), the demise of an adversary (1 Sam. 31:9), or the salvation of God (Isa. 52:7). There is no specific attribution of God's activity by the lepers, but when they use the term good news it must signal to the reader that Elisha's word has been fulfilled.

Dutifully proceeding back to the gate from where they came, the four lepers report their remarkable find. Announcement of the report succeeds in rousing the sleeping king (v. 12), who does not hesitate in sharing his own theory of the abandoned camp: "I will tell you what Aram has done to us: they know that we are famished, and they have gone out of the camp to hide themselves in the open field, saying, 'When they come out from the city we will capture them alive, and to the city we can go!'" Owing to the long-standing animosity with the Arameans, the king of Israel has a policy of suspicion: Naaman's arrival with his retinue and royal letter in 1 Kings 5 was, in the king's opinion, a cynical ploy. Now, in the context of a protracted siege where the city is desperate, the king mimics Elisha and attempts his own type of mind-reading. He interprets the empty camp as a logistical maneuver designed finally to end the siege, and hoodwink the residents of Samaria into opening the *gate* themselves. The king does not entertain any possible connection with Elisha's bold declaration about the imminent rescue of the city, and Elisha's recent track record of accurately predicting Aramean troop movements does not factor in the king's nocturnal deliberation. As the king is speaking in the middle of the night, the reader recalls that Elisha's economic forecast about the drastic price reduction at the gate specified the next day (7:1). Daylight, so we infer from the context, is rapidly approaching.

---

[34] Moore, *God Saves*, 97–8.

THE PRICE IS RIGHT

By misreading the situation with the desolate Aramean camp, it calls to mind the king's earlier misreading of the woman's plea during his walk on the city wall. When the woman called out, the king assumed she wanted provisions from the (empty) storehouses, but actually she wanted legal intervention in her claim against the other mother. Without resolving that dispute, the king issues a warrant for another death, yet, instead of Elisha's execution, the king hears a prophetic word about systematic deflation of prices—in light of the cannibalism and eighty-five shekel donkey heads, such a word is startling. If the king resisted Elisha's word about the immediate supply of food, then he likewise does not hear the good news of its fulfillment, and his statement about an Aramean subterfuge is definitive. The impasse is resolved, however, in a now customary manner: just as the king of Aram is convinced of a traitor in his corps but is put right by the acumen of one of his long-suffering servants in 6:12, so the king of Israel is given an option in 7:13 by "one from his servants" (אחד מעבדיו), who proposes an experiment: "Let them take five of the horses that remain—those that remain in the city. For behold, they will be like the multitude of Israel who are remaining in it—behold they will be like the multitude of Israel who have been consumed! Thus we'll send and see."

It is possible that the servant's words contain a veiled rebuke, but certainly there is frantic syntax and repetitions that cause many translators to opt for emending the text. Whether or not the king is concerned with the rebuke or the awkward syntax is not stated, but he does acquiesce and authorizes the mission. The servant advises that "horses" be taken to investigate the camp, recalling the Arameans abandoning their horses when fleeing from the sounds of horses, chariots, and a great army. Further, Marvin Sweeney remarks that the number *five* "highlights the desperation of the Israelites, who were down to their last five horses from the once-powerful Israelite chariot corps," and the servant does hint at a drastic reduction, with only a small number of remaining animals.[35] It is certainly dismal to imagine what the (former) warhorses were used for during the bleakest hours of the siege.

---

[35] Sweeney, *1 & 2 Kings*, 313.

With the servant's advice taken and the scouting mission dispatched, the result (v. 15) is even better than the lepers testified: the king's representatives follow the trail as far as the Jordan, "and behold, the entire road was full of clothing and equipment that Aram had hurled away in their terror!" When the messengers return to announce their discovery, the king believes them, and soon the people—who I assume are the residents of the Samaria—go forth to the plunder (בזז) the Aramean camp. We guess that there is a vast amount of plunder, because the prices for flour and barley are listed exactly as Elisha forecasts, "according to the word of the Lord." The notice about the fulfillment of Elisha's word on the prices of commodities brings to mind the *other* word Elisha speaks in 7:2, relating to the skeptical adjutant. The last scene in this episode (7:17–20) recounts the fate of this officer: in the rush to obtain the bargain prices after the lengthy siege, the adjutant is trampled "by the parade of people on their way to the food he had doubted."[36] The king of Aram leans on Naaman's arm, and Naaman receives healing when he submits to the prophetic word; the king of Israel leans on this officer's arm, but, in a stunning contrast, this officer is stampeded by the crowd after scoffing at Elisha's utterance. The king's officer becomes a graphic illustration of the cost of resisting the prophetic word, reinforced by the spatial setting of his demise: the gate where he is trampled is, we surmise, the same place where the four lepers first embark on their journey that leads to the deserted Aramean camp, resulting in the financial windfall at the gate that Elisha had predicted.

---

[36] Brueggemann, *1 & 2 Kings*, 363. Cf. Hens-Piazza, *1–2 Kings*, 274: "Amid the restoration of well-being that is taking place for the city, the dark consequences of doubt and despair dare not be ignored."

6

Throne Calls

"Politics," muses Gerhard von Rad while summarizing Elisha's involvement in Israel's foreign and domestic affairs, "was very probably the real focal point of his whole life."[1] Interpreters may want to quibble or refine the details, but von Rad undeniably has a point when considering the last four episodes of Elisha's prophetic career. Taking place in four different locales and involving four different kings and regimes, the final installment of Elisha's public life is the most diverse in terms of time, space, and political involvement. In the first episode (2 Kings 8:1–6) Elisha is present only in the form of a narrative flashback, but his "great deeds" are the centerpiece of two interviews held by the king of Israel. Both of the king's interlocutors have made prior appearances in the narrative—Gehazi and the Shunammite woman whose son was restored to life—and both contribute to the indirect characterization of Elisha in this scene.[2] The second episode (2 Kings 8:7–15) features a journey to Damascus, where Ben-Hadad is ill and desires to inquire of the LORD through Elisha. In this portentous visit to Damascus, the reader is finally introduced to Hazael, who is mentioned way back in 1 Kings 19:15, where *Elijah* is instructed to anoint Hazael as king. There is no anointing in this account, but there is a memorable encounter between the Israelite prophet and the future instrument of destruction. The third episode (2 Kings 9:1–3) also has a reflex to 1 Kings 19:16, where Elijah is ordered to anoint Jehu as king of Israel. Unlike Hazael, Jehu actually *is* anointed, but by

[1] G. von Rad, *Old Testament Theology*, trans. D. M. G. Stalker (2 vols; New York: Harper & Row, 1962–5), ii. 28.

[2] The woman is not referred to as the Shunammite, but only as the woman whose son Elisha restores to life; see H. J. Marsman, *Women in Ugarit & Israel: Their Social and Religious Position in the Context of the Ancient Near East* (Leiden: Brill, 2003) 311.

a member of the company of the prophets rather than by Elisha himself. After these long-dormant anointing instructions have been activated, one might have thought that Elisha could retire (and maybe he does), but in the fourth episode (2 Kings 13:14–19) he makes a comeback after a long hiatus and re-enters the story in a scene that scarcely could have been predicted.

Collectively, these four episodes add a complicating dimension to Elisha's profile, with a number of aspects that are both very interesting but quite difficult to interpret. There are, moreover, some stark contrasts with the material analyzed in the previous chapter, the Aramean attacks of 2 Kings 6–7. The situations in that stretch of text provided some rich material for analysis: from the mind-reading to the trampled adjutant (sandwiching the cannibal mothers and four lepers discovering the open window), Elisha is presented with a number of elements common to the *trickster* tradition. In my view, these elements are more than simply entertaining (though they certainly are), but have an ideological utility and contribute to the larger dismantling of the Omrides that pervades this section of Kings. "Trickster-hero tales may function, in part, as a means to resist the status quo. In this context, the trickster disrupts or overturns prevailing structures and relations of power: the weak become strong and the strong become weak."[3] Along these lines, characters like the four lepers emerge as messengers of good news and waggish opposites of the king who refuses to countenance Elisha's prophetic utterance. There are no equivalents of the four lepers in this next installment of the story, and any trickster side to Elisha is comparatively absent. Instead, the reader is taken to various staterooms and clandestine locations as the story turns to new kings and dynasties, and the Omrides fade from view. During this last phase of Elisha's prophetic career there is more weeping and ambiguity than at any previous point. Some serious questions arise over the course of these episodes. If Elisha warns the Shunammite family about an impending famine, why not warn the royal family of Israel? Does Elisha essentially sanction Hazael's lie to Ben-Hadad (abetting regicide in the process)? Is the prophet guilty of seditious conduct when entrusting the

---

[3] M. L. Humphries, "Trickster," in D. N. Freedman (ed.), *Eerdmans Dictionary of the Bible* (Grand Rapids: Eerdmans, 2000), 1336. On the potential for a trickster to disrupt power relations, see D. Jobling, T. Pippin, and R. Schleifer (eds), *The Postmodern Bible Reader* (Oxford: Blackwell, 2001), 171.

anointing of Jehu to a young subordinate? If there are numerous comic moments in the previous section, there is much more anguish in this section, as both Elisha and a king of Israel are reduced to tears.

SEVEN-YEAR SEQUEL

After the Aramean offensives in 2 Kings 6–7, the next episode (8:1–6) is decidedly lower key, as the reader is privy to a set of royal interviews conducted by the king of Israel. But the first two verses set the stage for the interviews by means of a flashback to an instruction given by the prophet to the Shunammite woman:

> Now Elisha had spoken to the woman whose son he had brought back to life, saying, "Arise and go, you and your house. Sojourn wherever you can, for the LORD has called for a famine, and for seven years it will be on the land." So the woman arose, and did according to the word of the man of God: she went with her house, and sojourned in the land of the Philistines for seven years.

Much is hidden from the reader in this exchange, but Elisha is specific about the certainty and duration of the famine. We are not sure when the conversation between Elisha and the woman takes place, but there have been two famines in recent memory. The first occurs in 4:38, located immediately after the long episode with the Shunammite and her son. The placement of the famine in such close proximity to the Shunammite episode has caused some scholars to connect the two events, meaning that Elisha warns the woman about the impending famine not long after her son is restored to life.

Of course it is possible that there were lots of famines, and in 2 Kings 8:1 there could be an intentional lack of specificity. But it should be noted that another famine occurs during the Aramean siege (6:25) and lasts for an extended period. Several implications emerge if this is the famine Elisha warns the Shunammite about, not least that the famine (brought on by the siege, or merely coinciding?) lasts seven years, explaining both the desperation of the mothers and the deliberation of the lepers. At the same time, questions surround the king: why does Elisha not warn him, or why does the king not seek Elisha's help earlier instead of waiting for seven years? When Elisha warns the Shunammite, is he subverting the king? Does he not believe that she (and her family) will survive the famine? For her part, the woman heeds the prophet's counsel and sojourns in the land of the Philistines. Several commentators note that Philistine territory is adjacent to Israel, yet the reader infers the famine is not a factor there; does this continue the subtle polemic directed at the ideology of the Omride kings? With a glance forward to Jehu's purge, Marvin Sweeney notes: "Insofar as the house of Omri is identified with the worship of Baal, the Canaanite/Phoenician god of fertility, the seven-year famine during the reign of Jehoram functions as part of the religious polemic against the house of Omri to justify his assassination as an act of YHWH."[4] If the famine stems from divine judgment on the Omrides, then the narrative could be underscoring the point that corrupt kings drive Israelites away from their land and into exile.

In one of his early conversations with the Shunammite woman, Elisha offers to speak to the king or the army commander on her behalf. The woman politely declines the offer, stating that she dwells "in the midst of my people" (2 Kings 4:13). Because she was then willing to heed Elisha's warning, to depart from her land is a testament to her confidence in the prophet's word, as she abandons her house, country, and people. But many things can happen over the course of seven years, and, as the flashback ends (and the main storyline resumes) in 8:3, some unidentified party has taken possession of the property during the woman's absence. There is speculation among some scholars that the king has appropriated the land, and this kind of tactic is not unheard of with the Omrides (see the affair of Naboth's vineyard in 1 Kings 21).[5] No crime is mentioned, but the woman does approach the king to "cry out" (צעק) for an apparent injustice while she was away during the famine. The verb is also used in 6:26, when one of the mothers cries out to the king to help resolve her legal issue near the end of the famine associated with the Aramean siege—possibly the same famine Elisha warns the woman of at the outset. What then transpires can only be described as the most incredible timing (8:4–5). As the woman approaches the king, he is engaged in a phenomenal conversation:

Now the king was speaking with Gehazi, the lad of the man of God, saying, "Please recount for me all the great deeds that Elisha did." Just as he was recounting to the king about restoring the dead to life, suddenly [הנה] the

---

[4] Sweeney, *1 & 2 Kings*, 316.
[5] Cf. I. W. Provan, *1 and 2 Kings* (NIBC 7; Peabody, MA: Hendrickson, 1995), 205.

woman whose son was restored to life was crying out to the king concerning her home and field! Gehazi said, "My lord the king, this is the woman and this is her son whom Elisha restored to life!"

During our analysis of the previous chapter we noted the literary technique of simultaneity: as the four lepers deliberate at twilight and amble toward the powerful Aramean camp ready to surrender, it turns out that at the same twilight moment the Arameans were deliberating and flee from their camp owing to the threat of a more powerful army. The purpose of this narrative design, I would submit, is to emphasize Elisha's prophetic word and the discovery of its fulfillment over and against the recalcitrance of the king. Here in chapter 8 the same technique of simultaneity is used, as Gehazi's report coincides with the woman's arrival: the same king who not so long ago asked "Can I kill or restore life" is now being told that Elisha has done exactly that, and the evidence shows up at that precise moment. Yet, even as the reader appreciates the narrative artistry, it is strange that the king seeks information on Elisha's great deeds (he has already seen many of them), and that he requests the data from Gehazi. One may have thought that Gehazi drifted off into a leprous sunset, with not much to look forward to but some hidden silver and bleached descendants. Periodically in history a disgraced politician may be tempted to launch a comeback, but the re-emergence of Gehazi ranks as a genuine surprise. The obvious question scholars struggle with—those who are reading sequentially, that is, and not dismissing the episode as a redactional insertion—is the matter of Gehazi's leprosy. If Gehazi is still inflicted with leprosy, how does he enter the king's presence? Conveniently, there is a precedence for such a royal audience, as illustrated by Naaman prior to his healing. But the strangeness persists, as the king of Israel is asking Gehazi about the great deeds of Elisha, and Gehazi's inheritance of Naaman's leprosy must rank among them. Whether or not Gehazi includes this personal detail is unknowable, but for the second episode in a row the king has a leper share news about miraculous happenings.

The denouement of this episode—as with many in the Elisha narrative—features a restoration (8:6), as the king turns from Gehazi and interviews the woman directly: "The king asked the woman, and she recounted it for him. Then the king appointed a eunuch to her, saying, 'Give back all that she had, and all that the field produced from the day she left the land until now.'" Quite conceivably the woman is better off because she heeds Elisha's warning: not only has she survived the famine, but now the king orders that all her assets and the income accrued in her absence be restored.[6] The contrast between this woman and the cannibal mothers of the previous episodes cannot be more stark. Those mothers are bereft of their offspring, whereas this woman has a legacy to bequeath. She appears before the king with her son, who I assume is the inheritor of the land that has just been restored to her. There is another contrast: when the woman stands before the king, the reader appreciates that these two figures have completely different futures. The woman was childless, but gives birth to a son who by every estimation will occupy the family land; the opposite situation faces the Omrides, a now sterile dynastic line soon coming to an end as Elisha's dismantling reaches its apogee.

Consequently, it is symbolically appropriate that the king appoints a *eunuch* (סריס) to handle her case, and in this instance I certainly agree with Wesley Bergen: "The inclusion of a eunuch in a story concerning a woman, her son and her inheritance is both humorous and interesting. It forms a definite contrast between the action of the king (restoration of produce) and the action of Elisha (production of children)."[7] The eunuch also epitomizes the Omrides, an emasculated kingly line without reproductive organs. By means of a eunuch, the king appears more magnanimous than any previous occasion. This is essentially the last scene of his career that features any dialogue or meaningful characterization; in the next chapter he only shouts a warning to his nephew Ahaziah that the manic Jehu has him in his sights. Does this episode function as a positive "parable," a glimpse of how events might have unfolded differently if the king had acted on the prophet's counsel more often? Robert Cohn understands the king's actions toward the woman in this kind of positive manner: "On a strictly natural plane, it is an act of revivification as surely as Elisha's resuscitation of the boy. It shows a king transformed by the miracle of the man

---

[6] For a different angle, see Roncace, "Elisha and the Woman of Shunem: 2 Kings 4.8–37 and 8.1–6 Read in Conjunction," 121: "The fact that the woman's land was productive in her absence, evidenced by her receiving the land's produce from the seven years when she returns (8.6), causes one to wonder how severe the famine was and whether it was worth her leaving home."

[7] Bergen, *Elisha and the End of Prophetism*, 153.

of God and willing to carry on his legacy."[8] If so, then Gehazi's role becomes more intriguing, as he appears to speak much more respectfully about Elisha than his interior monologue of 2 Kings 5:20, and resembles Naaman's attitude after he is healed.

HAZAEL EYES

If Elisha is only present in a flashback in the previous episode, he now returns to the main narrative sequence. The manner of the conversation between Gehazi and the king may have conveyed the impression that Elisha retired, but the next interval (8:7–15) indicates that this is not the case. As the next scene opens, he is entering Damascus, a journey that might raise an eyebrow: in chapter 6 a phalanx of soldiers from this region marched to Dothan to arrest Elisha, who now walks into the city unmolested. It is entirely possible that Elisha's timing is intentional, for his arrival coincides with a state of emergency: "Elisha came to Damascus, where Ben-Hadad king of Aram was ill. It was reported to him, saying, 'The man of God has come here.'" For the second time, a high-ranking Aramean is faced with a medical exigency: first the leprosy of Namaan, now an unspecified but serious illness (חלי) that threatens the king. Upon news of Elisha's arrival, there is an interesting development. Ben-Hadad does not issue an arrest order as on a previous occasion, but tenders a quite different kind of supplication: "The king said to Hazael, 'Take in your hand a present, and go to meet the man of God, and seek the Lord from him, saying, "Will I live through this illness?"'"

Recent commentators have noted the irony that foreigners know enough to seek the Lord, yet Israel's leadership seeks other deities. More specifically, some interpreters see an inversion between this scene and 2 Kings 1, where the Omride king Ahaziah has an "illness" (חלי) but seeks Baal-zebub for an inquiry rather than Elisha. Here Ben-Hadad seeks a word from Elisha in the midst of his illness (חלי) instead of Rimmon, whose temple he visits (according to Naaman

---

[8] Cohn, *2 Kings*, 56. Cf. Pyper, "Judging the Wisdom of Solomon: The Two-Way Effect of Intertextuality," 30: "Ultimately, the disasters that lead to the destruction of the monarchy are the product of its own internal dynamics as much as they are the result of God's vengeance or the activities of Israel's political enemies."

in 5:18). The courier of the king's message is Hazael, making his first formal appearance in the story. Readers have been anticipating the arrival of this character for a long while, ever since God instructed Elijah way back in 1 Kings 19:15: "Go, return on your way to the wilderness of Damascus. When you arrive, anoint Hazael king over Aram." Of course, Elijah has long since vanished from the scene, and so we assume that Elisha inherited this commission (along with the double portion of his master's spirit). For all of that, an immediate tension arises when Elisha enters the city of Damascus: how can Hazael reign if Ben-Hadad still lives and breathes, and if he recovers from his illness?

To set aside that thorny issue for a moment, Hazael's first action (v. 9) in the story is positive, in that he closely follows his king's directive: "So Hazael went to meet him, and took a gift in his hand, and all the good things of Damascus, a load for forty camels. He came and stood before him, and said, "Your son, Ben-Hadad king of Aram, sent me to you, saying, 'Will I live through this illness?'" The king asks Hazael to take a gift, which he certainly does—a lavish one, that exceeds even Naaman's massive present by a considerable amount. Whether the king intends a gift of this size, or whether this is Hazael's improvisation, is uncertain. It might betoken loyalty on Hazael's part, but, as with many items in this episode, there is a latent ambiguity. Some interpreters suggest that Hazael has royal ambition, but when he refers to the king as "your son" to Elisha he cannot be accused of misrepresenting his master in the first instance. If Hazael is eyeing the throne—with the monarch sick in bed—he is holding his cards close to the chest. Still, there are substantial ambiguities in the interview that follows, during what has to be classified as the most volatile and mystifying conversation of Elisha's career:

Elisha said to him, "Go, say to him,[9] 'You will indeed recover!' But the Lord has shown me that he will indeed die." He made his face to stand, that he set until the point of shame, and the man of God wept. Hazael said, "Why is my lord weeping?" He said, "Because I know what evil you will do to the Israelites: to their fortresses you will send fire, their choice young men you will kill with the sword, their infants you will smash, and their pregnant women you will rip open." Hazael said, "But what is your servant, but a dog,

---

[9] Reading the *Qere* of the MT, לו.

that he should do this great thing?" Elisha said, "The LORD has shown me *you* as king over Aram."

Among the numerous controversies in this exchange between Elisha and Hazael, what has raised the ire of interpreters more than anything else is Elisha instructing Hazael to deceive his sick king and tell him about a recovery that will never happen. Similar to the charges of false prophecy leveled against Elisha back in 2 Kings 3 during the Moabite campaign, scholars have accused Elisha of impropriety here: bearing false witness, and abetting regicide in the process, are serious charges indeed.[10] But, apart from troubling some modern readers, Seow remarks that other factors need to be considered: "The man of God apparently tells Hazael to lie and, whether he had intended it or not, is complicit in the assassination of the king. Within the narrator's larger view of history, however, this event fulfills the word of the Lord that promises an end to the horrible reigns of the apostate kings of the north." Seow concludes, "God's larger purpose will be worked out, it seems, even through human deceit (cf. 1 Kings 22) and unjustified death."[11] The reference to 1 Kings 22 is helpful, and we have had occasion to note other comparisons with the Micaiah incident, where the prophet's speech is brimming with duplicity, indirection, and a penetrating vision of the heavenly council. This scene in Damascus adds another layer of significance to this interplay: given that Micaiah is subverting an Omride king, it should be acknowledged that Elisha is also subverting the Omride regime through this dialogue with Hazael of Damascus, finally accelerating the divine instructions to Elijah back in 1 Kings 19:15 toward fulfillment.

After the instructions to deceive Ben-Hadad, Elisha then engages in some facial gymnastics, and, although the syntax is not the easiest, I am assuming that Elisha stares until Hazael feels decidedly uncomfortable ("until shamed," עד בש). The same expression is used in Judges 3:25 to capture the embarrassment of Eglon's courtiers. Inhaling the noxious fumes wafting from the locked upper chamber, the courtiers wait "until shamed," but their master does not open the door (because

---

[10] For an appraisal of past scholarship, see P. J. Kissling, *Reliable Characters in the Primary History: Profiles of Moses, Joshua, Elijah and Elisha* (JSOTSup 224; Sheffield: Sheffield Academic Press, 1996), 168–70. Note especially Kissling's review of C. J. Labuschagne, "Did Elisha Deliberately Lie?—A Note on II Kings 8.10," *ZAW* 77 (1965) 327–8.

[11] Seow, "1 & 2 Kings," 215.

he had been stabbed by Ehud). The expression also occurs in 2 Kings
2:17 when the company of the prophets are nagging Elisha himself
"until shamed" about the search for Elijah, and he finally relents. On
the basis of these two instances, the reader infers that Hazael feels the
full weight of the stare from the prophet Elisha, who knew the very
words uttered in the King of Aram's bedchamber (cf. 2 Kings 6:12).
For some interpreters the stare and the shame indicate that Hazael is
already designing his bid for the crown. But nothing is stated by
Elisha; instead, the stare ends with weeping. Robert Cohn believes
that the weeping prophet fares badly in comparison with his forerun-
ners such as Ahijah and Elijah: "Elisha is depicted pathetically, as the
agent of a drama he is powerless to prevent."[12] In term of Elisha's
overall configuration, this scene is unique, and this is the first time the
reader has seen tears like these. But, rather than Elisha seeming
pathetic, one could argue that, in the twilight of his career, he is
privy to a vision of Israel's future where kingly violence takes on new
dimensions. A glimpse of this devastation is provided in Elisha's
response to Hazael's question, when he outlines the inevitable carn-
age. In 1 Kings 19:17 the divine word mentions that Hazael has a
"sword." Based on Elisha's utterance here, it will be a well-used sword,
ripping open (בקע) pregnant women without mercy. The mothers of
Bethel had their sons ripped open (בקע) in chapter 2, but many more
sons will be destroyed by the sword of Hazael. If Hazael's name
means something like "God perceives" (חזהאל), as has been proposed,
then Elisha's weeping can be understood in the context of a prophetic
vision of Hazael's brutality.[13]

Hazael's reaction to this oracle of doom for Israel (at his expense) is
apparent incredulity, though he has been poker-faced so far. One term
stands out, however, as Hazael refers to himself as a dog. Varying
reactions to this designation can be found among scholars. Most
commonly, the canine reference is viewed as either "self-effacing," or
an expression of "false modesty."[14] Within the Deuteronomistic

---

[12] Cohn, "Convention and Creativity in the Book of Kings," 612.

[13] Note the discussion in Aucker, "Putting Elisha in his Place," 227–8. See, e.g.,
2 Kings 17:13, "The LORD solemnly warned Israel and Judah by every prophet and
seer (חזה), saying, 'Turn from your evil ways and keep my commandments, my
statutes, according to all the law that I commanded your ancestors, that I sent to
you through my servants the prophets.'"

[14] Fretheim, *First and Second Kings*, 164; Bergen, *Elisha and the End of Prophetism*,
158.

History, however, there is another side to this term, and an unusual distribution that locates Hazael in an exclusive fraternity: usurpers. Jeremy Schipper goes so far as to render Hazael's locution as "dead dog" following the LXX, and, surveying other instances where there is similar usage, concludes that "it is not long before those characters claim the throne."[15] When the reader makes this connection, further insight into Elisha's weeping is gained, as now Hazael's destiny as a usurper moves into sharper focus. In case there was any doubt, Elisha punctuates the matter with an emphatic declaration that Hazael will be king; there is no formal anointing, but a speech act without ambiguity. If Hazael felt suffocated by the prophet's gaze, and asked him why he was weeping, it is noticeable that no further words or reactions are recorded. Instead, Hazael returns to his ailing master: "He went from Elisha and came to his lord. He said to him, 'What did Elisha say to you?' He said, 'He said to me, "You will indeed recover."' The next day he took a cloth, dipped it in water, covered over his face, and he died. Then Hazael reigned in his place."

The final scene with Hazael portrays him as more loyal to Elisha's instructions than to his master. He sounds dutiful enough, but in his interview with the king he repeats the lie, stating it with deadpan accuracy. Even though the subject is not explicitly marked in the Hebrew text, it seems clear that Hazael is the one who takes a cloth of some sort, and dips it in water. For the second, an Aramean "dips," as the same verb is used earlier in 2 Kings 5:14 when Naaman dips (טבל) in the Jordan. When Hazael dips (טבל) the cloth in water, he then covers the royal face, and we assume cuts off King Ben-Hadad's breathing supply and completes the assassination in Shakespearian style. To be sure, Herbert Brichto draws a poignant comparison with the weird sisters of *Macbeth*: did the witches incite the Thane of Cawdor to murder Duncan, or did they merely fan nascent desires into a consuming fire?[16] With Hazael, commentators can be found on both sides: some are persuaded that he was ambitious from the outset, while others are convinced that Elisha inculcates the idea of kingship in him through the power of prophetic suggestion. Either way,

---

[15] J. Schipper, "'Why Do You Still Speak of Your Affairs?': Polyphony in Mephibosheth's Exchanges with David in 2 Samuel," *VT* 54 (2004), 348, tracing the usage in the books of Samuel.

[16] H. C. Brichto, *Toward a Grammar of Biblical Poetics: Tales of the Prophets* (New York: Oxford University Press, 1992), 219.

Hazael's methodical execution indicates that he has understood Elisha with perfect clarity. Hazael's regicide foreshadows that of Jehu, who also puts his king in a coffin, and is likewise instigated by Elisha's prophetic activity. But Hazael is a foreigner who quotes the words of an Israelite prophet to his bedridden monarch: "you will surely recover!" This duplicitous utterance puts the king at ease with an assurance of recovery, and thus Ben-Hadad comfortably falls into a deep sleep from which he never awakes.

FROM DOG TO FLASK

Political affairs in Judah have not been mentioned for a considerable time, but the narrative focus now switches to the south in 2 Kings 8:16–29, after the murder of Ben-Hadad by Hazael. In this material there are two items relevant for this study, the marriage of the southern king (v. 18) and the activities of Hazael (vv. 28–9). First, there is a short account of King Jehoshaphat's son and successor, also named Jehoram. King Jehoram of Judah is indicted for walking in the ways of the northern monarchs, no doubt exacerbated by his marriage to the daughter of Ahab. Comingling with the house of Omri through a marriage alliance did not bring positive results for Jehoshaphat, and it will be even worse for his successor. "The family of Ahab has now deeply infected both kingdoms," writes Terence Fretheim, "and Jehu's purge catches up the South as well."[17] Second, for better or worse, the intermarriage means that the two kingdoms are further intertwined, and, when Ahaziah (grandson of Jehoshaphat) assumes the throne of Judah in 2 Kings 8:25, there is a joint march against Hazael at Ramoth-Gilead. During this campaign Hazael injures the northern king of Israel—a foretaste of his later brutality and a preface to the fatal injury on the northern king inflicted by Jehu. Such events are not entirely unexpected, as back in 1 Kings 21:29 God announced to Elijah that "evil" will visit Ahab's house during the days of his son.[18] Furthermore, Elijah was instructed to anoint Jehu son of

[17] Fretheim, *First and Second Kings*, 166.
[18] For a discussion of how Ahab's son Jehoram is included within the purview of this prophetic utterance, see Otto, "The Composition of the Elijah–Elisha Stories and the Deuteronomistic History," 497.

Nimshi as king of Israel, in the same sequence where Elijah is told to anoint Hazael. With Elisha having carried out the Hazael task, the upheaval and toppling of regimes continues as Elisha's attention now turns to Jehu, albeit indirectly:

> But Elisha the prophet called to one of the sons of the prophets, and said to him, "Gird up your loins, take this flask of oil in your hand, and go to Ramoth-Gilead. When you arrive there, look for Jehu son of Jehoshaphat son of Nimshi. Then go in and make him arise from the midst of his brothers, and bring him into an inner room. Then take the flask of oil, pour it out on his head, and say, 'Thus says the LORD, I have anointed you as king of Israel.' Then open the door, flee, and don't wait!"

The scene in 2 Kings 9:1 begins with disjunctive syntax, implying a continuation from 8:29, where the reader learns the king of Israel has departed from Ramoth-Gilead to recuperate in Jezreel and is joined by his southern counterpart Ahaziah. In 9:1 Elisha is called "the prophet" by the narrator, yet he appoints a member of the company of the prophets to carry out the anointing of Jehu. Opinions vary among scholars as to why Elisha did not go himself, with the most common being that it is too dangerous: the king of Israel still lives and breathes, so this seditious activity is best kept below the radar. Sending a neophyte has some covert advantage, then, as the chances of Elisha being recognized must be higher than this unnamed character (who is described in the next verse as "young"). The notion that anointing Jehu is a hazardous mission is heightened by means of the instrument of anointing oil, the flask. The only other king to be anointed with a flask is Saul, and, likewise, Samuel seems intent on keeping the ceremony private (1 Samuel 10:1). The flask, one guesses, is less conspicuous than the horn of oil used to anoint David and Solomon, and even in contemporary English parlance a *flask* suggests a concealed liquid that the user is not particularly keen to advertise. Considering the recent usurpation of Hazael—who refers to himself as a dog—the flask of oil similarly implies concealment from the incumbent king and his allies. In this case, Elisha wishes to camouflage another hostile takeover of a throne, this time the throne of Israel. Moreover, the location of Ramoth-Gilead itself is not without significance for the house of Omri: Ahab dies in Ramoth-Gilead, and now the plot against his heir begins in the same locale.[19]

---

[19] Cf. Leithart, *1 & 2 Kings*, 219.

After the succinct commissioning, Elisha fades from view for the rest of this scene—indeed, he is absent for the execution of Jehu's manic purge—and it is left to the young apprentice to use the flask for its intended task. Elisha's words to the young prophet are extremely efficient, with a sense of urgency. The lad, however, takes a long time: he takes Jehu into the house, pours out the oil, and eventually opens the door and departs, but not before he utters a comprehensive and sweeping oracle well beyond Elisha's instructions (vv. 7–10). As Burke Long summarizes, the young prophet's speech transforms "the simple word of anointing-designation, 'I anoint you king over Israel,' into an elaborate announcement of judgment and, at the same time, evoke[s] much of the connective tissue belonging to the larger story of the northern monarchs."[20] A close analysis of the expansion lies outside the scope of my study here, but two aspects of the oracle need to be considered.

First, in the young man's long speech about vengeance against Ahab's house, there is special mention (on two occasions in the speech) of a character who has not been active in the narrative for quite some time: Jezebel. Wesley Bergen reflects on the surprising absence of Jezebel throughout Elisha's career, and, because of her prominence earlier in 1 Kings, such narrative silence is striking:

> Readers are left to wonder about her influence as queen mother on the reign of Jehoram in Israel and as queen mother-in-law on Jehoram and Ahaziah of Judah. How can she have been alive this whole time, given the silence of Elisha and the disappearance of Baal? For the narrative still accords her a place of considerable prominence in its rogues' gallery.[21]

Regarding her absence, one could be forgiven for thinking that, during Elisha's career, Jezebel is effectively neutralized, and she makes no appearance after the property annexation of Naboth and the divine condemnation in 1 Kings 21. Perhaps a useful byproduct of the *double portion* inherited by Elisha is that Jezebel's threat is marginalized. But at the end of this chapter Jezebel will make one final leap in the narrative (see 9:30–7), when Jehu's lunatic driving

---

[20] Long, *2 Kings*, 119. The speaker is referred to as a "student prophet" in F. O. García-Treto, "The Fall of the House: A Carnivalesque Reading of 2 Kings 9 and 10," *JSOT* 46 (1990), 55: "The student prophet calls Jehu to overthrow his master, echoing not Elisha's but Elijah's voice, and the effect is incongruous, as if a masquerading 'sorcerer's apprentice' had unwittingly pronounced a spell he cannot control."

[21] Bergen, *Elisha and the End of Prophetism*, 165.

takes him to Jezreel (where she apparently lives in the palace) to continue his purge of the Omrides. With an alliance in mind, Jezebel arranges her hair and paints her eyes, only to skydive without a parachute courtesy of a couple of nearby eunuchs who throw her down. I suppose it is possible that "eunuch" reinforces the symbol of sterility of the Omride line, but, more practically, a eunuch is less likely to be influenced by the seductive charms of arranged hair and painted eyes. Consequently, Jezebel ends up as food for rabid dogs and fertilizer for the fields of Jezreel more or less as the student prophet declares as he creatively expands the terse words of Elisha into an oracle of queenly doom.

Second, the student prophet's oracle contains several layers of justification for the obliteration of Ahab's house, not least being retribution for the slain prophets over the course of this murderous reign. The ruin of the house is captured with a catchphrase used occasionally in the Deuteronomistic History, and incomparably rendered in the King James Version: "For the whole house of Ahab shall perish: and I will cut off from Ahab him that pisseth against the wall" (9:8).[22] Most relevant for my purposes is that the last figure to use this catchphrase is Elijah, when predicting the termination of Ahab's house in 1 Kings 21:21. When the student prophet expands Elisha's instructions, there is a recycling of Elijah's earlier oracle to Ahab. Scholars disagree on how best to adjudge this aggressive and tessellated speech of the young prophet, with some opting for a later redactional insertion, while others understand the neophyte as taking initiative—providing Jehu with no margin of ambiguity—and ensuring the complete destruction of the regime that has claimed so many members of the prophetic guild.[23]

---

[22] Note 1 Sam. 25:22, 34, 1 Kings 14:10, 1 Kings 16:11, 1 Kings 21:21, and see the discussion in L. M. Wray Beal, *The Deuteronomist's Prophet: Narrative Control of Approval and Disapproval in the Story of Jehu (2 Kings 9 and 10)* (LHBOTS 478; New York and London: T & T Clark, 2007), 65–6. Cf. NRSV: "For the whole house of Ahab shall perish; I will cut off from Ahab every male, bond or free, in Israel."

[23] For summaries of arguments in favor of secondary expansion, see P. T. Cronauer, OSB, *The Stories about Naboth the Jezreelite: A Source, Composition, and Redaction Investigation of 1 Kings 21 and Passages in 2 Kings 9* (LHBOTS 424; London: T & T Clark, 2005), 53–4; cf. D. T. Lamb, *Righteous Jehu and his Evil Heirs: The Deuteronomist's Negative Perspective on Dynastic Succession* (Oxford Theological Monographs; Oxford: Oxford University Press, 2007), 54–6, who notes that Jehu's summation (v. 12) is closer to Elisha's instruction than the young member of the "sons of the prophets."

A question that immediately arises is whether Elisha *plans* it this way: does he know or expect that his appointee will expand a terse command into a litigious utterance? Just as Hazael's personality seems a necessary component of the prophetic word, so in all likelihood there is a parallel situation here as Elisha allows a young member of the company to unveil the last word on the house of Omri. For James Mead, Elisha's instructions are intentionally laconic: "If Elisha is hesitant to come and anoint Jehu himself, then this young prophet will speak what must be spoken in order to carry on the plan Yahweh gave to Elijah."[24] To take this point in a slightly different direction, I would say this expansion implies that Elijah's words are common knowledge in the guild, and, when Elisha chooses a young lad to anoint Jehu, such fusion ought to be expected. As with Hazael, Elisha's recruitment of the student prophet becomes a moment of prophetic suggestion, and consistent with the recent throne call in Damascus. Peter Miscall has argued: "Fulfillment of prophecy can be carried out and conditioned by the character of the fulfiller."[25] An anonymous member of the guild is chosen by Elisha, and his personality infuses Jehu's anointing and results in the hybrid oracle. Elisha the double agent appoints a young man of the prophets, who now recycles the original oracle of Elijah, setting the stage for the final act in the Omride drama.

Elijah's words—spoken many years previously—are only now reaching fulfillment, after a highly circuitous journey and in unexpected ways; one of Elisha's last moments in the story results in Elijah's oracle being brought to its termination. It should also be noted that the youngster's actions prove effective, as in short order Jehu is proclaimed king and wastes no time in setting in motion the program of annihilation. As several recent commentators have observed, this is the last exploit of the sons of the prophets.[26] With Jehu's usurpation, then, the reader senses the end of an era: Elisha has been both the head and the last of the class. Now that they have been absorbed into the larger storyline, we sense that the company of the prophets—almost exclusively associated with Elisha—were raised up in Israel for

---

[24] Mead, "'Elisha Will Kill'? The Deuteronomistic Rhetoric of Life and Death in the Theology of the Elisha Narratives," 126.

[25] P. D. Miscall, "Elijah, Ahab, and Jehu: A Prophecy Fulfilled," *Prooftexts*, 9 (1989), 79.

[26] e.g., Beal, *The Deuteronomist's Prophet*, 51–2.

a more specific (rather than a general task), and, once their job is done and the Omrides are dismantled, they fade from view. Their *de facto* head, Elisha, is also nearing the end of his run, but, like the borrowed axe-head, resurfaces after a period of absence.

THREE STRIKES

After delegating Jehu's anointing to a young apprentice, Elisha may have been thought to have drifted away, much like the other sons of the prophets. Indeed, 2 Kings 10–12 feature some momentous disruptions and changes in regimes, and the absence of Elisha during this period could cause the reader to surmise that his memorable career has concluded. But, reminiscent of Gehazi in chapter 8, Elisha makes a comeback in 2 Kings 13:14–19 for an exchange with Jehu's grandson, Jehoash king of Israel.[27] One problem scholars have with this comeback is the age of Elisha, as Wesley Bergen assays: "Jones notes that the chronology of the narrative makes Elisha about 85 or 90 years old," says Bergen, "a detail like this is only likely to be noted by the most chronology-fixated reader."[28] Regardless of the precise chronology—lest I be accused of an unwanted fixation—one could have expected Elisha's obituary to have already been written several chapters earlier. So why does this extraordinary prophet resurface here in 2 Kings 13:14 for yet another enigmatic conversation with a king? In my view, by means of this interview in chapter 13 there is no doubting that Elisha the prophet outlives the royal line of Omri. Moreover, he also survives long enough to speak words directed to the ambivalence of a Jehu legatee (third in the succession), and in this regard Elisha is no respecter of northern dynasties.

Estimating the age of Elisha has preoccupied many interpreters, but more interesting is the narrative dynamic in this scene, presented in the form of a flashback to an unspecified earlier point in Jehoash's otherwise undistinguished sixteen-year tenure. 2 Kings 13:10–12 briefly describes the reign of Jehoash, who is guilty of the same infractions as Jeroboam yet manages to fight heroically against the

---

[27] Note the variant spelling of J(eh)oash among translators; I am simply following the NSRV with the full spelling throughout.

[28] Bergen, *Elisha and the End of Prophetism*, 167, citing Jones, *1 and 2 Kings*, 501.

southern king Amaziah (further details are given in 14:8–14). This report is followed by notice of his death and burial (also repeated in 14:15–16), and then the flashback: "Now Elisha was ill (with the illness from which he died), and Jehoash king of Israel went down to him, wept upon his face, and said, 'My father, my father! The chariots and horsemen of Israel!'" Robert Cohn comments on the strange narrative structure: the report on Jehoash's reign finishes with his burial notice, only to have him return to the stage through a flashback for a meeting with Elisha. But, as a result, the chronology of Elisha's career is bracketed by episodes that are configured outside of royal time: "Just as Elisha's assumption of the prophetic role (2 Kings 2) took place outside any royal file, so too does his death. This placement suggests that Elisha is not under the thumb of any king, that his power operates independently of royal authority. So in Elisha's final appearance, Joash becomes a creature of his tale rather than the reverse."[29] Peter Leithart has a similar point about the narrative concluding Jehoash's reign with the standard regnal formula, but also adds that the king's figurative return to life foreshadows the later events in verses 20–1 of an actual resurrection: "This disturbance in the text's order is yet another indication that the work of prophets cannot be reduced to the chronicled history of Israel, but bursts the bounds of time, change, and death."[30]

The reader also notices an inversion of an earlier scene: in 2 Kings 8:7–15 there was an ill king who is visited by a weeping prophet, but now there is an ill prophet who is visited by a weeping king.[31] An even more striking intertextual reflex is the king's speech, beginning with "my father." No motivation is provided for the king's visit, but we recall that the same title is used in 2 Kings 6:21 by the Omride king, in probably the best moment of his reign: seeing the captured Aramean soldiers, he asks Elisha's permission to strike. For Jehu's descendant Jehoash in this scene, striking the Arameans likewise is a central concern, with Israel's political stability seemingly hanging in the balance. The rest of the king's speech has also been heard before, as Elisha himself once exclaimed the same cry as Jehoash, "My father, my father! The chariots and horsemen of Israel!" The reader is thus taken back to the place where Elisha's career begins, and reminded,

---

[29] Cohn, *2 Kings*, 87.
[30] Leithart, *1 & 2 Kings*, 233.
[31] Aucker, "Putting Elisha in his Place," 220.

not only of the prophet's longevity, but also of the fulfillment of the request: having witnessed Elijah's departure, Elisha receives the double portion that he asked for. Of course the fiery host also surrounded Elisha in Dothan, a celestial army that *could* consume the Arameans, we guess, at will. Is this what the weeping king is acknowledging? When the king sobs and cries out in verse 15, the majority of scholars take it as a sincere moment, and a recognition of the prophet's involvement and the necessity of divine protection. But what is less certain is how the king's demeanor toward Elisha can be reconciled with his negative verdict in 2 Kings 13:11, where he refuses to turn aside from the sins of Jeroboam. Considering the king's overall record, it is notable that he is afforded the privilege of Elisha's last official interview, in a scene replete with sign language and prophetic forecasting:

Elisha said to him, "Take up a bow and arrows." So he took up a bow and arrows. He said to the king of Israel, "Mount your hand on the bow." He mounted his hand, and Elisha put his hands on the hands of the king. He said, "Open the window to the east," and he opened it. Elisha said, "Shoot!" and he shot. He said,

> "The arrow of salvation from the LORD,
> The arrow of salvation over Aram.
> You will strike Aram at Aphek until the finish!"

There are grounds for supposing that King Jehoash has reasons for fear after surveying the whole of 2 Kings 13. In the light of Elisha's prediction of Hazael's viciousness (including infanticide), such fear is not out of order considering texts such as 2 Kings 13:22, describing the era of Jehoash's father: "Now Hazael king of Aram oppressed Israel throughout the days of Jehoahaz." In this flashback scene of 13:14–19, Jehoash's earthly father is dead, having been continually harassed by Hazael, and so Jehoash calls on Elisha the spiritual father of the nation anticipating a crisis during his reign. Just as Elisha has a request for the departing Elijah, so the king now cries out for assistance as Elisha's departure through illness is imminent.[32] In response

---

[32] Hens-Piazza (*1–2 Kings*, 322) speaks of "the king's desperation and fear at facing the future without the power and presence of the one departing," so it stands to reason that he is asking something much like Elisha asks his soon-to-be-departing master for the double portion. Cf. Cohn, *2 Kings*, 88: "Elisha reacts as if Joash were asking for prediction and protection and offers two symbolic actions that issue in oracles."

to the king's tacit plea for divine aid, Elisha's sign language with the bow indicates a decisive victory at Aphek over the Arameans. The exact location of Aphek is disputed—there seems to have been more than one location with the same name—but in all likelihood this must refer back to 1 Kings 20:26–9, where Aphek is the site of an improbable victory by Israel over the vast Aramean host, likewise predicted by a prophetic word in 20:28 by an unnamed figure: "The man of God drew near to speak to the king of Israel, and he said, 'Thus says the LORD, "On account of the fact that Aram is saying 'A god of the mountains is the LORD, but not a god of the valleys is he,' I will give all this great commotion into your hand, and you all will know that I am the LORD."'" Even though Israel inflicts losses of 100,000 soldiers, Ahab does not quite finish the task by failing to eliminate Ben-Hadad.[33] This failure comes back to haunt Ahab by means of a prophetic illustration (see 1 Kings 20:35–42). Jehoash might enjoy success against Aram at Aphek, but a more somber mood accompanies the next phase of Elisha's sign language:

He said, "Take up the arrows," and he took them up. He said to the king of Israel, "Strike the ground!" He struck it three times, and stopped. The man of God was angry with him, and said, "By striking five or six times, you would then have struck Aram until the finish! But now three times you will strike Aram."

Some interpreters have a low opinion of Elisha's anger management as this scene concludes, and the seeming disconnect between the two signs: the first is quite encouraging, followed by the second that is disheartening by comparison, given the prophet's contentious language with the king. Was Jehoash simply to assume he should have kept striking the ground with the arrows? But, for James Mead, the issue is not so much the number as the fact that the king stops: "The narrator could have said that he 'smote three times' if the reporting of a mere quantity was at issue; but by adding the phrase, 'and he stopped,' the narrator calls attention to the *cessation* of the striking as much as to the *amount* of striking."[34] Again there is an inversion of an earlier episode, as back in 2 Kings 6:21 the Omride king is not

---

[33] Seow, "1 & 2 Kings," 238: "The mention of Aphek recalls Ahab's victory over the Arameans at that same site, although Ahab did not completely destroy the Arameans, as he was supposed to do in a holy war (1 Kgs 20:26–43)." Jehu's heir stops short of complete victory, just like his Omride predecessors.

[34] Mead, "'Elisha Will Kill'? The Deuteronomistic Rhetoric of Life and Death in the Theology of the Elisha Narratives," 86.

allowed to strike the Arameans. Now Jehoash does not strike enough completely to defeat the Arameans. Possibly the king is being tested by Elisha through the arrows, and this prior event helps to make sense, in retrospect, of the king's negative evaluation in 13:12. Failing the test has consequences for both the king and the nation: "Note that the action of the king (and not just the prophetic word) shapes the nature of Israel's history. Jehoash had a chance to succeed fully; he failed, and in effect determined his own future. It is likely that this failure has such effects, not simply because of this one test, but because the test reveals the shape of a life."[35]

Jehoash's three strikes anger Elisha and create the dissonance between the two signs. Shooting the bow out of the eastern window signaled victory at Aphek, but the aborted striking results in Elisha predicting only limited overall success against the Arameans. When considering the issue of Jehoash's failure, one tactile detail in verse 16 is often neglected by interpreters: "Elisha put his hands on the hands of the king." Perhaps the point is that the king is successful when working in tandem with the prophet, or indeed under the guidance of the prophet's hand. But, when the king acts independently or without the hand of the prophet, there is not nearly the same degree of success, as the Omride monarch in 2 Kings 3–8 also discovered. There are far-reaching implications resulting from Jehoash's ultimate inability to eliminate the Aramean threat, as Marvin Sweeney outlines: "Although Jehoash recovered the cities of Israel lost by his father Jehoahaz, he was not able to destroy Aram completely, which enabled Aram to play a role in Israel's later destruction by backing Pekah's coup against Pekahiah and by drawing Israel into the Syro-Ephraimite War."[36] Chiding Jehoash for giving up before reaching the finish line is characteristic for Elisha: on his deathbed he still has a stinging riposte for a wayward king. But, as we will see, even buried, Elisha had still not completed his eventful career.

---

[35] Fretheim, *First and Second Kings*, 183–4.
[36] Sweeney, *1 & 2 Kings*, 361.

Postscript: Double Take

> And Elisha died, and they buried him. Now raiding parties of
> Moab entered the land in the spring of every year. As they were
> burying a man, behold they saw the raiding party, and threw the
> man in the grave of Elisha. The man went, touched the bones of
> Elisha, lived, and arose to his feet.
>
> 2 Kings 13:20–21

Comparisons between Elijah and Elisha have been inevitable from the
outset, and so it is with the last incident of Elisha's career and the
manner of his final departure from the narrative. Elijah is dramatically transported in a fiery chariot, whereas Elisha simply dies of the
illness mentioned in 2 Kings 13:14, and is buried (by whom?) in an
uncertain location. But, if Elijah's leave-taking is unique, Elisha's
"afterlife" is also distinctive.[1] Moreover, just as there are comparisons
between Elijah and Elisha, so too are there contrasts between Elisha
and royal figures in the story, also occurring in this last scene. Jehoash
dies and is buried in 13:13; then he is the subject of an extended
reflection by means of a flashback with Elisha. The king fails, reminiscent of the Omrides before him, to finish a task necessary for the
security of God's people. Elisha too is buried, but after he dies
something rather different happens: he may not be given the royal
funeral of Jehoash, but, when a corpse touches his bones, the dead
man rises to his feet. The interview with King Jehoash in 2 Kings
13:14–19 is presented by means of a flashback to the time of Elisha's
illness. But the final scene involving Elisha—or at least what remains
of him—in verses 20–1 are presented by means of a modest

---

[1] Cohn, *2 Kings*, 89.

flashforward, as the mention of his "bones" implies steady decomposition. Therefore the last scene transpires at some point in the future, after the interview with the king. This temporal dislocation is similar to the narrative of Elisha's succession in 2 Kings 2, and again attests to the prophetic character standing outside of royal time, neither bound nor beholden to the world where kings hold sway.

The setting for Elisha's encore performance is a graveyard, during the interment of an unnamed man. There are no clues as to the identity of the deceased, but the funeral is suddenly interrupted by Moabite raiders. To judge from the Hebrew syntax, such an incursion is a regular occurrence, though the undertakers seem caught off guard. But the frequency of the raids would explain the sense of fear that is conveyed in the text, as the visual angle is refracted from the undertakers' perspective: "behold (הנה), they saw the raiders!" The nationality of the marauding band has elicited different reactions among commentators: is there any significance to *Moabites* here? Some interpreters dismiss any significance, and claim that the Moabite factor is a mere plot contrivance. Others, such as John Gray, sense an opportunism at work: "By raiding at the end of the year in late summer the Moabites, like the Midianites of Gideon's time (Judg. 6.11), found plenty to loot on the threshing-floors and storage-pits. The reduced state of Israel after the campaigns of Hazael and Benhadad no doubt encouraged the Moabites."[2] It would be appropriate, on these grounds, to note that a dead man springs to life during the spring season, the time of perennial rebirth. It is also worth remembering that the Moabites feature prominently in Elisha's first exploits on the international stage. Back in 2 Kings 3 the king of Israel does not fully execute his task, and the Moabite campaign ends with a horrible sacrifice on the wall. The present story about Moabite raiders immediately follows an account of another Israelite king who likewise does not finish an assigned task. As it stands, Moabites form a bookend to Elisha's international career.

But, for the mourners in 2 Kings 13:21, figuring out the Moabite role in the narrative structure is not their highest priority. Instead, the Moabites' arrival aborts the memorial service, and they hastily throw (שלך) the body into Elisha's grave. Again considering the lineaments of Elisha's career, from first to last he has items tossed in his direction:

---

[2] Gray, *I & II Kings*, 600.

Elijah throws (שלך) his mantle at him in his first formal appearance, now a body is throw at him during his last. When Elijah throws the mantle in 1 Kings 19, it is a symbol of succession, as Elisha will both carry on and complete the work begun by his master. When the dead man rises to his feet in 2 Kings 13 after his thrown corpse touches the bones of Elisha, there also are several symbolic layers that can be perceived. Immediately after this scene, the reader is told of Hazael's oppression in verses 22–5, with verse 23 providing a theological reflection: "The LORD was gracious with them and compassionate with them. He turned toward them on account of his covenant with Abraham, Isaac, and Jacob, and was not willing to destroy them or throw them (שלך) from his presence until now." Pushed to its limits, however, this divine patience eventually is exhausted and Israel is "thrown" (שלך) from God's presence by the Assyrian invasion (2 Kings 17:20). The message of Elisha's last scene, according to James Mead and Iain Provan, is that, even if the nation is thrown into exile by a foreign invader, the prophetic word is not defeated: "If contact with the great prophets of the past is maintained, through obedience to their teachings (we presume), death may yet be followed by unexpected resurrection (cf. Ezek. 37:1–14), defeat by victory."[3]

The closest analogue to this scene in the Deuteronomistic History is probably 1 Samuel 28, where the deceased prophet scolds the doomed King Saul. But 1 Samuel 28 is a deadly serious episode, and Samuel himself is in a decidedly irritable mood.[4] There is a different ambiance in 2 Kings 13:20–1, and several scholars point to the comical side of the scene.[5] The gravity of the situation is not in dispute—Moabite raiders no doubt are menacing and are inflicting suffering on the Israelites—but there is a certain jocularity to the interrupted funeral. The mourners, hoping to avoid their own

---

[3] Provan, *1 and 2 Kings*, 230 (cited by Mead, "'Elisha Will Kill'? The Deuteronomistic Rhetoric of Life and Death in the Theology of the Elisha Narratives," 94). Cf. Otto, "The Composition of the Elijah–Elisha Stories and the Deuteronomistic History," 504: "The announcements of the prophets were aimed not at Israel's destruction but at Israel's conversion to Yahweh as the only God and its consequent salvation. The author shows that after the time of judgment, the way to live in peaceful communion with God is open for everybody—one needs only to give up the other gods and return to the way of Yahweh."

[4] See A. G. Auld, *I & II Samuel: A Commentary* (OTL; Louisville, KY: Westminster John Knox Press, 2011), 327–9.

[5] e.g., Seow, "1 & 2 Kings," 238–9; Kissling, *Reliable Characters in the Primary History*, 198.

(premature) burials as they see the approaching raiders, hurl the body on Elisha's skeleton, restoring the bewildered corpse to life. It is not stated whether the Moabites witness this event, and they recede into the background. The scene concludes on a note of suspended animation: no reaction from the now-standing man is provided, though I would recommend that he join his colleagues and efficiently depart the graveyard. The man's lack of identity is surely intentional so that the central focus remains on Elisha, as Yael Shemesh explains: "The narrator is silent about the subsequent adventures of the living dead after his miraculous resurrection because he has absolutely no interest in his fate. The man's sole narrative function is to serve as the object of a miracle that provides final evidence of the holiness and greatness of the deceased prophet."[6] Consequently, the final scene provides a neat structural arrangement to the prophet's career: Elisha is introduced while tilling the soil and providing food for the living, and concludes his tenure *in* the soil and providing life to the dead.

POETICS AND PROPHECY

When the king asks Gehazi about the deeds of Elisha during their interview in 2 Kings 8, only a fragment of that singular conversation is preserved, and punctuated by that moment of extraordinary timing when the Shunammite arrives along with her resurrected son. But one suspects that, if Gehazi were to include even a short list of highlights during Elisha's career, the catalogue would be a lengthy one, ranging from healed water to opened eyes, in numerous settings with some interesting characters at every juncture. From start to finish Elisha engages a host of different figures from all walks of life, with many miles of travel along the way (both inside and outside the land of Israel). In what remains of this short postscript I would like to provide a summary of some major literary techniques that are used in the narrative, those elements that are deployed to great effect in this sector

---

[6] Y. Shemesh, "The Elisha Stories as Saints' Legends," *JHS* 8 (2008), 35. Hens-Piazza (*1–2 Kings*, 323) emphasizes a different facet of the scene, and, in the aftermath of Jehoash's weeping, she understands Elisha's grave to mark a *terminus* in the narrative: "The power of the Lord over life and death, which was present among them in the person of the prophet, is now gone."

of 2 Kings. Moreover, I will also revisit some members of the support-ing cast in the story, as well as the surrounding context of the fall of the northern house of Omri that is central to Elisha's prophetic task. Finally, I will summarize the characterization of Elisha in light of our analysis of those portions of Kings where he is a major participant.

At the beginning of Chapter 4 I cited Dennis Olson's essay, where the point is made that biblical narrative is highly amenable to literary appreciation in the classic sense. Furthermore, literary approaches have enjoyed a surge in popularity over the past several decades, directing the interpreter's gaze toward ways of reading and appreciat-ing biblical narrative "by training attention on its artfulness—how it orchestrates sound, repetition, dialogue, allusion, and ambiguity to generate meaning and effect."[7] My own interest in narrative criticism in this book has a practical utility, and I would hope can be used alongside other kinds of studies and methods. Focusing on the artistic elements of the narrative—from the level of sound play and verbal repetition all the way to intertextuality and structural design—can itself generate useful insights, because these are technical strategies used to make Elisha such an intriguing personality. Whoever was ultimately responsible for this section of Kings utilizes a rich variety of literary techniques and devices for the delineation of character and event.

To review several examples that emerged during our analysis of the famine in Samaria, consider first the configuration of *simultaneity* in the episode. The four lepers arise at twilight (נֶשֶׁף) to surrender to the Aramean camp, and soon after the reader discovers that the Ara-means had surrendered their camp at twilight (נֶשֶׁף) when hearing the sounds of a great army. Far from mere ornamentation or cleverness on the part of the ancient writer(s), this technique of simultaneity is used to underscore the correspondence between the prophetic utter-ance and its fulfillment, a theological concern that is central to the larger Deuteronomistic History.[8] The correspondence is further

---

[7] S. Weitzman, "Before and After *The Art of Biblical Narrative*," *Prooftexts*, 27 (2007), 191. Note also the theoretical discussion of Y. Amit, "Narrative Analysis: Meaning, Context, and Origins of Genesis 38," in J. M. LeMon and K. H. Richards (eds), *Method Matters: Essays on the Interpretation of the Hebrew Bible in Honor of David L. Petersen* (Atlanta: Society of Biblical Literature, 2009), 271–91.

[8] On the prophecy and fulfillment schema, see G. von Rad, *Studies in Deuteron-omy*, trans. D. M. G. Stalker (SBT 9; London: SCM Press, 1953). Note the extension of this schema by Otto, "The Composition of the Elijah–Elisha Stories and the Deuter-onomistic History," 492.

emphasized in the wordplay between the *four* (ארבע) lepers and the *window* (ארבה) sarcastically mentioned by the king's adjutant: "Behold, the LORD is about to make windows in heaven! How can this thing be?" The unwillingness of the adjutant to consider any notion of the famine ending contrasts with the lepers' willingness to venture outside their comfort zone, so the intransigence of the one becomes a foil to the journey of the others.

Even if the four lepers are clowns (in the Shakespearian sense), they become an important source of insight in the story: the group of four illustrate that the windows described incredulously by the adjutant have already been opened, and so the lowliest ones of the besieged city are the first to taste the fulfillment of Elisha's bold declaration. In fact, the first inklings of fulfillment are refracted from the lepers' point of view, as it gradually dawns on them that there is no human presence in the camp. Even after a lengthy parenthetical digression (where the narrator explains *why* the camp is empty in vv. 6–7), the lepers' perspective is picked up again as they tentatively skirt the edges of the camp before discovering the empty tents, tethered donkeys, and great plunder. Through the modulations in point of view, the reader is given a tour of the vacated camp; rather than simply being told about the fulfillment of Elisha's word, there is a visual and tactile experience through the eyes of the four lepers. Each of these literary elements (simultaneity, wordplay, point of view) used in the story-telling combines for a vivid reading, confirming the critical appraisal of Robert Alter:

The fact of the matter is that the biblical writers chose to cast a very large part of what they wanted to say, however fervid their religious aims, in narrative and poetry, and without a good grasp of how the narrative and poetry work as vehicles of literary expression, one is bound to have a rather imperfect understanding of what is going on in these texts.[9]

In the architecture of the narrative, the four lepers (מצרעים) are contrasted with Gehazi: they share the good news about Aramean silver and clothes, whereas Gehazi hordes the same items and becomes a leper (מצרע) in the process.

---

[9] R. Alter, "Response," *Prooftexts*, 27 (2007), 369.

THE ENSEMBLE

In a concise article on minor characters in biblical narrative, Uriel Simon emphasized that insufficient attention has been directed towards such figures who fill a variety of "expressive auxiliary roles" in almost every episode.[10] Apart from the obvious functions of advancing the story or filling in details, there are other purposes for minor characters:

> For beyond their function of furthering the plot (by providing advice and help, or through acts of disturbance and resistance), they have a definite expressive function—the indirect characterization of the protagonist and the implied evaluation of his deeds. This is done mainly through comparing and contrasting: the unexpected is set against the expected, the outstanding against the normal, and the scrupulous against the advantageous.[11]

If we review our analysis of the Elisha narrative, there are numerous figures in the story who have an expressive role of one kind or another. Supporting actors such as Gehazi appear in more than one scene, and he is presented as much more than a stock character with a stereotypical function. In 2 Kings 4 Gehazi has two qualities: he is observant enough to perceive the woman's lack of a child, and he can run (as evidenced by Elisha's directive, asking him to run and initiate the healing of the dead child). Both of these qualities are seen again in 2 Kings 5, but for unscrupulous ends: he perceives the wealth of Naaman as ripe for picking and runs to implement his scheme. Such chicanery rises above that of a standard flat character, as does Gehazi's interview with Elisha where he is given the leprosy of Naaman. Indeed, Gehazi's final scene in 2 Kings 8:4–6 where he is rehearsing the prophet's "great deeds" implies a measure of character development, as Gehazi (whose descendants are cursed with the skin disease) influences the king (whose dynasty has no hope) to make a decision to reinstate the property.

Along with Gehazi, one recalls that characters such as the Shunammite woman and Namaan the Aramean are supporting actors with attenuated roles in the narrative. Even Hazael of Damascus

---

[10] U. Simon, "Minor Characters in Biblical Narrative," *JSOT* 46 (1990), 14. Cf. the longer study of A. Reinhartz, *Why Ask My Name?: Anonymity and Identity in Biblical Narrative* (New York: Oxford University Press, 1998).

[11] Simon, "Minor Characters in Biblical Narrative," 18.

formally appears in only one scene, but his tense engagement with the prophet is fraught with tears and regicidal dialogue. The majority of minor characters in the Elisha narrative, however, are anonymous. There is a vast range of these figures—with representatives from virtually every age group and socio-economic station—and whose narrative importance should not be minimized. As indicated in Simon's research, these minor figures are often strategically placed in the narrative: "Another way of illuminating the situation or the main character is the use of irony: clever and true words uttered by a servant or by an adviser place in an ironic light the vacillations and blunders of his master or his king."[12] Not long after crossing back over the Jordan, Elisha stays in Jericho, where the residents present their hydrology crisis to the prophet. Their actions form a contrast with the miscreants of Bethel in the next episode and the later kings who eschew prophetic counsel during times of emergency. Still on the subject of water problems, some irony is certainly at work in 2 Kings 3:11, where King Jehoram's courtier knows about Elisha during the thirstiest phase of the Moabite campaign: "Elisha son of Shaphat is here, who poured water on the hands of Elijah." In the oil episode of 2 Kings 4:1–7—where the two sons are threatened by a creditor—the widow cries out not to the king but to the prophet, and likewise the farmer of Baal Shalishah brings a gift of first fruits not to any member of the royal circle, but instead to Elisha the man of God.

Another noteworthy character is the Aramean advisor who speaks up in the rather comical moment of 2 Kings 6:12, explaining to the king that the prophet is privy to the very words whispered in the royal bedchamber. This advisor is similar to the captured Israelite girl (2 Kings 5:2–3), in that both characters understand something unique about the prophet and relay this information to the highest-ranking Aramean leaders. There is also an example of group characterization when the elders of Samaria gather at the prophet's house seemingly in defiance of the king, who in turn visits the same house with a decidedly more homicidal agenda.[13] Taking all the figures collectively, I would conclude by reasserting that the reader is exposed to a

---

[12] Simon, "Minor Characters in Biblical Narrative," 16.

[13] Note the discussion on the role of the elders both in 2 Kings 6 and 2 Kings 10 (at the height of Jehu's purge) in G. W. Ahlström, "King Jehu—A Prophet's Mistake," in A. L. Merrill and T. W. Overholt (eds), *Scripture in History & Theology: Essays in Honor of J. Coert Rylaarsdam* (Pittsburgh: Pickwick, 1977), 47–69.

range of different kinds of minor figures in the Elisha narrative, from cannibal mothers to a neophyte prophet who unleashes a rabid oracle against the house of Ahab. Far from diverting focus away from Elisha, these actors shine light on different facets of the main character; even (as we have seen in this postscript) the dead man walking, a former corpse who rises from the grave and stands on his feet when he touches the bones of Elisha.

CLASHING CROWNS

Within the sweeping narrative context of Joshua to 2 Kings, the rise and fall of the house of Omri occupies a prominent position. Like a television mini-series, the story has memorable characters, multiple plotlines, layers of conflict, and even a (prophetic) superhero with exceptional capabilities. Indeed, there is not much in 1 Kings 17 to 2 Kings 13 that does not somehow involve the presence or words of Elijah and Elisha.[14] The prophets inevitably have confrontations with the wayward kings, whom they indict on charges of corruption and compromise. Borrowing a label from John Goldingay, one might refer to Elijah and Elisha as "troublemakers" who regularly cause inconvenience to any person or group opposed to the God of Israel, whether foreign or domestic, kings or servants.[15] But the Omrides are the main objects of prophetic harangue in this section. Omri establishes Samaria as his capital in 1 Kings 16, and the city remains the seat of the northern monarchs until the fall of the kingdom in 2 Kings 17. Historians and archaeologists are quick to point out that Omri was a successful king in material terms; although Omri's reign is not given much press in 1 Kings, William Dever notes that his reign and dynasty were "in fact so prominent that for nearly 150 years the Neo-Assyrian annals refer to the Kingdom of Israel as 'the house (dynasty) of Omri.' Are the biblical writers' 'stories' then mere fiction, invented centuries later? Obviously not," Dever continues, "but the writers are highly selective, as well as highly judgmental, in what they have chosen from their sources to tell us. In short, these writers were

---

[14] Cf. Grabbe, "The Kingdom of Israel from Omri to the Fall of Samaria," 58–9.
[15] J. Goldingay, *Old Testament Theology*, i. *Israel's Gospel* (Downers Grove, IL: InterVarsity Press, 2003) 685.

not charlatans, but simply typical ancient historians, often more sophisticated than we give them credit for being."[16] Without sifting through every layer of Dever's comment, we can surely apply the notion of selective literary judgment and sophistication to both the prophetic portraits and those of the Omrides kings, as the conflict unfolds in a manner that is anything but predictable.

A textbook example is the last of the Omride royal house, Jehoram. Although not always explicitly named in 2 Kings 3–8, in my view Jehoram is the king associated with Elisha during this stretch of text. Over the duration of his twelve-year reign Jehoram appears numerous times, but remains somewhat of an elusive figure. Summarizing Martin Noth's classic work on the Deuteronomistic History, Flemming Nielson discusses the sense of "divine justice" that pervades the work, most evident when "the heroes, those who adhere to Yahweh, are rewarded, while villains are punished."[17] Conceding the general point, I would nonetheless submit that Jehoram's villainy is sketched with considerably more vitality than some commentators have allowed. No mere caricature, the highs and lows of Jehoram's career elevate him above the category of a one-dimensional evil king.[18] Ahaziah has no heir (2 Kings 1:17), and at his death—caused by an injurious fall, and augmented by Elijah's denunciation—Jehoram accedes the throne of Samaria. Based on the mixed appraisal in his regnal formula (2 Kings 3:1–3), it becomes clear that Jehoram is a conflicted character: his evil is less than his parents (as he removes the Baal pillar), but still walks in the ways of Jeroboam son of Nebat. Jehoram inherits the Omride crown around the same time as Elisha inherits Elijah's mantle, setting up an inevitable collision between king and prophet in this crowded section of the narrative. The Moabite campaign provides the arena for the first confrontation as the king's despair is trumped by the prophet's announcement of both water and victory.

---

[16] W. G. Dever, "Archaeology, the Israelite Monarchy, and the Solomonic Temple," in L. G. Perdue (ed.), *The Blackwell Companion to the Hebrew Bible* (Oxford: Blackwell, 2001), 186–206, at 194.

[17] F. A. J. Nielson, *The Tragedy in History: Herodotus and the Deuteronomistic History* (JSOTSup 251; Sheffield: Sheffield Academic Press, 1997), 86.

[18] On the complexity of Jehoram and his inability to cope with maternal pressures, see Otto, "The Composition of the Elijah–Elisha Stories and the Deuteronomistic History," 496.

The strains that are evident between Elisha and Jehoram continue throughout the storyline, with Elisha almost invariably having the upper hand. Another instance is 2 Kings 5, when the king of Aram sends a letter with Naaman: Jehoram's suspicions of mischief are tempered by Elisha, who instructs the king to send Naaman to him in order that "he may know there is a prophet in Israel." After this episode of healing their general, the Arameans are increasingly prominent in an adversarial capacity. Elisha foils their raids with frustrating consistency, and (in a comical scene) leads blind captives into downtown Samaria. Matters become much less amusing and more miserable with the siege of Samaria in 2 Kings 6–7, and I am referring here primarily to the relationship between king and prophet. The king—whom we infer was not keen to release the captives that Elisha orders set free—is angry with the prophet, since those same captives are now among those Aramean soldiers besieging the city. Of course, it seems ludicrous that the king blames Elisha for the famine, given that Elisha earlier was able to lead blinded captives in the first place, and also provided all those warnings about Aramean troop movements. The king puts a price on Elisha's head, but is foiled by the *prices* at the gate, just as Elisha predicts, again with uncanny precision.

The king's interview with Gehazi in 2 Kings 8:4–6, where he entreats the (former?) leper to recite the great deeds of Elisha, is hard to interpret in the aftermath of the death threat and confrontation at the prophet's house on the eve of the bargain prices at the gate. The scene must take place at some unspecified point in the future; but, still, the question as to why the king wants to hear about Elisha's deeds—from Gehazi of all people—is a strange conversation. Any reason why the king wants to hear this report is unstated, though perhaps it is somewhat akin to removing the Baal pillar: a half-measure not fully implemented over the duration of his reign. Asking Gehazi about Elisha's deeds may function as an overture to Jehoram's last scenes in the narrative, where the fulfillment of the prophetic word is in full operation. Just as Jehoram's brother Ahaziah was injured and in need of healing in the moments leading up to his death, so Jehoram himself is wounded by Hazael at Ramoth-Gilead, the same site where Ahab was fatally injured (1 Kings 22:34: "Then a man speculatively drew his bow, and struck the king of Israel between the appendages and the body armor. He said to his charioteer, 'Turn your hand, get me out of the camp, for I'm wounded!'"). There is a convergence of plotlines in Jehoram's final moments, emanating from the prophetic word directed at the house of Omri. An early act of Hazael's kingship is the offensive against Ramoth-Gilead, and, though Jehoram narrowly avoids death, he does not escape from the sword of Jehu. Of course, in 2 Kings 9:24 it is Jehu's well-placed arrow that pierces Jehoram's heart, but, when his body is thrown on the plot of ground belonging to Naboth the Jezreelite, it brings down the final curtain on the Omrides.

DOUBLED OVER

When reflecting on the ultimate dismantling of the house of Omri as a central narrative thrust, we can reconsider earlier episodes in Elisha's career. For instance, consider the sordid incident with the bears from the forest near Bethel (2 Kings 2:23–5) we examined in the opening moments of this book. When Elisha curses the lads of Bethel and forty-two of them are ripped apart by the pair of female bears, it may seem a somewhat arbitrary or random number. But that number, we later discover, corresponds to Jehu's destruction of forty-two relatives of Ahaziah king of Judah in 2 Kings 10:12–14. This group from Judah, comingled with the northern royal house, is en route to Samaria to extend peace to the princes and Jezebel, but Jehu cancels their trip and, one assumes, throws the forty-two corpses into a pit before continuing with his purge. Consequently, with a larger narrative horizon in view, Elisha's curse on the Bethelites can be seen to have an anticipatory function. In several ways, it could be argued that the bears of Bethel episode is configured to foreshadow the destruction unleashed against the Omrides and all whom that house has infected (for example, Ahaziah's forty-two relatives). The circle now closes on the word(s) given to Elijah during his prophetic ministry, as Elisha finishes "the job of overthrowing the house of Omri" that is started by Elijah.[19] To return to the episode with Elisha and the bears, it seems to me that a morality tale, as has been suggested by some interpreters, is precisely what this story is *not*. Elisha's actions quite often have a different end in view, and in retrospect encompass more than the reader may initially suspect.

---

[19] Sweeney, *I & II Kings*, 275.

In an earlier chapter of this book we had occasion to assay the idea of Elisha as a type of Joshua-figure, commissioned to (re)claim the land after a period of apprenticeship with his master.[20] During the era of the conquest, Joshua embarks on a sweeping program to remove the Canaanite religious presence, while Elisha works to remove the ideology adopted by the Omride kings. Joshua assumes leadership over the people after a long period as Moses' assistant, and early in his career commemorates the crossing of the Jordan by erecting a monument of twelve stones (Joshua 4:1–9). Elisha is first mentioned by God at Mount Horeb, and first appears in the story plowing with twelve yoke of oxen. He is then accosted by the mercurial Elijah, thrown the mantle, and gives a communal supper. The feast is a miniature overview of his career, as he both provides for the people and burns through the Omride political stranglehold on the land. Both Moses and Elijah are absorbed in mystery, with the funeral of Moses attended only by God, and Elijah's celestial transport conducting him skyward; by contrast, both Joshua and Elisha are buried in the promised land. A further comparison can be made in terms of logistics, as both Joshua and Elisha sometimes resort to *trickery* in military situations. Though an ambush is a common feature in battle accounts of the Hebrew Bible, Richard Patterson suggests that Joshua 8:1–29 (where the king and citizenry of Ai are fooled by Joshua and the Israelites and lured out of the city) has similar contours to 2 Kings 6:15–20 (where the Aramean infantry is struck with sudden blindness, then led to Samaria) and 2 Kings 7:6–7 (where the Aramean troops hear the sound of a mighty cavalry, then abandon their camp outside Samaria).[21]

Both Joshua and Elisha are closely associated with the spirit (רוח), and this pneumatic instrumentality provides unique empowerment

---

[20] On translating the phrase "a prophet in your place" (לנביא תחתיך) in 1 Kings 19:16 as "a prophet under you," see D. T. Lamb, "'A Prophet Instead of You' (1 Kings 19.16): Elijah, Elisha and Prophetic Succession," in J. Day (ed.), *Prophecy and the Prophets in Ancient Israel* (LHBOTS 531; New York: T & T Clark, 2010), 172–87.

[21] R. D. Patterson, "The Old Testament Use of an Archetype: The Trickster," *JETS* 42 (1999), 387. In the 2 Kings account, the humorous elements could serve a further purpose, recalling theorist Peter Berger: "The comic transcends the reality of ordinary, everyday existence; it posits, however temporarily, a different reality in which the assumptions and rules of ordinary life are suspended." See P. Berger, *Redeeming Laughter: The Comic Dimension of Human Experience* (New York: Walter de Gruyter, 1997), 14, cited in M. Jackson, "Lot's Daughters and Tamar as Tricksters and the Patriarchal Narratives as Feminist Theology," *JSOT* 98 (2002), 44.

for these major figures in the Deuteronomistic History. In Elisha's case, as we have discussed at length, the request for a double portion of his master's spirit becomes the defining moment of his career and enables him to complete the project of subverting the Omrides set in motion by Elijah. In my opinion, labeling Elisha as a double agent is a convenient designation because it draws attention to the inherent cohesiveness of these two intertwined prophets, who are raised up at this pivotal time in history for just such an occasion. For Rachel Havrelock: "The answer to whether or not Elisha receives a double portion, never addressed directly, can be surmised only by textual clues that contain contradictions and evade a definitive conclusion."[22] It is true that the story relies on understatement, inviting the reader's participation while avoiding heavy-handedness, but I would maintain that the textual clues inexorably lead to the verdict that Elisha does receive the parting gift that he requests. "The language," so Jon Levenson prompts us once more, "recalls the law that specifies the 'double portion' as the firstborn son's inheritance (Deut. 21:17) and thus underscores Elisha's status as the sole successor to the man he calls 'father' (2 Kgs 2:12)."[23] Asking for the spirit at Elijah's departure acts as a kind of promissory note for the narrative future, hinting that Elisha will both follow and advance the work of his forerunner. Havrelock's comment, however, underscores the lack of a definitive conclusion about the numbers, or the precise calculation of the doubling according to Jewish tradition: "Elijah's promise to bestow a double portion of his wondrous spirit upon his disciple was realized instantaneously. During his life Elisha performed sixteen miracles, and eight was all his master had performed."[24]

Even if the interpreter resists a carbon-copy "eight versus sixteen" doubling—after all, one could employ different criteria to define a miracle and then massage the data to conform numerically—the essential insight remains intriguing. The proposition of Elisha as the prophetic successor who replicates and enhances strikes me as the most fruitful way of understanding the relationship between the activities of the two figures. Rather than a mechanical facsimile, Elisha

---

[22] R. Havrelock, *River Jordan: The Mythology of a Dividing Line* (Chicago: University of Chicago Press, 2011), 157.

[23] K. J. Madigan and J. D. Levenson, *Resurrection: The Power of God for Christians and Jews* (New Haven and London: Yale University Press, 2008), 99–100.

[24] Ginzberg, *The Legends of the Jews*, iv. 239.

receives his portioning in order creatively to amplify the *métier* of Elijah. A case in point is the resurrected sons of 1 Kings 17 and 2 Kings 4. Elijah raises the son of a foreign widow while hiding from Ahab and Jezebel in Sidonian territory. Elisha raises the dead son of a married woman inside the boundaries of Israel, a son who is poised to inherit the land of his ancestors—land that was threatened and restored by the son of Ahab and Jezebel in a subsequent episode, where Elisha plays a starring role even when he is offstage. The "doubling" in this case is an extension and (as it turns out) enhancing of his predecessor's actions, and, as we have seen, the pattern of magnification and enlargement is subtly woven throughout the narrative. Elijah speaks the prophetic utterance about the end of the Omrides and inaugurates the process, but it is brought to completion by his double agent and successor in a story thick with plot and character. A compelling and mysterious figure, Elisha makes a memorable contribution to the story from start to finish, first as the prophet who heals the waters of Jericho, and finally as the one whose bones can disrupt a funeral.

Bibliography

Ahlström, Gösta W., "King Jehu—A Prophet's Mistake," in Arthur L. Merrill and Thomas W. Overholt (eds), *Scripture in History & Theology: Essays in Honor of J. Coert Rylaarsdam* (Pittsburgh: Pickwick, 1977), 47–69.

Alter, Robert, *The Art of Biblical Narrative* (New York: Basic Books, 1981).

Alter, Robert, "How Convention Helps Us Read: The Case of the Bible's Annunciation Type-Scene," *Prooftexts*, 3 (1983), 115–30.

Alter, Robert, "Response," *Prooftexts*, 27 (2007), 365–70.

Amit, Yairah, "A Prophet Tested: Elisha, the Great Woman of Shunem, and the Story's Double Message," *BibInt*, 11 (2003), 279–94.

Amit, Yairah, "Narrative Analysis: Meaning, Context, and Origins of Genesis 38," in Joel M. LeMon and Kent Harold Richards (eds), *Method Matters: Essays on the Interpretation of the Hebrew Bible in Honor of David L. Petersen* (Atlanta: Society of Biblical Literature, 2009), 271–91.

Aucker, W. Brian, "Putting Elisha in his Place: Genre, Coherence, and Narrative Function in 2 Kings 2-8" (Ph.D. diss., University of Edinburgh, 2000).

Aucker, W. Brian, "A Prophet in King's Clothes: Kingly and Divine Re-Presentation in 2 Kings 4 and 5," in Robert Rezetko, Timothy H. Lim, and W. Brian Aucker (eds), *Reflection and Refraction: Studies in Biblical Historiography in Honour of A. Graeme Auld* (VTSup 113; Leiden: Brill, 2007), 1–25.

Auld, A. Graeme, "The Deuteronomists and the Former Prophets, or What Makes the Former Prophets Deuteronomistic?" in Linda S. Schearing and Steven L. McKenzie (eds), *Those Elusive Deuteronomists: The Phenomenon of Pan-Deuteronomism* (JSOTSup 268; Sheffield: Sheffield Academic Press, 1999), 116–26.

Auld, A. Graeme, *I & II Samuel: A Commentary* (OTL; Louisville, KY: Westminster John Knox Press, 2011).

Avioz, Michael, "The Book of Kings in Recent Research (Part II)," *CBR* 5/1 (2006), 11–57.

Babcock-Abrahams, Barbara, "'A Tolerated Margin of Mess': The Trickster and his Tales Reconsidered," *Journal of the Folklore Institute*, 11 (1975), 147–86.

Barré, Lloyd M., *The Rhetoric of Political Persuasion: The Narrative Artistry and Political Intentions of 2 Kings 9–11* (CBQMS 20; Washington: Catholic Biblical Association of America, 1988).

Barrick, W. B., "Elisha and the Magic Bow: A Note on 2 Kings xiii 15–17," *VT* 35 (1985), 355–63.

Bartlett, John R., "The 'United' Campaign against Moab in 2 Kgs 3.4–27," in J. F. A. Sawyer and D. J. A. Clines (eds), *Midian, Moab and Edom: The History and Archaeology of Late Bronze and Iron Age Jordan and North West Arabia* (JSOTSup 24; Sheffield: JSOT Press, 1983), 135–46.

Beal, Lissa M. Wray, *The Deuteronomist's Prophet: Narrative Control of Approval and Disapproval in the Story of Jehu (2 Kings 9 and 10)* (LHBOTS 478; New York and London: T & T Clark, 2007).

Begg, Christopher T., "Unifying Factors in 2 Kings 1:2–17a," *JSOT* 32 (1985), 75–86.

Bergen, Wesley J., *Elisha and the End of Prophetism* (JSOTSup 286; Sheffield: Sheffield Academic Press, 1999).

Berger, Peter, *Redeeming Laughter: The Comic Dimension of Human Experience* (New York: Walter de Gruyter, 1997).

Berlin, Adele, *Poetics and Interpretation of Biblical Narrative* (Bible and Literature Series; Sheffield: Almond Press, 1983).

Boda, Mark J., "Chiasm in Ubiquity: Symmetrical Mirages in Nehemiah 9," *JSOT* 71 (1996), 55–70.

Bodner, Keith, "The Locutions of 1 Kings 22:28: A New Proposal," *JBL* 122 (2003), 533–43.

Bodner, Keith, *Jeroboam's Royal Drama* (Oxford: Oxford University Press, 2012).

Boyce, Richard N., *The Cry to God in the Old Testament* (SBLDS 103; Atlanta: Scholars Press, 1988).

Brenner, Athalya, and Radday, Yehuda T. (eds), *On Humour and the Comic in the Hebrew Bible* (JSOTSup 92; Sheffield: Almond Press, 1990).

Brichto, H. C., *Toward a Grammar of Biblical Poetics: Tales of the Prophets* (New York: Oxford University Press, 1992).

Brooks, Peter, *Reading for the Plot: Design and Intention in Narrative* (Cambridge, MA: Harvard University Press, 1984).

Bronner, Leah, *The Stories of Elijah and Elisha as Polemics against Baal Worship* (Leiden: Brill, 1968).

Brodie, Thomas L., *The Crucial Bridge: The Elijah–Elisha Narrative as an Interpretive Synthesis of Genesis–Kings and a Literary Model for the Gospels* (Collegeville, MN: Liturgical Press, 2000).

Britt, Brian, "Prophetic Concealment in a Biblical Type Scene," *CBQ* 64 (2002), 37–58.

Bruckner, James K., *Implied Law in the Abraham Narrative: A Literary and Theological Analysis* (JSOTSup 335; London: Sheffield Academic Press, 2001).

Brueggemann, Walter, *1 & 2 Kings* (Macon: Smyth & Helwys, 2000).

Burnett, Joel S., "'Going Down' to Bethel: Elijah and Elisha in the Theological Geography of the Deuteronomistic History," *JBL* 129 (2010), 281–97.

Carroll, Robert P., "The Elijah–Elisha Sagas: Some Remarks on Prophetic Succession in Ancient Israel," *VT* 19 (1969), 400–15.

Chiffolo, Anthony F., and Hesse, Rayner W., Jr, *Cooking with the Bible: Biblical Food, Feasts, and Lore* (Westport, CT: Greenwood Press, 2006).

Chisholm, Robert B., Jr, "Israel's Retreat and the Failure of Prophecy in 2 Kings 3," *Biblica*, 92 (2011), 71–80.

Christian, Mark A., "Middle-Tier Levites and the Plenary Reception of Revelation," in Mark Leuchter and Jeremy M. Hutton (eds), *Levites and Priests in Biblical History and Tradition* (Atlanta: Society of Biblical Literature, 2011), 173–97.

Cogan, Mordechai, *I Kings: A New Translation with Introduction and Commentary* (AB 10; New York: Doubleday, 2001).

Cogan, Mordechai, and Tadmor, Hayim. *II Kings: A New Translation with Introduction and Commentary* (AB 11; New York: Doubleday, 1988).

Coggins, Richard, "What Does 'Deuteronomistic' Mean?," in Linda S. Schearing and Steven L. McKenzie (eds), *Those Elusive Deuteronomists: The Phenomenon of Pan-Deuteronomism* (JSOTSup 268; Sheffield: Sheffield Academic Press, 1999), 22–35.

Cohn, Robert L., "The Literary Logic of 1 Kings 17–19," *JBL* 101 (1982), 333–50.

Cohn, Robert L., "Form and Perspective in 2 Kings V," *VT* 31 (1983), 171–84.

Cohn, Robert L., "Convention and Creativity in the Book of Kings: The Case of the Dying Monarch," *CBQ* 47 (1985), 603–16.

Cohn, Robert L., *2 Kings* (Berit Olam; Collegeville, MN: Liturgical Press, 2000).

Conroy, Charles, "Hiel between Ahab and Elijah–Elisha: 1 Kgs 16, 34 in its Immediate Literary Context," *Biblica*, 77 (1996), 210–18.

Cronauer, Patrick T., OSB, *The Stories about Naboth the Jezreelite: A Source, Composition, and Redaction Investigation of 1 Kings 21 and Passages in 2 Kings 9* (LHBOTS 424; London: T & T Clark, 2005).

Day, John, *Yahweh and the Gods and Goddesses of Canaan* (JSOTSup 265; Sheffield: Sheffield Academic Press, 2000).

Dever, William G., "Archaeology, the Israelite Monarchy, and the Solomonic Temple," in Leo G. Perdue (ed.), *The Blackwell Companion to the Hebrew Bible* (Oxford: Blackwell, 2001), 186–206.

DeVries, Simon J., *1 Kings* (WBC 12; Waco, TX: Word, 1985).

Dorn, Christopher, "The Ways of God in the World: The Drama of 2 Kings 6:8–23," in J. Harold Ellens and John T. Greene (eds), *Probing the Frontiers of Biblical Studies* (Princeton Theological Monograph Series 111; Eugene, OR: Pickwick, 2009), 9–20.

Edelman, Diana V., "Abel-Meholah," in David Noel Freedman (ed.), *The Anchor Bible Dictionary* (New York: Doubleday, 1992), i. 11–12.

Exum, J. Cheryl, *Tragedy and Biblical Narrative: Arrows of the Almighty* (Cambridge: Cambridge University Press, 1992).

Fewell, Danna Nolan, "The Gift: World Alteration and Obligation in 2 Kings 4:8–37," in S. M. Olyan and R. C. Culley (eds), *A Wise and Discerning Mind: Essays in Honor of Burke O. Long* (Providence, RI: Brown Judaic Studies, 2000), 109–23.

Fishbane, Michael, *Haftarot: The Traditional Hebrew Text with the New JPS Translation* (Philadelphia: Jewish Publication Society, 2002).

Frei, Hans W., *The Eclipse of Biblical Narrative: A Study in Eighteenth and Nineteenth Century Hermeneutics* (New Haven: Yale University Press, 1974).

Fretheim, Terence E., *First and Second Kings* (Louisville, KY: Westminster John Knox, 1999).

Fritz, Volkmar, *1 & 2 Kings* (Continental Commentary; Minneapolis, MN: Fortress, 2003).

García-Treto, Francisco O., "The Fall of the House: A Carnivalesque Reading of 2 Kings 9 and 10," *JSOT* 46 (1990), 47–65.

Gass, Erasmus, "Topographical Considerations in 2 Kings 3," *JBL* 128 (2009), 65–84.

Gilmour Rachelle, "Suspense and Anticipation in 1 Samuel 9:1–14," *JHS* 9 (2009), 1–16.

Ginzberg, Louis, *The Legends of the Jews*, iv (Philadelphia: The Jewish Publication Society, 1913, 1941).

Goldingay, John, *Old Testament Theology*, i. *Israel's Gospel* (Downers Grove, IL: InterVarsity Press, 2003).

Gottwald, Norman K., *All the Kingdoms of the Earth: Israelite Prophecy and International Relations in the Ancient Near East* (New York: Harper & Row, 1964).

Grabbe, Lester L., "The Kingdom of Israel from Omri to the Fall of Samaria: If We Had Only the Bible . . . ," in Lester L. Grabbe (ed.), *Ahab Agonistes: The Rise and Fall of the Omri Dynasty* (LHBOTS 421/ESHM 6; New York and London: T & T Clark, 2007), 54–99.

Gray, John, *I & II Kings* (2nd edn; OTL; London: SCM, 1970).

Guillaume, Philippe, "Miracles Miraculously Repeated: Gospel Miracles as Duplication of Elijah–Elisha's," *BN* 98 (1999), 21–3.

Halpern, Baruch, and Lemaire, André, "The Composition of Kings," in Baruch Halpern, André Lemaire, and Matthew J. Adams (eds), *The Books of Kings: Sources, Composition, Historiography and Reception* (VTSup 129; Leiden: Brill, 2010), 123–53.

Hauser, Alan J., "Yahweh versus Death: The Real Struggle in Kings 17–19," in Russell Gregory and Alan J. Hauser, *From Carmel to Horeb: Elijah in Crisis* (JSOTSup 85; Sheffield: Almond Press, 1990), 11–89.

Havrelock, Rachel, *River Jordan: The Mythology of a Dividing Line* (Chicago: University of Chicago Press, 2011).

Hendel, Ronald, "Cultural Memory," in Ronald Hendel (ed.), *Reading Genesis: Ten Methods* (New York: Cambridge University Press, 2010), 28–46.

Hens-Piazza, Gina, *Nameless, Blameless, and without Shame: Two Cannibal Mothers before a King* (Interfaces; Collegeville, MN: Liturgical Press/ Michael Glazier, 2003).

Hens-Piazza, Gina, *1–2 Kings* (Nashville: Abingdon, 2006).

Hobbs, T. R., "2 Kings 1 and 2: Their Unity and Purpose," *SR* 13 (1984), 327–34.

Houtman, Cornelis, "Elijah," in Karel van der Toorn, Bob Becking, and Pieter W. van der Horst (eds), *Dictionary of Deities and Demons in the Bible* (2nd edn; Leiden: Brill, 1999), 282–5.

Humphries, Michael L., "Trickster," in D. N. Freedman (ed.), *Eerdmans Dictionary of the Bible* (Grand Rapids: Eerdmans, 2000), 1335–6.

Hutton, Jeremy M., *The Transjordanian Palimpsest: The Overwritten Texts of Personal Exile and Transformation in the Deuteronomistic History* (BZAW 396; Berlin: Walter de Gruyter, 2009).

Jackson, Melissa, "Lot's Daughters and Tamar as Tricksters and the Patriarchal Narratives as Feminist Theology," *JSOT* 98 (2002), 29–46.

Jobling, David, "A Bettered Woman: Elisha and the Shunammite in the Deuteronomic Work," in Fiona Black, Roland Boer and Erin Runions (eds), *The Labour of Reading: Desire, Alienation and Biblical Interpretation* (Semeia Studies 36; Atlanta: Scholars Press, 1999), 177–92.

Joblin, David, Pippin, Tina, and Schleifer, Ronald (eds), *The Postmodern Bible Reader* (Oxford: Blackwell, 2001).

Johnson, Benjamin J. M., "What Type of Son is Samson? Reading Judges 13 as a Biblical Type-Scene," *JETS* 53 (2010), 269–86.

Jones, Brian C., "In Search of Kir Hareseth: A Case Study in site Identification," *JSOT* 52 (1991), 3–24.

Jones, Gwilym H., *1 and 2 Kings* (NCB; Grand Rapids: Eerdmans, 1984).

Kalmanofsky, Amy, "Women of God: Maternal Grief and Religious Response in 1 Kings 17 and 2 Kings 4," *JSOT* 36 (2011), 55–74.

Kaltner, John, "What Did Elijah Do to his Mantle? The Hebrew Root *GLM*," in John Kaltner and Louis Stulman (eds), *Inspired Speech: Prophecy in the Ancient Near East: Essays in Honor of Herbert B. Huffmon* (JSOTSup 378; London: T & T Clark, 2004), 225–30.

Keil, Carl F., *I & II Kings, I & II Chronicles* (Commentary on the Old Testament, 10 vols), ed. C. F. Keil and F. Delitzsch (Peabody, MA.: Hendrickson, 1996) (originally published 1866–91).

Keinänen, Jyrki, *Traditions in Collision: A Literary and Redaction-Critical Study on the Elijah Narratives 1 Kings 17–19* (Helsinki: The Finnish Exegetical Society; Göttingen: Vandenhoeck & Ruprecht, 2001).

Kim, Jean Kyoung, "Reading and Retelling Naaman's Story (2 Kings 5)," *JSOT* 30/1 (2005), 49–61.

Kissling, Paul J., *Reliable Characters in the Primary History: Profiles of Moses, Joshua, Elijah and Elisha* (JSOTSup 224; Sheffield: Sheffield Academic Press, 1996).

LaBarbera, Robert, "The Man of War and the Man of God: Social Satire in 2 Kings 6:8–7:20," *CBQ* 46 (1984), 637–51.

Labuschagne, C. J., "Did Elisha Deliberately Lie?—A Note on II Kings 8.10," *ZAW* 77 (1965), 327–8.

Lamb, David T., *Righteous Jehu and his Evil Heirs: The Deuteronomist's Negative Perspective on Dynastic Succession* (Oxford Theological Monographs; Oxford: Oxford University Press, 2007).

Lamb, David T., "'A Prophet Instead of You' (1 Kings 19.16): Elijah, Elisha and Prophetic Succession," in John Day (ed.), *Prophecy and the Prophets in Ancient Israel* (LHBOTS 531; New York: T & T Clark, 2010), 172–87.

Landy, Francis, Review of "D. A. Nicholas, *The Trickster Revisited: Deception as a Motif in the Pentateuch*," *CBQ* 73 (2011), 132–3.

Lanner, Laurel, "Cannibal Mothers and Me: A Mother's Reading of 2 Kings 6.24–7.20," *JSOT* 85 (1999), 107–16.

Lasine, Stuart, "Jehoram and the Cannibal Mothers (2 Kings 6.24–33): Solomon's Judgment in an Inverted World," *JSOT* 50 (1991), 27–53.

Lasine, Stuart, "The Ups and Downs of Monarchical Justice: Solomon and Jehoram in an Intertextual World," *JSOT* 59 (1993), 37–53.

Lasine, Stuart, "Matters of Life and Death: The Story of Elijah and the Widow's Son in Comparative Perspective," *BibInt*, 12 (2004), 117–44.

Leithart, Peter J., *1 & 2 Kings* (Brazos Theological Commentary on the Bible; Grand Rapids: Brazos, 2006).

Leuchter, Mark, and Klaus-Peter, Adam (eds), *Soundings in Kings: Perspectives and Methods in Contemporary Scholarship* (Minneapolis: Fortress, 2010).

Levine, Nachman, "Twice as Much of your Spirit: Pattern, Parallel, and Paronomasia in the Miracles of Elijah and Elisha," *JSOT* 85 (1999), 25–46.

Long, Burke O., *2 Kings* (FOTL 10; Grand Rapids: Eerdmans, 1991).

Long, Jesse C., Jr, "Elisha's Deceptive Prophecy in 2 Kings 3: A Response to Raymond Westbrook," *JBL* 126 (2007), 168–71.

Long, Jesse C. Jr, and Sneed, Mark, "'Yahweh Has Given These Three Kings into the Hand of Moab': A Socio-Literary Reading of 2 Kings 3," in John Kaltner and Louis Stulman (eds), *Inspired Speech: Prophecy in the Ancient Near East. Essays in Honor of Herbert B. Huffmon* (JSOTSup 378; London: T&T Clark, 2004), 253–75.

Lundbom, J. R., "Elijah's Chariot Ride," *JJS* 24 (1973), 39–50.

McKenzie, Steven L., "A Response to Thomas Römer, *The So-Called Deuteronomistic History*," in Raymond F. Person, Jr, "In Conversation with

Thomas Römer, *The So-Called Deuteronomistic History: A Sociological, Historical and Literary Introduction* (London: T. & T. Clark, 2005)," *JHS* 9 (2009), article 17.

McLaughlin, John Leo, "Baal Zebub," in D. N. Freedman (ed.), *Eerdmans Dictionary of the Bible* (Grand Rapids: Eerdmans, 2000), 136–7.

Madigan, Kevin J., and Levenson, Jon D., *Resurrection: The Power of God for Christians and Jews* (New Haven and London: Yale University Press, 2008).

Marsman, Hennie J., *Women in Ugarit & Israel: Their Social and Religious Position in the Context of the Ancient Near East* (Leiden: Brill, 2003).

Matthews, Victor H., "Back to Bethel: Geographical Reiteration in Biblical Narrative," *JBL* 128 (2009), 149–65.

Mead, James K., "'Elisha Will Kill'? The Deuteronomistic Rhetoric of Life and Death in the Theology of the Elisha Narratives" (Ph.D. diss., Princeton Theological Seminary, 1999).

Mercer, Mark K., "Elisha's Unbearable Curse: A Study of 2 Kings 2:23–25," *Africa Journal of Evangelical Theology*, 21 (2002), 165–98.

Miscall, Peter D., "Elijah, Ahab, and Jehu: A Prophecy Fulfilled," *Prooftexts*, 9 (1989), 73–83.

Moore, Rick Dale. *God Saves: Lessons from the Elisha Stories* (JSOTSup 95; Sheffield: JSOT Press, 1990).

Montgomery, J. A., and Gehman, H. S., *A Critical and Exegetical Commentary on the Books of Kings* (ICC; Edinburgh: T & T Clark, 1951).

Morschauser, Scott, "A 'Diagnostic' Note on the 'Great Wrath upon Israel' in 2 Kings 3:27," *JBL* 129 (2010), 299–302.

Mulder, Martin J., *1 Kings* (HCOT; Leuven: Peeters, 1998).

Nelson, Richard D., *First and Second Kings* (Interpretation; Atlanta: John Knox Press, 1987).

Nelson, Richard D., "A Response to Thomas Römer, *The So-Called Deuteronomistic History*," in Raymond F. Person, Jr (ed.), "In Conversation with Thomas Römer, *The So-Called Deuteronomistic History: A Sociological, Historical and Literary Introduction* (London: T. & T. Clark, 2005)," *JHS* 9 (2009), article 17.

Niditch, Susan, "Samson as Culture Hero, Trickster, and Bandit: The Empowerment of the Weak," *CBQ* 52 (1985), 608–24.

Niehoff, Maren, "Do Biblical Characters Talk to Themselves? Narrative Modes of Representing Inner Speech in Early Biblical Fiction," *JBL* 111 (1992), 577–95.

Niehr, Herbert, "'Israelite' Religion and 'Canaanite' Religion," in Francesca Stavrakopoulou and John Barton (eds), *Religious Diversity in Ancient Israel and Judah* (London: T & T Clark, 2010), 23–36.

Nielson, Flemming A. J., *The Tragedy in History: Herodotus and the Deuteronomistic History* (JSOTSup 251; Sheffield: Sheffield Academic Press, 1997).

Noll, K. L., "Deuteronomistic History or Deuteronomic Debate? (A Thought Experiment)," *JSOT* 31/3 (2007), 311–45.

Noth, Martin, *The Deuteronomistic History*, trans. E. W. Nicholson (JSOTSup 15; Sheffield: JSOT Press, 1981) (originally published 1943).

O'Brien, D. P., "'Is this the Time to Accept...?' (2 Kings V 26B): Simply Moralizing (LXX) or an Ominous Foreboding of Yahweh's Rejection of Israel (MT)?" *VT* 46 (1996), 448–57.

O'Brien, Mark A., "The Portrayal of Prophets in 2 Kings 2," *ABR* 46 (1998), 1–16.

Oeming, Manfred, *Contemporary Biblical Hermeneutics: An Introduction*, trans. Joachim Vette (Aldershot: Ashgate, 2006).

Olley, John W., "YHWH and His Zealous Prophet: The Presentation of Elijah in 1 and 2 Kings," JSOT 80 (1998), 25–51.

Olson, Dennis T., "Literary and Rhetorical Criticism," in Thomas B. Dozeman (ed.), *Methods for Exodus* (Methods in Biblical Interpretation; Cambridge: Cambridge University Press, 2010), 13–54.

Otto, Susanne, "The Composition of the Elijah–Elisha Stories and the Deuteronomistic History," *JSOT* 27 (2003), 487–508.

Parker, Simon B., *Stories in Scripture and Inscriptions: Comparative Studies on Narratives in Northwest Semitic Inscriptions and the Hebrew Bible* (New York: Oxford University Press, 1997).

Patterson, Richard D., "The Old Testament Use of an Archetype: The Trickster," *JETS* 42 (1999), 385–94.

Provan, Iain W., *1 and 2 Kings* (NIBC 7; Peabody, MA: Hendrickson, 1995).

Pyper, Hugh S., "Judging the Wisdom of Solomon: The Two-Way Effect of Intertextuality," *JSOT* 59 (1993), 25–36.

Pyper, Hugh S., "The Secret of Succession: Elijah, Elisha, Jesus, and Derrida," in A. K. M. Adam (ed.), *Postmodern Interpretations of the Bible: A Reader* (St Louis: Chalice, 2001), 55–66.

Rad, Gerhard von, *Old Testament Theology*, trans. D. M. G. Stalker (2 vols; New York: Harper & Row, 1962–5).

Rad, Gerhard von, "Naaman: A Critical Retelling," in *God at Work in Israel* (Nashville: Abingdon Press, 1980), 47–57.

Rad, Gerhard von, *Studies in Deuteronomy*, trans. D. M. G. Stalker (SBT 9; London: SCM Press, 1953).

Radday, Yehuda T., "Chiasmus in Hebrew Biblical Narrative," in J. W. Welch (ed.), *Chiasmus in Antiquity* (Hildesheim: Gerstenberg, 1981), 50–117.

Reinhartz, Adele, *Why Ask My Name?: Anonymity and Identity in Biblical Narrative* (New York: Oxford University Press, 1998).

Rendsburg, Gary A., "Confused Language as a Deliberate Literary Device in Biblical Hebrew Narrative," *JHS* 2 (1999) <www.purl.org/jhs> (accessed December 2010).

Rentería, Tamis Hoover, "The Elijah/Elisha Stories: A Socio-Cultural Analysis of Prophets and People in Ninth-Century BCE Israel," in Robert B. Coote (ed.), *Elijah and Elisha in Socioliterary Perspective* (Atlanta: Scholars Press, 1992), 75–126.

Robinson, J. C., "Narrative," in Stanley E. Porter (ed.), *Dictionary of Biblical Criticism and Interpretation* (New York: Routledge, 2007), 236–7.

Robinson, Joseph, *The Second Book of Kings* (CBC; Cambridge and New York: Cambridge University Press, 1976).

Rofé, Alexander, "The Classification of the Prophetical Stories," *JBL* 89 (1970), 427–40.

Rofé, Alexander, "Elisha at Dothan (2 Kgs 6:8–23): Historico-Literary Criticism Sustained by the Midrash," in Robert Chazan, William W. Hallo, and Lawrence H. Schiffman (eds), *Ki Baruch Hu: Ancient Near Eastern, Biblical, and Judaic Studies in Honor of Baruch A. Levine* (Winona Lake: Eisenbrauns, 1999), 345–53.

Rollston, Christopher A., *Writing and Literacy in the World of Ancient Israel: Epigraphic Evidence from the Iron Age* (Atlanta: Society of Biblical Literature, 2010).

Roncace, Mark, "Elisha and the Woman of Shunem: 2 Kings 4.8–37 and 8.1–6 Read in Conjunction," *JSOT* 91 (2000), 109–27.

Roth, Wolfgang, *Hebrew Gospel: Cracking the Code of Mark* (Oak Park, IL: Meyer-Stone Books, 1988).

Ryan, Marie-Laure, "Toward a Definition of Narrative," in David Herman (ed.), *The Cambridge Companion to Narrative* (Cambridge: Cambridge University Press, 2007), 22–35.

Satterthwaite, Philip E., "The Elisha Narratives and the Coherence of 2 Kings 2–8," *TynBul*, 49 (1998), 1–28.

Savran, George W., *Encountering the Divine: Theophany in Biblical Narrative* (JSOTSup 420; London: T & T Clark, 2005).

Schipper, Jeremy, "'Why Do You Still Speak of your Affairs?': Polyphony in Mephibosheth's Exchanges with David in 2 Samuel," *VT* 54 (2004), 344–51.

Schulte, Hannelis, "The End of the Omride Dynasty: Social–Ethical Observations on the Subject of Power and Violence," trans. Carl S. Ehrlich, *Semeia*, 66 (1994), 133–48.

Schwartz, Saundra C., "From Bedroom to Courtroom: The Adultery Type-Scene and the Acts of Andrew," in Todd C. Penner and Caroline Vander Stichele (eds), *Mapping Gender in Ancient Religious Discourse* (BIS 84; Leiden: Brill, 2007), 267–311.

Scott, James C., *Domination and the Arts of Resistance: Hidden Transcripts* (New Haven: Yale University Press, 1990).

Seow, Choon Leong, "1 & 2 Kings," in L. E. Keck et al. (eds), *The New Interpreter's Bible*, iii (Nashville: Abingdon, 1999), 1–295.

Sharp, Carolyn J., *Irony and Meaning in the Hebrew Bible* (Bloomington: Indiana University Press, 2009).

Shemesh, Yael, "Elisha and the Miraculous Jug of Oil (2 Kgs 4:1–7)," *JHS* 8 (2008), 1–18.

Shemesh, Yael, "The Elisha Stories as Saints' Legends," *JHS* 8 (2008), 1–41.

Shields, Mary E., "Subverting a Man of God, Elevating a Woman: Role and Power Reversals in 2 Kings 4," *JSOT* 58 (1993), 59–69.

Siebert-Hommes, Jopie, "The Widow of Zarephath and the Great Woman of Shunem: A Comparative Analysis of Two Stories," in B. Becking and M. Dijkstra (eds), *On Reading Prophetic Texts: Gender-Specific & Related Studies in Memory of Fokkelien van Dijk-Hemmes* (BIS 18; Leiden: Brill, 1996), 231–50.

Simon, Uriel, "Minor Characters in Biblical Narrative," *JSOT* 46 (1990), 11–19.

Simon, Uriel, *Reading Prophetic Narratives* (Bloomington: Indiana University Press, 1997).

Smelik, Klaas A. D., "The Literary Function of 1 Kgs 17, 8–24," in C. Brekelmans and J. Lust (eds), *Pentateuchal and Deuteronomistic Studies* (Leuven: Peeters, 1990), 239–43.

Smelik, Klaas A. D., *Writings from Ancient Israel: A Handbook of Historical and Religious Documents* (Edinburgh: T & T Clark, 1991).

Smith, Morton, *Palestinian Parties and Politics that Shaped the Old Testament* (New York: Columbia University Press, 1971).

Sparks, James T., *The Chronicler's Genealogies: Towards an Understanding of 1 Chronicles 1–9* (Academia Biblica 28; Atlanta: Society of Biblical Literature, 2008).

Stern, P. D., "Of Kings and Moabites: History and Theology in 2 Kings 3 and the Mesha Inscription," *HUCA* 64 (1993), 1–14.

Sternberg, Meir, *The Poetics of Biblical Narrative: Ideological Literature and the Drama of Reading* (Indiana Studies in Biblical Literature; Bloomington: Indiana University Press, 1985).

Sweeney, Marvin A., "On the Literary Function of the Notice concerning Hiel's Reestablishment of Jericho in 1 Kings 16.34," in M. A. O'Brien and H. N. Wallace (eds), *Seeing Signals, Reading Signs: The Art of Exegesis* (JSOTSup 415; Sheffield: Sheffield Academic Press, 2004), 104–15.

Sweeney, Marvin A., *I & II Kings* (OTL; Louisville, KY: Westminster John Knox Press, 2007).

Talmon, Shemaryahu, "The Presentation of Synchroneity and Simultaneity in Biblical Narrative," in J. Heinemann and S. Werses (eds), *Studies in Hebrew Narrative Art throughout the Ages* (Scripta hierosolymitana 27; Jerusalem: Magnes Press, 1978), 9–26.

Thatcher, Tom, "Anatomies of the Fourth Gospel: Past, Present, and Future Probes," in Tom Thatcher and Stephen D. Moore (eds), *Anatomies of*

Narrative Criticism: The Past, Present, and Futures of the Fourth Gospel as Literature (Atlanta: Society of Biblical Literature, 2008), 1–37.

Tiemeyer, Lena-Sofia, "Prophecy as a Way of Cancelling Prophecy—The Strategic Uses of Foreknowledge," *ZAW* 117 (2005), 329–50.

Valeta, David M., "Polyglossia and Parody: Language in Daniel 1–6," in Roland Boer (ed)., *Bakhtin and Genre Theory in Biblical Studies* (Semeia Studies; Atlanta: Society of Biblical Literature, 2007), 91–108.

Walsh, Jerome T., "The Elijah Cycle: A Synchronic Approach" (Ph.D. diss., University of Michigan, 1982).

Walsh, Jerome T., *1 Kings* (Berit Olam; Collegeville, MN: Liturgical Press, 1996).

Walsh, Jerome T., "The Organization of 2 Kings 3–11," *CBQ* 72 (2010), 238–54.

Watson, Wilfred G. E., *Classical Hebrew Poetry* (Sheffield: JSOT Press, 1986).

Weitzman, Steven, "Before and After *The Art of Biblical Narrative*," *Prooftexts*, 27 (2007), 191–210.

Westbrook, Raymond, "Elisha's True Prophecy in 2 Kings 3," *JBL* 124 (2005), 530–2.

White, Marsha C., *The Elisha Legends and Jehu's Coup* (BJS 311; Atlanta: Scholars Press, 1997).

Woods, Fred E., "Elisha and the Children: The Question of Accepting Prophetic Succession," *BYU Studies*, 32 (1992), 47–58.

Wright, Jacob L., "Warfare and Wanton Destruction: A Reexamination of Deuteronomy 20:19–20 in Relation to Ancient Siegecraft," *JBL* 127 (2008), 423–58.

Zakovitch, Yair, "Humor and Theology or the Successful Failure of Israelite Intelligence: A Literary–Folkloric Approach to Joshua 2," in Susan Niditch (ed.), *Text and Tradition: The Hebrew Bible and Folklore* (Atlanta: Scholars Press, 1990), 75–98.

Index

2016. 07. 06   99.95 (49.10)